BRITISH–EGYPTIAN RELATIONS
FROM SUEZ TO THE PRESENT DAY

ISBN: 978-0-86356-685-1

A full CIP record for this book is available from the British Library.
A full CIP record for this book is available from the Library of Congress.

Manufactured in Lebanon

SAQI

26 Westbourne Grove, London W2 5RH
825 Page Street, Suite 203, Berkeley, California 94710
Tabet Building, Mneimneh Street, Hamra, Beirut

www.saqibooks.com

in association with

The London Middle East Institute

ol of Oriental and African Studies, Russell Square, London WC1H 0XG
www.lmei.soas.ac.uk

SOAS MIDDLE EAST ISSUES

British–Egyptian Relations

from Suez to the Present Day

Edited by

Noel Brehony and Ayman El-Desouky

SAQI

in association with

**LONDON
MIDDLE EAS**
INSTITUT
SOAS

Schoo

Contents

Part Three: Cultural Relations

Contents

Acknowledgments

The origins of this book lie in a forum jointly organised by the British Egyptian Society (BES) and the London Middle East Institute (LMEI) of the School of Oriental and African Studies (SOAS) in November 2006 under the title *50 years since Suez: from conflict to collaboration*. The forum took almost two years in the planning and execution. It was agreed from the outset that we should publish a book based on its proceedings to bring the issues discussed to a much wider audience. This is the result.

The editors would like to acknowledge the contribution made, in particular, by a sub-group from the BES and SOAS. Its members were Professor Robert Springborg of the LMEI with Dr Ahmed El-Mokadem, Professor Magdy Ishak-Hanna, Mr Peter Mackenzie Smith, Professor Amir Azmy, Dr Noel Brehony and Mr Noel Rands of the BES.

It was impossible for an event such as this to take place without major sponsorship. We were fortunate to be supported by *Allam Marine Limited, BAE Systems, the British Council, BG Egypt, the British Museum, BP, Dr Ahmed El-Mokadem, EgyptAir, HSBC Global Banking, HSBC Private Banking*, the late *Dr Ashraf Marwan, Professor Magdy Ishak-Hanna, Menas Associates, Orascom Telecom* and *Transform Cosmetic Surgery*.

The publication of this book would not have been possible without the assistance provided by Louise Hosking of the LMEI. The editors would also like to thank Vincenzo Paci and other members of the LMEI staff for their assistance.

Finally, the editors of this book would like to pay tribute to the late Sir Michael Weir, chairman of the British Egyptian Society from its formation in 1990 until just before his death in 2006, whose initial help and support enabled the conference to take place.

Editorial Note

The majority of the chapters in this book are based on papers delivered at the *50 years since Suez: from conflict to collaboration* conference. Some have been kept in the form in which they were delivered at the conference; others have been reworked into longer articles. Two further articles were especially commissioned to address important aspects of the British–Egyptian relationship: one by Gamon McLellan on the role of the BBC Arabic Service in Egypt and another by Stephen Quirke on joint archaeological efforts.

The editors have decided not to standardise the transcription of Egyptian names, choosing to keep them in the various forms used by different authors. All of these are easily recognisable and work to convey the authors' frames of reference. Penelope Lively's French-inspired renditions, for example, reflect the times and discourses feeding into her memoirs.

Noel Brehony and Ayman El-Desouky

Preface

The fiftieth anniversary of the Suez Crisis provided an opportunity to assess the subsequent evolution of the British–Egyptian relationship, which was one of the most intense of the entire colonial era. Although there were no British colonial settlers in the fashion of French settlers in North Africa, the duration of the British presence, combined with its depth and breadth, meant that the political, economic and social systems of the two interacted extensively. Not surprising, then, was the emotion and hostility brought by both sides to the cataclysmic termination of British influence at Suez. But what seems puzzling is how quickly the bitterness passed and how effective both sides have been at building a new relationship that draws upon the positive legacies of the colonial encounter. On more considered reflection this is hardly surprising, for once the unequal relationship that was the cause of the conflict was equalised, it became possible for both sides to capitalise effectively on the wide-ranging relationships that had been built in the previous era.

This book, based virtually entirely on a conference convened in London in November 2006 by the British Egyptian Society and the London Middle East Institute at the School of Oriental and African Studies, illustrates how the bilateral relationship has flourished over the past half-century, without avoiding some of the persisting difficulties it has confronted. While many of the chapters deal directly with examples of the relationship between the two countries, whether in the area of economics, politics or culture, others illustrate the relationship and its effects indirectly by assessing particular phenomena in one or the other country, especially in Egypt. Occurences and developments in Egyptian economy and polity, for example, have the potential to impact on relations with the United Kingdom, so it makes sense to evaluate such developments separately, as several chapters do.

The approach has been to consider elements of the countries' political and economic relations first, then to take up various aspects of their cultural relations. In both areas the range of interactions, as reflected in the diversity of subject matter covered in this book, is remarkable. As regards politics and economics, for example, some idea of the extensiveness of diplomatic cooperation between the two countries is conveyed by an insightful investigation of collaboration on the sensitive issue of weapons of mass destruction within the Middle East region. An assessment of UK support for democracy promotion in Egypt reveals how the two countries deal with an issue that has the potential to damage the relationship at either or both government and popular levels. As regards cultural relations, the range of topics suggests just how intensive colonial and post-colonial encounters have been. Whether in the area of literature, education, film, broadcasting or cultural heritage preservation, contributors to the volume have found ample evidence of mutual impact.

The contributors to this volume are prominent policy makers, officials, academics, businessmen, journalists, archaeologists and producers of popular culture. Precisely because they are drawn from such different professional backgrounds – and hence examine topics from varied perspectives – the volume as a whole is able to reflect the enormous diversity of the bilateral national relationship and its penetration into everyday lives. This, in sum, is not just an analytical work, but a book that reflects the first-hand engagement of many of its authors in the subjects under consideration. As such, it not only fills the gap in scholarly literature on British–Egyptian relations, but it does so with a strong sense of personal commitment and knowledge on the part of those who have contributed to it.

Preface

The London Middle East Institute, supported by the British Egyptian Society and assisted by Saqi editorial staff, has produced this book. Opinions expressed in it are those of the individual authors and do not necessarily reflect the views of the Institute or Society.

Robert Springborg
Director, London Middle East Institute
MBI Al Jaber Chair in Middle East Studies, SOAS

PART ONE

Salutatory Remarks

AHMED MAHER EL SAYID

Salutatory Remarks

The relationship between Egypt and the United Kingdom has gone through different phases in modern times. Some have been related to manifestations of a naturally tense relationship between colonialists and colonised. Others resulted from the determination of a new regime to reform a deteriorating internal situation through a revolutionary process. This took place against the background of a world torn between the ideals of the United Nations Organisation based on the right to freedom and self-determination, and cooperation among nations on the basis of equality and mutual respect; and the memories of a past domination, which had not yet faded. Old empires found it difficult to change their ways and relinquish their influence. Consequently they saw in the defiance of a new young leadership, led by an unknown colonel, an unacceptable challenge that could alter the balance of the new world order created by the emergence of the Soviet Union, once an ally against the Axis, now a powerful adversary. Moscow pursued a strategy based on ideology, which held some attraction for the poor and weak. In challenging established American power it went beyond ideological competition and sowed the seeds of a new war – cold and then hot. In this context, any country which took a position that had the potential to alter the new and fragile balance, where geographic as well as ideological frontiers were challenged, would constitute a danger which had to be nipped in the bud. In my opinion, this is the background against which the events of 1956 took place. It was a war between a past which did not want to fade away or pay the price of adapting to the new world, and a future which was trying to emerge. This confrontation was pregnant with hopes and fears, resentments and worries, dreams and nightmares. In this war, the past was defeated – an outcome which would change the world and herald a new era. Soon the winds of change would blow all over the Middle East, Africa and beyond. The future appeared, beyond the clouds of disappointments to come, with the growing brightness of a rising sun. Of course, problems remained and there were ups and downs, but there was a capacity to heal.

Having presented these general observations and considerations I would like to make two points. First of all, I would like to pay tribute to the country that was on the wrong side of history in the battle of Suez, and yet felt able to host the *50 years since Suez* conference. It was this sense of fairness that made the event possible. During the conference, harsh judgements were passed – and mostly justifiably so – on the actions and reactions of the British government. They were received with the characteristic response of a people who can face criticism and adversity with magnanimity and a solid respect for truth. This may have been made easier – and this is my second observation – by the fact that, since that sad and dramatic episode, relations between Egypt and the United Kingdom have significantly improved. There are still differences, sometimes wide and deep, concerning important matters such as the invasion of Iraq four years ago. Egypt opposed this, not out of any sympathy for the regime which had both harmed Arab solidarity and added to the problems faced by an Arab world trying to build a highway to progress, but from the point of view of international law as well as from a correct and accurate assessment of the negative repercussions of such an invasion. Despite these differences the general trend of the relationship has been positive and beneficial to both sides. Economic relations have improved significantly, both bilaterally and in the context of the Euro-Med connection. Trade has increased to the benefit of both countries, and

British investments seem to be on the right path, although they could and should do better. Political consultations are continuous and the two countries have been able to create a good atmosphere of mutual understanding by expanding the scope of agreements and allowing frank and open, though sometimes vigorous, discussion of points of disagreement. These are the characteristics of a healthy and sound relationship which looks to the future with optimism and is based on mutual and hopefully equal benefits. Details of the relationship will be given by other eminent contributors to this book. They reach the same conclusion; that while we are entitled to be pleased with what has been achieved, more progress must and should be made through constant dialogue and consultation. Beyond bilateral interactions, I believe that our relationship, based on mutual knowledge of each other through a long and sometimes tumultuous past can help bridge the gap between East and West. That gap unfortunately has widened over the last few years, for which both parties have at times been to blame. It poses serious threats to the stability, progress and prosperity of both East and West. The world – now a big village – cannot afford a clash of civilisations which could harm the future of humanity, and which is certainly avoidable if we all show the same good will towards working and living together as is displayed in this book.

Salutatory Remarks

I was delighted to be elected chair of the British Egyptian Society in April 2006. It has meant that I have been able to maintain the great interest in fostering British–Egyptian relations that I developed whilst working as a minister responsible for trade relations between the two countries and then as Minister of State for the Middle East. Without doubt the highlight of last year was *Fifty Years since Suez: from Conflict to Collaboration*, the joint forum we organised with the London Middle East Institute of the School of Oriental and African Studies. It commenced with a stunning reception in the Egyptian Sculpture Gallery at the British Museum. During the course of the forum we had forty-two speakers from the United States, Egypt and the United Kingdom. Keynote speakers were Professor Roger Owen from Harvard and Mr Ahmed Maher El Sayid, the former Egyptian Foreign Minister. We were determined from the outset that we should produce this book to make available some of the discussions to a wider audience. I would like to thank all those who have contributed.

As my good friend Ahmed Maher notes, the relationship between Egypt and Britain has passed through good and less good phases – as happens in any interaction between peoples. The two countries have over centuries developed their own distinct national identities and ways of organising their politics and societies. The United

Kingdom has longstanding global interests which in its imperial phase led it to attempt to impose itself on Egypt. Suez was the final act. In the twenty-first century Britain maintains its global interests by working in the closest collaboration with Egypt. Egypt, too, has global interests and thanks to the excellence of its diplomatic service it makes its voice felt throughout the world.

This book shows the depth and diversity of the relationship. Britain is the biggest non-Arab investor in Egypt. Over a million British tourists visited Egypt last year. The British Council presence in Egypt is one of the largest in the world. There is a British University presided over by Dr Mostafa El-Feki, who has contributed a typically lively chapter. There are thousands if not tens of thousands of Egyptians working in the UK and they make major contributions to many aspects of British life, not least in the field of medicine. British and Egyptian scholars collaborate in archaeological and historical research and in the conservation of historical monuments and artefacts. This book examines how British and Egyptian writers, artists and filmmakers inspire each other. Penelope Lively gives an extraordinarily evocative memoir of her childhood in Egypt. The cultural interchange has continued to grow despite the vicissitudes of politics. It is these activities that give substance to the relationship and build the numerous individual links that have brought about its recent flowering.

This gives me the greatest confidence in the future of our collaboration. Several writers in this book have noted that there is something unique about how Egypt and the UK regard each other compared with the interaction between Egypt and other countries. I have certainly felt this on my visits to Egypt and in meeting its people. There may be historical and cultural bonds but there is special warmth in the way that day-to-day contacts are conducted. This makes my chairmanship of the British Egyptian Society such a pleasure. This book and the forum on which it was based are the first steps in a dynamic series of events that we plan for the future. We want to involve more of the British and Egyptian people in the society and in doing so give the relationship even greater depth and breadth.

PART TWO

─────────

Political and Economic Relations

NOEL BREHONY

The Political and Economic Context of the British–Egyptian Relationship

At the height of the cold war and the emergence of the Non-Aligned Movement, President Nasser sought a new role for his country in what he described as the three circles – Arab, African and Islamic. He wanted to drive out of Egypt and then out of the three circles those vestiges of imperialist influence that appeared to threaten the security of his state. Like his successors, he was constrained by the problems caused by rapid population growth and limited resources. The number of Egyptians increased threefold from 1956 to reach 76 million in 2006. Egyptian governments have had to ensure that the country received a strong inflow of external funds, whether loans, grants or investment, to deal with this. Nasser proved adept at playing off the major powers against each other in an era of East–West competition. He was able to turn the latent nationalism and anti-imperialism in his three circles to Egypt's advantage, and yet still manage to attract funds needed for Egypt's internal development. Under Nasser Egypt became the leading force in the Arab world. He created a socialist state that promised its citizens a better life. However, his policies also led to repression at home, to a costly and unsuccessful intervention in Yemen and to the shattering defeat of 1967. For most of his presidency Britain and Egypt had poor and difficult relations.

President Sadat took Egypt in a different direction, as soon as he had consolidated his power. He expelled Soviet advisers in 1972 and repositioned Egypt as a potential ally of the United States. The 1973 war led to the 1979 peace treaty with Israel. The USA became Egypt's major source of political, military and economic support. Sadat's policies led to the isolation of Egypt in the Arab world and put an end to its claims to the leadership of Arab nationalism. His opening of the economy, the Infitah, paved the way for greater Western involvement and was the first step in dismantling the socialist state. (This process continues: in March 2007 Egypt finally removed much of the socialist rhetoric from its constitution.) The UK played a role in helping consolidate the peace process. In 1981 President Sadat even visited the British Embassy to meet the Duke of Edinburgh and see the room in which one of the unequal treaties of the colonial past was signed.

President Mubarak has continued along the same path, but has been more successful in balancing the conflicting pressures. The relationship with Washington has remained crucial. US civil and military assistance has flowed into Egypt. Cairo has supported American policies in the region, at least where these were seen in Egyptian eyes to foster stability. The relationship with Israel has remained intact. Egypt has successfully re-established its relations with the rest of the Arab world even though it was one of the first Arab states to join the US-led coalition in 1990–1 to throw Iraqi troops out of Kuwait. Whilst the relationship with the US has been fundamental, President Mubarak has sought to build up links with other powers that can both bolster and provide potential substitutes for the central relationship with Washington. Within these efforts, Western Europe has been a major target and the UK receives special attention because it is close to the US whilst being influential in the EU.

The domestic scene

The 1952 revolution started as a military coup against a monarchical system that had lost its legitimacy even before the disastrous war of 1948. The armed forces were central to the regime at the outset. All the presidents since 1952 have come from the army or air force. In that period Egypt fought the wars of 1967 and 1973 against Israel, and the support of the military leadership was crucial in helping President Sadat to negotiate the 1979 peace treaty with Israel and in holding Egypt to that peace in subsequent years. In the last twenty years or so the political influence of the armed forces has diminished as civil institutions developed, but behind the scenes the army's function remains that of safeguarding the regime.

President Mubarak was elected in the aftermath of the assassination by Islamists of President Anwar Sadat on 6 October 1981. Political Islam in both its moderate and extreme forms had taken root in the 1970s, in part because President Sadat needed it to counter the power of the left within the system. He had faced an early crisis in his presidency when his authority was challenged from the left in what he called 'the centres of power'. President Mubarak quickly imposed a State of Emergency, which remains in force today pending its anticipated replacement by new anti-terror laws. In the 1980s and 1990s Egypt had to deal with terrorism from the Islamic Jihad and the Gama'at Islamiya, culminating in the killing of over sixty tourists in Luxor in 1997. The threat from those organisations has receded, but there were terrorist attacks in Sinai in 2004, 2005 and 2006 in which foreign tourists and Egyptians died. The Egyptian government has insisted that the State of Emergency or its equivalent should stay in force to fight terrorism. Many Egyptians and foreign governments and NGOs argue that anti-terrorist measures are misused to curb freedoms and limit the opportunities for non-violent opposition and protest. The government says that the new anti-terror law will address these concerns.

Since the early days of the revolution the Egyptian constitution has conferred on the president widespread executive power. Though the constitution has been amended several times – most recently in 2007 – there has been virtually no reduction in the power of the presidency. Article 141 of the constitution states 'The President of the Republic shall appoint the Prime Minister, his deputies, the Ministers and their deputies and relieve them of their post'. The president appoints senior figures in the military and civil service, and provincial governors. Some ministers report directly to the president (for example defence, interior and foreign affairs) rather than to the prime minister, whose main responsibilities are for the economy, internal administration and delivery of services. The cabinet is responsible to the president, and presidential advisers can have more influence than ministers, especially in defence and security.

President Mubarak, who was born in 1928, was re-elected in 2005 to a fifth term. This expires in 2011. Unlike his predecessors he has never appointed a vice-president. The question of succession dominates Egyptian politics at present, as might be expected given the powers of the office. The widely-held belief that his son Gamal will succeed is regularly denied by the President and his family.

There are two houses of parliament. The People's Assembly currently has 454 elected members, plus ten appointed by the president (normally to ensure that women and Christian minorities are given some representation). Constitutionally it has considerable powers, though in practice the executive initiates legislation, and defence and security matters are off limits, while budgetary supervision is minimal. The constitution gives it the power to overturn decisions of the president by a majority of two thirds but all parliaments have been dominated by a government party that itself has controlled more than two thirds of the assembly. The constitution assigns the upper house, the Shoura Assembly, a special role in safeguarding the principles of the revolution. Two thirds of its members are elected and one third selected by the president.

Elections for the People's Assembly take place every five years (the last was in late 2005) and, like elections for the upper house and local councils, are contested by political parties and often a large number of independents. The National Democratic Party has had an overwhelming majority in all these bodies. Turnout is usually very low. The electoral process is criticised inside and outside Egypt as being less than fair to the opposition.

From the outset the regime created a political movement to encompass the ideas of the revolution and to mobilise and organise support for the regime and its policies. The early versions – the Liberation Rally (1952–6), the National Union (1956–62) and the Arab Socialist Union (1962–76) – operated in a system that did not tolerate opposition parties. President Sadat began a process of liberalisation in 1976 that has been continued by President Mubarak. The core of the Arab Socialist Union developed into the National Democratic Party, which has branches throughout the country and can use its powers of organisation, its patronage and the official media to overwhelm the opposition. In the last few years a younger leadership, based around the Policies Committee of the NDP, has sought to make the NDP function as a conventional political party, taking advice from the British Labour Party among others. Policy ideas, particularly on economic and social affairs, are increasingly developed within the Policies Committee and then taken to government. The key figure in the Policies Committee is Gamal Mubarak, and a number of its most influential members are now in the cabinet – including the current prime minister and the main economic team. However, the NDP, headed by President Mubarak, remains a party of the regime.

When President Sadat dissolved the ASU he created from it, in addition to the NDP, two other parties: the National Rally for Unity and Progress (known as the Tagammu) and the Liberal Party (al-Ahrar), both then led by Nasser's Free Officers. They were quickly joined by the Socialist Labour Party and the New Wafd Party – a descendant of the party that had dominated Egyptian politics before the revolution. These parties have formed since then the main opposition groups and they have all achieved some representation in parliament. They have been joined in recent years by others so that now there are twenty-three political parties. New parties have to apply for registration from the People's Parties Committee, which is chaired by the speaker of the Shoura Assembly, who is also a key figure in the NDP. There is a judicial appeal process that rejected parties can use.

The overwhelming presence of the NDP and its links to the regime and local elites restricts the space available to others. The opposition parties themselves have limited appeal and their effectiveness has been reduced by often bitter internal divisions over policies and personalities. The electoral system, especially for local councils, disadvantages the opposition. In the words of the International Crisis Group, 'Regardless of the intentions of their leaders and members, they cannot be said to constitute serious opposition forces'.[1]

The main challenge in recent years has come from the Muslim Brotherhood. This group is not recognised by the government either as a political party or a social organisation. It exists outside the law, but is tolerated. It has a known leadership, is organised on a national basis, and is good at providing, at a local level, the sort of social support services that government cannot always deliver. It is a powerful political force, as its performance in the parliamentary elections of December 2005 demonstrated: it won eighty-eight seats despite putting up a limited number of candidates and facing restrictions as well as partial supervision of elections. The changes to the constitution approved in March 2007 will ban political parties based on religion and are expected to be followed by legislation that will make it more difficult for independents to contest future elections. These measures are likely to reduce the presence of the Muslim Brotherhood in national and local assemblies. It is uncertain how the Brotherhood will respond. The most hopeful sign is that several of its leaders, like their equivalents in other Arab countries, are seeking to develop coherent policies to deal with the main political issues.

The influence of the Muslim Brotherhood is not balanced by a secular opposition movement, as the weakness of the political parties shows. A popular movement called the Egyptian Movement for Change (Kifaya) emerged in the run-up to the September 2005 presidential elections, but it has failed to retain its initial momentum. Some observers have noted a lack of political interest in Egypt among the masses, so that politics is confined to the small elite.

Hugh Roberts, in his chapter, discusses the implications for both Egypt and the UK of the current strength of the Muslim Brotherhood. His views would be contested by many in Egypt. There is substantial support for his argument that the Egyptian regime should give more power and accountability to parliament. Whilst this is clearly a desirable end in itself, Dr Roberts argues that it would help to engage the Brotherhood in political debate and encourage the established parties, including the NDP, to counter the Brotherhood's arguments in an open political process. It would provide a potent stimulus to political life in Egypt. However, there is still distrust in Egypt of the Brotherhood's real commitment to democratic change and a fear that once it had attained power through the ballot box it would not be prepared to relinquish it. There is also support for the banning of political parties based on Islam in a country where there are strong secular traditions within parts of the elite and a substantial Coptic minority. Dr Roberts also discusses how Britain should deal with the emergence of the Brotherhood in Egypt and other countries. There is a need within the UK to foster a greater understanding of political Islam and to find a way of engaging with it in a form that is acceptable to governments and people in both the UK and Egypt.

Civil society

Political party behaviour needs to be set against the background of the lively media and civil society. Though the role of the state is prominent in all forms of media, there is an opposition and an independent press. There has been a long tradition of active civil society in Egypt, as shown by the role in the twentieth century of the trade unions and professional syndicates. Since the revolution, the trade unions have become virtually part of the state and are no longer directly involved in political work. The professional syndicates expanded under the revolution and became politicised under Sadat. In the 1980s and 1990s there were often fiercely-fought contests for control of the syndicates by the opposition parties and the Muslim Brotherhood. In recent years, as a result of new restrictive legislation, they have become less controversial and less effective. There has been a proliferation of human rights groups and NGOs in recent years and the Egyptian Human Rights Organisation, created by the government and chaired by Butrous Butrous Ghali, has established itself as a credible organisation locally and internationally.

Economic and social factors

Heba Handoussa's chapter looks at the social problems that Egypt faces today. The main thrust of her argument, which the government has accepted, is that Egypt needs a new social charter to deal with poverty. She considers that Egypt must utilise its foreign policy to alleviate poverty and enhance human development. Successive Egyptian presidents have struggled to find the resources to tackle these immense problems. Many of the current generation of leaders had seared into their minds the bread riots of 1977. Egypt's population has nearly doubled during President Mubarak's term of office. Investment is needed to generate at least 750,000 new jobs every year in a country where half the population is under twenty-five. The long-term stability of Egypt depends on the success of the government in meeting these demands.

Fiona Moffitt assesses the performance of the current Egyptian government, whose competence to manage the economy is widely acknowledged. Led by businessmen and others with a background in international finance and private sector companies, the Ahmad Nazif government has implemented extensive reforms. This process must continue if Egypt is to raise the living standards of its people whilst at the same time gradually removing the subsidies that help keep families above the breadline. As the Minister of Finance said in London in March 2007, it is essential to ensure that the poor receive some of the fruits of reform if they are to continue to support the long-term and at times painful process involved.[2] David Lubin's chapter explores the critical importance of foreign exchange reserves in giving the Egyptian government the confidence to press forward with difficult and challenging reforms.

The reform process still has a long way to go, as the Egyptian government itself acknowledges. The educational system, once the best in the Arab world, has fallen behind as institutions have been forced to cope with the huge numbers passing through the system. There are issues linked to commercial dispute resolution and the transparency of decision-making that still need to be tackled. The state is still too large and intrusive. Egypt, nevertheless, has substantial assets. It has emerged as a leading supplier of gas to the world market and particularly to Europe. There has been a major inflow of new investment in recent years, much of it now going to sectors other than oil and gas.

The Egyptian government has shown great skill in managing the delicate balancing act of meeting the demands of the International Monetary Fund and international donors. It must increase the living standards of the poor without increasing living costs, whilst dismantling the socialist state created by Nasser. One major change in recent years has been the re-emergence of the Egyptian private sector. Not only are Egyptian businessmen investing in Egypt, but some, such as Neguib Sawaris, are now operating on the world stage.

Egypt's foreign policy

Egypt's relations with the UK must be seen within the broader context of Egyptian foreign policy. Geography and history help determine its policies. The Suez attack of 1956 was merely the last of many attempts by external powers to control Egypt, the land bridge between the Mediterranean and the Indian Ocean. Egypt, with its long history and large population, has historically sought to dominate its regional environment to neutralise threats that might arise from within it. It is dependent on the Nile waters, so must take a close interest in developments in Sudan and the east African headwaters of the river.[3] More recently, rapid population growth and limited resources mean that it must seek external support for economic development. As noted above, Egypt has adopted different policies under its previous three presidents to manage its external relations.

The daily preoccupation of the Egyptian government is with the country's regional problems. The core issue is management of the relationship with Israel to further the peace process that is so essential for long-term regional security. Cairo is deeply concerned about the future of Iraq, Iranian ambitions and the problems that constantly arise in the region, such as those of Darfur and Lebanon. Beyond this, Egypt's weight in the Muslim world and in international fora give it a significant interest in and influence on how the world deals with major issues of the day, from weapons of mass destruction (as Mohammed Shaker's chapter describes) to terrorism and the protection of the world environment.

The relationship with the United States is paramount. US support is essential to Egypt's strategic, security and economic objectives. It will remain central, but it is an uncomfortable relationship at times. There are disagreements over US policies on Palestine, Iraq and democracy promotion. The Egyptian regime understands the need for the close relationship with Washington, but public opinion does not. It is thus in Egypt's interests to build up relations with others. When Nasser spoke of three circles he might have added a fourth – Europe and the Mediterranean – if they had not at that time been a source of threat rather than friendship. Today Egypt has an association agreement with the EU and excellent relations with the major European states. There have been recent visits by the heads of state of Russia and China as Egypt extends the field of international cooperation. The effectiveness of Egypt's foreign policy has been greatly enhanced by what is widely acknowledged to be one of its best assets: the quality of its diplomatic service.

The British–Egyptian relationship

Britain and Egypt are probably closer to each other today than at any time in the last hundred years. Mostafa El-Feki describes Suez as the last on a list of traumatic events that began with the British occupation in 1888. Roger Owen points out that Britain and Egypt recovered from the Suez attack remarkably quickly. Both show that Britain has abandoned its imperial pretensions as a world power and Egypt its attempts to impose itself on the Arab world. Ahmed El-Mokadem sees the UK as a 'great power' that has retained a global presence and influence and significant interests in the Middle East. He sees Egypt as a 'pivotal' state that can exercise great influence in the Middle East, Africa and the Islamic world. Britain and Egypt work closely with the United States, the sole superpower, on the major issues of the day.

Both Professor Ali E. Hillal Dessouki and Mostafa El-Feki argue that Britain should be more, not less, active in dealing with the issue that most affects Egypt: the Arab–Israeli peace process. They stress that Britain should have a special role because of the strong bonds between Cairo and London and also because of Britain's special interest in and understanding of the Middle East. They, and others, write of a shared understanding and sympathy for each other that are not so evident in Egypt's relations with the USA and France. Ahmed Maher El Sayid speaks of the role that Cairo and London can play in reducing the gap in understanding between the East and the West.

These writers also draw attention to difficulties. There are some international issues on which the two countries can work together, and others on which they take opposing stands. The US-led war against Iraq in 1991 was an example of the former and the attack on Iraq in 2003 of the latter. There can be problems when one country seeks to bring about a change of policy in the other's domestic affairs. Egypt, for example, objected to the presence in the UK in the 1980s and 1990s of Egyptian Islamic extremists, whom it regarded as posing a threat to Egyptian security. This was a view shared by others at the time who regarded the UK capital as 'Londonistan'. The UK at the time was not willing to change its laws, although later took a different stand.

The Foreign and Commonwealth Office lists on its website its major international priorities.[4] Those relevant to Egypt are:

1. Making the world safer from global terrorism and weapons of mass destruction;
2. Reducing the harm to the UK from international crime, including drug trafficking, people smuggling and money laundering;
3. Preventing and resolving conflict through a strong international system;
4. Building an effective and globally competitive EU in a secure neighbourhood;
5. Supporting the UK economy and business through an open and expanding global economy, science and innovation and secure energy supplies;
6. Achieving climate security by promoting a faster transition to a sustainable, low carbon global economy;
7. Promoting sustainable development and poverty reduction underpinned by human rights, democracy, good governance and protection of the environment;
8. Managing migration and combating illegal immigration.

The first two of these are clearly shared by both governments. Mohammed Shaker, ambassador to London for seven years and a leading expert on the international aspects of dealing with nuclear proliferation, looks at how the two countries have cooperated in seeking to ban weapons of mass destruction. They may have slightly different approaches, with Egypt focusing on the region and the UK on the global picture, but the general objectives are shared and close cooperation has occurred.

Egypt, like the UK, has experienced major terrorist attacks from Islamic extremists in recent years. Egypt has dealt with the problem through security measures and by seeking to isolate extremists by involving religious leaders in campaigns of education, an approach the UK is considering. The aim is to foster moderate Islam and engage leaders of the Islamic communities in the process. Mostafa El-Feki highlights the need for the Ulama in al-Azhar to learn English and other foreign languages so that al-Azhar can contribute more effectively to efforts in the UK and elsewhere to counter terrorism. Both countries understand they must also deal with the causes of extremism and terrorism, whether they are based on opposition to the foreign policies of a government, or on poverty, unemployment and a feeling of alienation. The UK and Egypt can learn from each other with a very strong emphasis on the need for positive, sustained action to prevent terrorism, rather than having to deal with its consequences.

The two countries can agree on the desirability of the other objectives on the UK's list, includingthe implication that the UK may support changes in Egyptian domestic policies. London has in fact joined with many other outside actors in helping to persuade Egypt of the need for faster economic reform. There has been a strong lobby for such reform in Egypt since the Sadat era but there are also major forces that have viewed the UK's efforts as interference. Today such resistance has all but vanished.

The UK, along with other governments, has also expressed unhappiness at the pace and depth of political reform, at the handling of parliamentary elections and at the fact that Ayman Nour, head of the al-Ghad Party who stood against President Mubarak in the 2005 elections, was later tried and sentenced. Britain prefers to make its criticisms in private directly to Egyptian ministers and officials on these political matters. It did not follow the path of Washington when the US government launched its Broader Middle East Initiative, aimed at bringing greater democracy to the Middle East, though it committed itself to the agenda agreed at the G8 Sea Island Summit of 2004. The UK has opted for more subtle methods of persuasion. Professor Mustapha Kamel al-Sayyid describes some of these, but he concludes they are unlikely to work and may be seen as mere gestures. The UK position is that it does not try to impose its views, but works at a practical level to help build institutions and organisations, including NGOs, that will contribute to the development of democracy and human rights. Its support may take the form of helping to develop the judiciary, the way that elections are managed and the empowerment of women and other citizens so they may participate in the political process. But there are limits to what a foreign government can do and London appears to recognise that reality.

The future

The British–Egyptian relationship has been remarkably enduring and successful, quickly recovering from crises and refocusing on shared interests, values and experience, and mutual admiration, a mixture – as Dr El-Feki points out – of love and hate. The chapters in this book illustrate the range and diversity of the relationship. The writers all seem confident that the relationship will flourish, despite concerns about potential disagreements over foreign and domestic policies. They also agree that the essential factors will not change. Egypt's geographical position and its shape, the squeezing of so many people into the Nile Valley and Delta, and limited resources will help determine the major strands of its policies. The United States will remain the most important strategic ally of both Britain and Egypt. Britain will need to understand the concerns and constraints on Egypt in responding to the regional, international and economic challenges it faces. Egypt will need to understand that foreign policy in countries like Britain must take account of the changing values within British society. The two share many interests and objectives and there is no reason to doubt that the extraordinary and diverse nature of the relationship examined in this book will continue. This book illustrates the quality and frankness of the dialogue between Britain and Egypt, providing a solid foundation for the next fifty years, when emerging issues like climate change will profoundly affect both countries and the world.

Notes

1. International Crisis Group, *Reforming Egypt: In Search of a Strategy*, Middle East/North Africa Report, no. 46, 4 October 2005.
2. Yousef Butrous Ghali speaking at 'Egypt: The Investors Conference', organised by Euromoney, London, 21 March 2007.
3. Raymond Hinnebusch, *The Foreign Policy of Egypt in the Foreign Policies of the Middle East States*, in Raymond Hinnebusch and Anoushiravan Ehteshami, eds, London: Lynne Rienner, 2002.
4. http://www.fco.gov.uk/servlet/Front?pagename=OpenMarket/Xcelerate/ShowPage&c=Page&cid=1007029394997.

ROGER OWEN

Suez 1956: Lessons We Thought We Had Learned and the Lessons Now

The Suez Crisis of October 1956 was one of those seminal twentieth century events that connected the emerging cold war with the early period of post-colonial independence. Beginning as a dispute between the Egyptian government, on the one hand, and Britain and France on the other, its impact spread rapidly to involve the United States, the Soviet Union, the United Nations and most of the states in the Middle East, North Africa and the developing world. It was also closely connected with Russia's bloody suppression of the Hungarian uprising against Soviet domination in Budapest during the same month, an event which many now argue might well not have taken place if the United States and two of its major European allies had not been otherwise occupied in either promoting, or trying to prevent, the tripartite Anglo-French and Israeli attack on the Suez Canal.[1]

On a more personal note, for many Britons of my generation the Suez Crisis of 1956 is still remembered as one of the most visceral political experiences of our young lives. Passions ran high, angry demonstrations took place, friendships were broken and, for those of us whose high ideals were still largely untarnished, it was our first encounter with the cynicism of great power politics, the first major event which suggested that, in spite of the creation of the United Nations and a growing movement towards post-colonial independence, the tide of world history was still capable of moving quite strongly in the wrong direction.

What shocked us most was the discovery of the Eden government's obvious collusion with Israel to try to hoodwink the Security Council and to create a specious pretext for war in late October. Yet few of us were able to take much comfort from Britain's humiliating withdrawal. Nor did we get any great satisfaction from the view, widely canvassed at the time, that Suez marked the last attempt at imperial re-conquest, even though, at least as far as the Middle East was concerned, it proved to be largely true, with no significant British military interventions in the second great Middle Eastern crisis set off by the union between Egypt and Syria in February 1958, followed by the scuttle from Aden in 1967, and the withdrawal of all British forces from the Gulf a few years later.

I also had my own personal reasons for being alarmed as well as upset. I had visited Egypt for the first time in June 1956, only a month before the start of the crisis, when the withdrawal of the last British troops from the Canal Zone, celebrated then and now as 'Evacuation Day', seemed to promise a new era of more friendly Anglo-Egyptian relations. Furthermore I had just finished my national service and, for a while, faced the possibility of being recalled to the army for service in Egypt, a recall I felt strongly I would have to oppose. Looking back on it, I now realise that it was also my peripheral involvement in the crisis that first prompted the interest in Anglo-Egyptian relations that was one of the primary reasons for my choosing a career in Middle East studies.

In what follows, I will draw on my own experience to try to sketch out, first, the lessons concerning the Suez Crisis that were drawn at the time and, then, how I think we might look at the crisis some fifty years later. I will conclude with some thoughts as to how the crisis itself fits into the long history of Anglo-Egyptian relations.

Lessons of the Suez Crisis drawn at the time

As far as both Britain and France were concerned the major lessons drawn from the Suez Crisis became clear within a very short period of time. For Harold Macmillan, who succeeded Anthony Eden as prime minister in January 1957, and his cabinet, the most pressing issue was how to re-establish a close relationship with the United States, something Macmillan was able to achieve within a few months. They were also of the strong opinion that Britain should never again endanger this relationship by embarking on a major military adventure without American support, a position to which succeeding governments have adhered up to the present day.

The French, on the other hand, drew quite the opposite conclusion, which was that they should reduce their dependence on the United States by developing their own independent nuclear deterrent, to be delivered by their own *force de frappe*, a policy strongly advocated by President de Gaulle on his return to power in 1958 and underlined by the French decision to withdraw from the integrated command structure of the North Atlantic Treaty Organisation (NATO) in 1959. France's turn away from its war-time alliance with the Anglo-Saxon powers was then completed by the first steps to construct an alternative alliance system in Europe in association with the Federal Republic of (West) Germany.

Nevertheless, for both Britain and France, and whether with the United States or against it, their proven inability to influence the Middle East by force had a knock-on effect in forcing them to recognise the rising power of local, anti-colonial nationalisms. This was demonstrated almost at once by Britain's low-key role in the Middle Eastern crisis of 1958.[2] Apart from providing a show of support for the beleaguered King Hussein of Jordan by sending some parachute troops to guard Amman airport, Britain allowed the United States to play the major Western role in defusing the threat thought to be posed to Lebanese independence by union between Egypt and Syria. Britain then made no move to try to overturn the revolutionary regime of Brigadier Qasim after its overthrow of the pro-British government in Baghdad in July of the same year. As for the French, although remaining deeply suspicious of President Nasser's support for the revolt against them in Algeria, President de Gaulle was prescient enough to see the writing on the wall and to move towards a rapid dismantling of the French position not only in Algeria itself but in the rest of its colonial empire as well.

If the brief invasion of Egypt in November 1956 was a chastening lesson in the decline in their world power for the British and the French, it had exactly the opposite effect for Egypt, allowing President Nasser to proclaim a famous victory against imperialism, to seize leadership of the Arab nationalist movement, and to begin that process of state-led industrial development which lasted for a good ten years before being brought to a sudden end by the equally sudden military defeat at the hands of the Israelis in June 1967.

As for the Israelis themselves, in spite of being forced to withdraw, prematurely from their point of view, from the Sinai peninsula which they had captured after the withdrawal of Egyptian troops once the British and the French had landed in Port Said, they achieved the major part of their objective, the destruction of the bulk of the new weaponry obtained by Egypt from the Soviet Union under the so-called 'Czech' arms deal of February 1955. Nevertheless, given the fact of Egypt's subsequent re-equipment with newer and better Soviet equipment after 1956, they began to arm themselves for a second round, taking advantage of their close association with France forged during the Suez war to purchase not only advanced tanks and planes but also help with the technology which allowed them to begin to produce nuclear weapons in the early 1960s.[3]

The immediate impact of the crisis on the Soviet and American governments is less clear, at least in some of its most important aspects. What was relatively well-understood at the time was its effect of bringing the Middle East further into the cold war, with the Russians emerging as the major military and economic supporters of Egypt and the Americans more heavily engaged in trying both to protect their local allies through the encouragements contained in the Eisenhower Doctrine proclaimed in 1957, and to build up Saudi Arabia as an Islamic anti-communist rival to the Egyptians.

What could not be known at the time by the general public, however, were the lessons drawn by governments, not just from the Egyptian crisis itself, but also from its close association with the anti-Soviet revolt in Hungary, especially its subsequent suppression by Soviet tanks during exactly the same days in October and November 1956. According to recently-revealed notes of the meetings of the Presidium, the Communist Party's top decision-making body, the new Russian leadership under Nikita Khrushchev saw these twin crises as particular threats both to its hegemony over Eastern Europe and to its new opening to the post-colonial world exemplified above all by its close ties with Egypt. Hence, it was the prospect of an Anglo-French overthrow of the Nasser regime as a result of the attack begun on 31 October that was enough to convince Khrushchev and his colleagues to change from their previous day's policy of non-intervention to one of violent repression of the revolt in Budapest that very same day.[4]

Russian efforts to demonstrate their support for Egypt by threatening to rain nuclear rockets on London and Paris, although known to be an empty threat even at the time, also had the somewhat paradoxical effect of alarming American officials in Washington to such an extent that they and their successors under President John F. Kennedy were adamant in their determination to prevent the establishment of Russian rocket-launching pads in Cuba during the missile crisis of late 1962.[5]

Lessons from the Suez Crisis now

Fifty years is a long time even in a nation's life and perhaps it is not surprising that so few young people, Egyptian as well as British and French, have even heard of the Suez Crisis, which had such an influence on their grandparents' world and on my own life.[6] It is not just that the world itself has changed so much, even from the end of the cold war, but that it has changed in such a way that many of the lessons we once thought had been learned for ever have now to be learned all over again, most notably, as far as Tony Blair's British government is concerned, those involving the problems awaiting anyone who feels compelled to invade, to occupy and to effect a change of regime in a third world country like Iraq in the face of world opinion.

By the same token, however, we can now see many things about the past much more clearly. As a result of the lessons learned from, for example, the invasion of Iraq, we know, or think we know, much more about the political obsessions which lead certain leaders to mislead their fellow nationals, about the role played by false historical analogy and the creation of Hitler-like international bogeymen – now a Gamal Abdel Nasser, now a Saddam Hussein – about political and military incompetence, and about the more general problems posed by attempts to impose an unwelcome change of regime. Take the case of Sir Anthony Eden. Although there are still some who continue to think, as many also did in 1956, that Eden had gone 'mad' as the result of a botched medical operation, this was not how he saw himself at the time, nor how we should now.[7] Too many leaders since those days have wanted to present a tough image, too many have persuaded themselves that there was 'no other way', for us to be able to ignore the contemporary existence of much the same type of compulsive behaviour exhibited by a variety of present-day political actors on the international stage.

The fifty years since 1956 have reinforced other lessons as well. It is now even more clear than it was then that the business of getting democracies into overseas wars which may necessitate the expenditure of blood, of treasure and, quite possibly, of a country's worldwide reputation requires the whole operation to be presented in a particular light, generally as a battle between good and an evil which can be confronted in no other way but by force. It is also clear how such a presentation requires a careful manipulation of the evidence, as well as a sometimes deliberate, sometimes unthinking ignorance of the real problems ahead, whether in terms of local resistance or international condemnation. Just as Anthony Eden shut almost all the senior members of the British Foreign Office out of his decision-making process, much the same happened with the State Department during President Bush's road to war in 2002–3.

What we do not know, and cannot know, because the Anglo-French military presence in Egypt was so short, is how many of these particular chickens might have come home to roost if the occupation had taken its hoped-for course; that is, the replacement of President Nasser's regime by one consisting of ancien régime politicians favourably disposed to the interests of the invaders. We can suppose, on the basis of what was later to happen in Iraq, that there would have been a very high level of confusion, of infighting between the British and French military and the political officers, of half-heartedness and shame on the part of many of those officials sent as midwives to the new order. We can also suppose, partly on the basis of what happened in southern Iraq in 2004, that, as a result of initial Egyptian resistance like that begun by armed members of the population of Port Said, there would have been a strong British disposition to hand over civil power as quickly as possible to any group that was able to legitimise itself in the first provincial and local elections, and then to withdraw its soldiers to the comparative safety of well-defended camps. These are all interesting historical hypotheses of the 'what if?' variety. But, of course, we cannot be sure.

What else might we do if we were to write the history of the Anglo-French and Israeli attack based on present concerns rather than by making an attempt to reconstruct the world exactly as it was then? In the interests of brevity let me suggest just a few avenues to explore: one looking from the point of view of the British invaders; a second from that of the country they invaded and the regime they tried to overthrow. As far as the former is concerned, I will do this by raising some of the questions prompted by our contemporary interest in the role of prior knowledge, or lack of it, of occupied Iraqi society; others by the equally conspicuous demonstrations of military and political incompetence; others again by related problems of why so much of what took place in Iraq after the invasion seemed so familiar, even if the particulars often seemed strange. Concerning the apparent victors, I will pose the very large historical question of what, in the long run, Egypt can be supposed to have gained.

Britain was in whole or partial occupation of Egypt for over seventy years, while its Canal Zone garrison had left the country only a few months before the autumn invasion. And yet, when coming to plan for its reoccupation in the summer and early autumn of 1956 the military made a number of crucial mistakes based, it would appear, on lessons wrongly learned from the experience of only a few years before. Of these, far and away the most significant was the over-importance attached to the fierce opposition put up by Egyptian urban guerillas against British troops in the Canal Zone fighting in 1951 and 1952, a memory which led the General Staff to demand an 'overwhelming' invasion force of 80,000 men, something which it took until September 1956 to assemble, allowing plenty of time for world opinion to unite in protest.[8]

The General Staff was almost equally remiss in choosing Port Said, a virtual island, as a landing ground once Alexandria, the invasion force's initial target, was ruled out on the grounds of the large amount of civilian casualties which its initial bombardment would entail. As Michael Thornhill points out, had the occupation lasted longer and the Egyptian army managed a counter-attack to cut the two causeways that connected the city to the rest of Egypt to the south and west, the British and French troops would quite easily have been bottled up.[9]

Meanwhile, as far as Britain's civilian leadership was concerned, Anthony Eden believed that the invaders would have no difficulty in finding Egyptians to form an alternative government, an idea based less on first-hand knowledge, or on any realistic sense of the pressures which such a quisling administration must certainly have faced, than on the simplistic assumption that the members of the country's ancien régime must have hated the Nasser regime as much as he did. Much the same set of colonialist assumptions underlay his belief that Egypt had no pilots capable of steering large ships through the canal once he had engineered the resignation of most of the company's foreign employees.

Given what we now know about Iraq, it is clear that what once seemed the false or unreasonable assumptions of a bygone age must have origins in something more persistent and well-structured than the particular agendas of individual statesmen or the particular blindness of this or that military planner. It has been said, for example, that when meeting a number of British Middle East experts just before the invasion of Iraq in late 2002, neither Tony Blair nor his foreign secretary, Jack Straw, showed much interest in either the country or the society they planned to attack.[10] Part of the explanation for this can be ascribed to the kind of deliberate ignorance so much in evidence in Washington at the same time, an ignorance that allowed the terra incognita of Iraq to be filled in with the broad brushstrokes of totalitarianism, religion and of a brutalised and undifferentiated society united in its yearning to be free. But it is also suggestive of what might be seen as a type of the still-prevalent negative racism by which Europeans tend to view non-European societies as too different and too unimportant to be worthy of serious study.

It is also worth asking what a better understanding of Iraqi society might have yielded, should the British and American leaders have thought it helpful to know more. If the lessons of earlier military invasions are anything to go by, for example the British occupations of Egypt in 1882 and lower Iraq in 1914, the main preoccupation of an invader's leaders is gathering intelligence of a fairly basic type; that is to say, an attempt to work out in advance which sections of the occupied population are likely to be hostile, which friendly and which trustworthy enough to be recruited for employment in a new regime.[11] This involves, in turn, a division of society into some fairly simple components, often based on such simple divisions as tribal persons, peasant agriculturalists and town dwellers, with the latter perhaps split by religion or a crude version of class.

No doubt Anthony Eden and his close advisers went in for something of the same kind. Although it also seems reasonable to assume that, in the end, their thinking was based almost exclusively on just two large assumptions: first, that the bulk of the population was hostile to Nasser's dictatorial ways, and second, that there were also enough members of the old monarchical political and business elite whose interests would have led them to form a type of alternative government once Nasser himself had been killed or chased away. Just what kind of 'knowledge' this constitutes remains an open question. It is certainly a convenient way of avoiding having to face up to questions about the type of national or patriotic feeling that unites populations rather than divides them. And so it seems to bear little relation to what most Egyptians actually felt, and to how most Egyptians behaved, when their country came under foreign attack.

Another line of inquiry is suggested by the notion of military occupation itself. Given its importance in nineteenth-twentieth-century imperial history it is still extraordinary small a role it plays in the study of colonialism, with much more interest shown in the creation of new 'native' armies than in the presence of the British, French or other troops which underpinned the whole project in the first place.[12] Occupations, we have now learned, are usually very messy operations, over which the civil and military authorities exercise an uneasy cooperation, in which jurisdictional and other conflicts in the metropolis are later replayed in the equivalent of the 'green zone' of the occupied capital, and in which there is an unresolvable tension between the high ideals with which the whole affair is justified before world opinion and the more grubby events on the ground. Not only do such conditions stoke up almost inevitable local opposition, but they are also productive of a high degree of confusion, muddle and administrative incompetence which, though often hidden by history, has been painfully obvious in Iraq since the occupation began.

In such circumstances, it would seem, it would be better to take such conditions as the norm, in 1956 just as much as the present day. Try as any set of leaders might to exercise a centralised leadership over the whole enterprise, the interests involved, not to speak of the aims to be pursued, are just too many and various to be reconciled under any one plan. Meanwhile, it is of the essence of such enterprises that the transition from the military imperatives underlying invasion to the more civilian and political ones involving occupation will be a messy business, as will the constant need to tailor the whole process either to make it more palatable or to meet actual or anticipated criticism from domestic or world opinion. Hence, just as the focus for the invasion of Egypt in 1956 was switched from Alexandria to Port Said halfway through for fear of its bloody impact on those Egyptians who might, otherwise, have been willing to support a change of regime, so President Bush suddenly vetoed Donald Rumsfeld's plan to install a puppet regime of Iraqi exiles on the grounds that this was contrary to his professed aim of replacing Saddam Hussein by a working, Western-style democracy.[13] Often what looks like sheer incompetence can be better explained by the conflicting interests and administrative logics created within complex modern political, administrative and military organisations.

Two other caveats can be entered here. First, although the Anglo-French invasion force was too large to be assembled quickly, if we remember the shortage of troops faced by the Americans in Baghdad in 2003, it might, if the invasion had succeeded, have been just what was required to occupy a restive country. Second, given the times in which the Suez invasion took place, regime change looked in some ways a much easier enterprise that it does now. Eden could certainly take heart from the successful overthrow of the Mossadeq government in Iran only three years before, with which he was closely associated, as well as from the successful British Abdin Palace coup, which forced King Farouk to return a cowed Wafd government to power in Egypt in 1942, also on his watch. The question then becomes, were these the right precedents to chose? In the event, and had the operation gone according to plan, Saad Zaghlul's successful call to boycott the Milner Mission's visit to Cairo in 1919–20 might have been a better guide to what would almost certainly have been a concerted effort by Egyptians of all types to prevent any collaboration with the new British puppet regime.

Turning now to the Egyptian side of the story, historians are still none the wiser about many of the military aspects of the Suez story than people were at the time. This is largely because none of the relevant archives are open in spite of the country's putative fifty-year rule. Hence, while almost everything can now be known about even the Soviet side of the story from newly-available records, the people of Egypt are left in a position in which, as Professor Khaled Fahmy has ruefully noted, they can learn more in their own archives about their army's two great military victories against the Ottoman army in the 1830s than they can about the famous battle of Port Said in 1956.[14] Hence, too, one of President Nasser's surviving confidants, Mohamed Hassanein Heikal, can still assert that Suez represented not just a political victory but also a famous military victory, without anyone else having the documentary evidence to contradict him.[15]

Putting together what we do know, it would seem likely that, at the time, President Nasser and his regime sought to compensate for the fact that they had decided, probably wisely, to withdraw all of their armed forces from the Sinai, in the face of the Israeli parachute drops in the central sector, by turning the popular resistance which they had sought to encourage in Port Said against the invading Anglo-French forces into a symbolic victory of the entire Egyptian people. This, at least, is the lesson to be learned from all the talk of Port Said as a 'martyr' city with its own museum of 'popular resistance', as well as the role assigned to it in the national 'Victory Day' celebrations held annually until 1973.

What is also clear, and much better known, is the way in which President Nasser used this victory against imperialism to seize leadership of the Arab nationalist movement and to institute that process of state-led industrial development which lasted for a good ten years before being brought to an end by the equally sudden military defeat at the hands of the Israelis in June 1967 when, rather than evacuating the Sinai peninsula in good order as they had done in 1956, the Egyptian forces retreated – whether on orders from Cairo or not we still do not know – in the kind of pell-mell confusion that seemed to symbolise the vast gap which had come to exist between its high-flown rhetorical aims and its less than spectacular achievements. As it says in the Charter of National Action, which Nasser presented in 1962, Port Said was to be seen not as the end of imperialism but as the beginning of a more glorious future marked by a concerted political, economic and scientific effort to develop Egypt's resources.[16]

In the event, the defeat of 1967 marked the beginnings of a forty-year retreat from Nasser's Egyptian socialism, via a partial victory against Israel in 1973 and then a slow process of liberalisation which has only now, in 2007, been brought rhetorically to an end with the final abolition of the word 'socialism' from the official Egyptian political vocabulary.[17] That it has taken so long is testimony to the fact that the Suez 'victory' provided the impetus to undertake such a wholescale, root and branch attempt to remodel Egypt's society and economy largely along East European lines that its structures and modes of behaviour have proved enormously resistant to change. Given the almost total absence of official records it still remains unclear just how and why such a thing should have happened, leaving President Nasser and his regime in something of a historical limbo, praised by a few, attacked by many and almost completely ignored by the majority of young Egyptians who know little about its achievements other than what they have seen in the repeats of such films as *Nasser 56* or *Port Said*, two of the few perennial memorials to those stirring times.[18]

Anglo-Egyptian relations before and after 1956

Relations between Britain and Egypt have as long and varied a nineteenth- and twentieth-century history as could possibly be desired. They began in earnest during the Napoleonic Wars for both military/strategic and cultural reasons. On one hand, there was Nelson's victory over the French fleet at what is variously known as the Battle of the Nile or of Aboukir Bay (near Alexandria) followed by the brief British military landings a few miles away in 1807; on the other, the vast fillip which Napoleon's continental blockade gave to extra-European tourism, with Egypt becoming an essential feature of the Britons' war-time 'grand tour', and so launching the first period of serious interest in the country's Pharaonic remains. Commercial relations were also important, with Egypt providing much of the cereal necessary to provision the British garrisons in Malta and other Mediterranean islands and then, from 1820 onwards, the fine cotton used in Manchester's upmarket spinning and weaving mills. Finally, finance followed trade with substantial British investments first providing the credit needed to expand the cotton trade after 1840, and then to pay for infrastructural projects like the establishment of Egypt's first modern international mail service and its first railway from Alexandria to Cairo and on to the town of Suez, built in the 1850s.

These three main themes – geo-strategic, tourist/cultural and financial/commercial – have continued to inform the two countries' relations ever since, cemented, if that is the right word, first by British interest in the Suez Canal and the role Egypt played in defending the route to its Middle Eastern and Indian empire, and now by Britain's growing dependence on Egypt's natural gas. And if they have sometimes been productive of considerable strife, they have also nourished a wide variety of memorable personal relations, and provided the inspiration for a considerable amount of important archaeological, historical and political literature.

In my own case, while I wrote my doctoral thesis about the role of cotton in Egypt's nineteenth-century economic development, and lecture regularly on Egypt's twentieth-century efforts to move from a monocultural economy to one based on industry and the provision of services, the themes that now interest me more come from the period of the British occupation, 1882–1956, of which three are of particular importance. One is the role played by the struggle against Britain in the Egyptian national narrative perfected during the Nasser years, in which the movements led by Colonel Urabi in 1881–2 and by Saad Zaghlul in 1919 prefigure the much more successful movement of Colonel Nasser himself in removing the last vestiges of the British military presence between 1954 and 1956. A second is the stimulus provided by the events leading up to the occupation of 1882 to the production of J. A. Hobson's influential theory of imperialism which, for the first time, provided a theory of imperial expansion based on what, for him, was the illegitimate exploitation of non-European resources by the agents of European powers dressed up in the rhetoric of bringing the local peoples the benefits of civilisation and progress.[19] Finally, my third and most recent interest concerns the way in which, out of the colonial encounter, came that first great flowering of Egyptian cultural, scientific and administrative talent – associated with names like Naguib Mahfouz, Taha Hussein and those of the engineers like Mohamed Younis who ran the post-1956 canal and designed the High Dam at Aswan – which had a major impact during the monarchical period before going on to provide much of the intellectual power of the Nasser regime.

I am fairly sure that it was the Suez Crisis of 1956 which not only prompted my interest in Anglo-Egyptian relations but also provided my first encounter with what I then believed to be an entirely meretricious appeal to the 'verdict' of history, first by Anthony Eden, then by my old boarding-school history master who seemed to have convinced himself that if Nasser was not 'stopped', whatever that might mean, he was hell-bent on handing his country over to the Soviets: witness the underground barracks which he said had been built in the Sinai to accommodate the incoming Russian troops. Happily I knew enough about the world even then to see that this was absurd, that the language used to create those late-imperial bogeymen, like Mohamed Mossadeq, Jomo Kenyatta, Archbishop Makarios and then Gamal Abdel Nasser was a necessary, if dangerous, fiction for those who could find no other way to understand Britain's loss of global power.

Other lessons followed, both good and bad. If I despaired then, and continue to despair now, at the ease with which politicians who should know better continue to describe any foreign politician who gets in their way as another tyrant like Hitler or Stalin, I also learned that for most of the world's population there is a huge distinction to be made between the leaders and their people, with the latter only tangentially responsible for the misdeeds of the former. This was certainly true of the Egyptians I met when I went back to teach and to conduct research in Cairo in the academic year 1962–3, only six years after Suez. There, near where I lived, was the Port Said school, once the English School for Girls. There were my Egyptian neighbours who, even if they supposed that I might just have been old enough to vote for Eden, could not possibly have blamed me for an attack with which, in their eyes, no ordinary Britain like myself could possibly have had anything to do.

Notes

1. Alexander Fursenko and Timothy Naftali, *Kruschev's Cold War: The Inside Story of an American Adversary*, New York, NY, 2006, ch. 5.
2. Roger Owen, 'Conclusion', in W. Roger Louis and Roger Owen, eds, *A Revolutionary Year: The Middle East in 1958*, London, 2002.
3. Avi Shlaim, 'The Protocol of Sèvres, 1956: Anatomy of a War Plot', *International Affairs*, vol. 73, no.3, 1997.
4. Fursenko and Naftali, *Krushchev's Cold War*, pp. 129–32.
5. Timothy Naftali, ed., *John F. Kennedy: The Great Crises*, vol. III, New York, NY, 2001, p. 11.
6. Dina Ezzat, 'Pride Recalled', *Al-Ahram Weekly*, 27 July–2 August 2006, p. 3.
7. Michael T. Thornhill, *Road to Suez: The Battle of the Canal Zone*, Stroud, 2006, p. 216.
8. Ibid., pp. 216–17.
9. Ibid., p. 217.
10. Charles Tripp, 'The Grammar of Violence in Iraq', *London Review of Books*, vol. 29, no.2, 23 January 2007, pp. 30–1.
11. For example, General Sir Aylmer Haldane, *The Insurrection in Mesopotamia 1920*, Nashville, TN, 2005, ch. 3.
12. See, for example, the very short passages relating to the British army of

occupation in Alfred Milner, *England in Egypt*, London, 1904, pp. 28, 119–20, and the Earl of Cromer, *Modern Egypt*, vol. I, London, 1908, pp. 420–1.

13. Michael R. Gordon and General Bernard E. Trainor, *Cobra II: The Inside Story of the Invasion and Occupation of Iraq*, New York, NY, 2006, pp. 275–7.

14. 'Fasal Dar al-Watha'iq 'an Dar al-Kutub darura qawmiyya', *Akhbar al-Adab*, no. 505, 16 March 2003, pp. 31–3.

15. 'A Moment of Revelation', *Al-Ahram Weekly*, 2–8 November 2006, p. 2.

16. UAR (Egypt), *Draft of the National Charter*, presented by President Gamal Abdel Nasser at the Inaugural Session of the National Congress of Popular Power, Cairo, 21 May 1962, p. 10.

17. Gamal Essam El-Din, 'Ridding Egypt of Socialism', *Al-Ahram Weekly*, 1–7 February 2007, p. 4.

18. Ezzet, 'Pride Recalled', p. 3

19. J. A. Hobson, *Imperialism: A Study*, London, 1902, pp. 223–46.

Britain and Egypt: Working Together

It gives me great pleasure to contribute to this book just as I did to the forum on which it is based, held at SOAS, from which I graduated. It is appropriate that we should look at the Egyptian–British relationship in the light of all that has happened in the last fifty years. I will not go deeply into the historical background, which is covered by the excellent contributions from His Excellency Ahmed Maher, the former Egyptian minister of foreign affairs and Professor Roger Owen. However, I would like to make three initial comments.

The first is that the image of Britain in the minds of Egyptians is formed of a strange mixture of love and hate. Egyptians admire the British style of life. They sometimes say, 'He's as sharp as the British'. The British are known for their firmness and objectivity. But there are certain events in our history that remain very much alive in the memory of the two nations, and resurface from time to time; such as those of 1807, 1882, 1906, 1919 and, of course, 1956. The British are more experienced than others in dealing with our region and our country. If we compare the British with the Americans we will discover that the latter are not able to understand the Arab mentality or Egyptian psychology. We sometimes quote the example of Henry Kissinger who, in his shuttle diplomacy between Washington and Cairo, used to arrive from London and leave via London because he took advice in the capital that is more specialised and knowledgeable about the Middle East than others. We feel that the British understand us better and we sometimes rely on them to explain issues to the Americans.

Secondly, we often say in our part of the world that most of the major problems in our region and adjacent ones are made by Britain – that is, created either at a time of British domination or shaped in some way through the influence of the British. The Kashmir dispute has bedevilled relations between India and Pakistan. The Palestinian problem has been the dominant issue in the Middle East. This is not to ignore other cases: Afghanistan, Iraq, Sudan and Somalia. I am not saying that the British created these major international problems deliberately, but they became deeply involved in all of them. The British were partnered by the French in controlling the key nerve centres in Asia and Africa, but the British always had the upper hand and the most pervasive influence. Much good came of this and the British were effective in different parts of the world. When I served in India from 1979 to 1983, I formed the impression that the Indians recognised this in the way that they viewed the history of Britain in their land and in the way they still admired the British.

Thirdly, I regret that I sometimes feel that the relationship between Egypt and Britain – especially on the political level – has been greatly influenced in the last two or three decades by the United States. We feel that whenever the British are asked to play a more effective or prominent role in the region they react sometimes with reservation and sometimes with reluctance. They usually say the Americans are doing it. This response is not viewed as encouraging in our part of the world. We do not like to be left in American hands as if they are the only people who count. The USA is, of course, the only superpower in our world. I believe, accept and admit that we are living in the era of the Pax Americana as our ancestors lived under the Pax Romana many centuries ago. However, there are other powers that are able to play a role. The EU can play such a role, but, in my view, it should be led by the British, because the British understand better than others Middle Eastern affairs, Islamic issues and the relationship between the

Western and Muslim worlds. The British know Islam, in particular, better than others. I will return to this point later.

We have to keep these three points in mind when trying to understand how our relations will develop in the future. We exist within an international community and other problems and events will intrude. As noted in Professor Roger Owen's chapter, the tripartite aggression of 1956 coincided with the US elections and the dramatic Soviet intervention in Hungary that led to the execution of the late Prime Minister Imre Nagy. Today we have a similar confluence of events. Arab–Israeli relations, American support for Israel, the double standards of policies applied in the region, are all reasons to reject American policy. I cannot envisage American policy ever being in a worse state than it is now, not just in the Middle East but also in South America and East Asia. We understand, of course, that American people are friendly. We like their style of life – which is very popular all over the world. Living under the Pax Americana, new generations are attracted to the style of life, the style of food, the manner of discussion and the quality of education in America. But American policy, especially in the last decade, is seen as too provocative in our region. I am not saying this merely to state a fact. I am saying it because Britain sometimes is associated with American policy and attitudes to the UK are influenced by the atmosphere of rejection in our region.

For this reason, I believe that an independent British policy, a more European British policy, is essential for us. In saying this I admit that I am a graduate from a British university. I admire London. I respect the British nation. I believe that Britain has a role to play and that this not sufficiently understood or given adequate attention in London. It sometimes seems that the relationship between the United States and Britain is like that of a father who has a rich son who is taking over his role and acting on his behalf. America should be seen as an extension of Anglo-Saxon culture. The British should use this to extend their influence. The French are deprived of such an advantage. The British need to exploit it.

There are several potential fields of cooperation between the two nations – the British and the Egyptian. We should look to Britain as a leading state in the EU and as one enjoying close relations with Washington. Nobody can deny that. The Americans often listen to the British more then they do others. Relations between France and the USA have their ups and downs. The French are inclined to respond with a 'yes' to an American request, but not very quickly. The British are different. This gives the British greater influence and can give us an additional advantage in promoting our policies in the region. I feel that we need greater effort from the British in dealing with the Middle East crises. The British tend to respond by saying that they are supporting the region through the EU. They show that they give aid, assistance and financial support to the Palestinians. But they know in their heart of hearts that they need to be more directly involved. I do not know how this can be done and I am sure that the Americans will not welcome such a role. They will express reservations, as they prefer to be the only player in the Middle East. However, it is we who are inviting the British to become more closely involved in dealing with the current situation in the Middle East.

If we look at the situation in Iraq, we can see that the British know best. That is why the situation in southern Iraq is less violent than in other parts of that country. Some people will say that this is because there is a clear majority of Shi'ites. This could be one reason but there are others. The British know how to deal with the tribes and the urban population. They know the mentality of the Iraqis. We should not forget that it was the British who sent Lawrence of Arabia to escort El-Sharif Hussein on his historic campaign. They also appointed General Glubb Pasha to be Chief of Staff of the Arab Legion in Jordan to build and shape that force. The British have always lived in the community itself. They have not sat at desks behind computer screens on which they play political games and make decisions, as our friends in Washington seem inclined to do. The British stay close to the ground. They mingle with the people. They know what is going on. That is why they know Iraq better than the Americans. They are sometimes accused of having given the Sunni Arabs the upper hand in the 1920s. The Americans are trying to rebalance this and compensate the Shi'ites in a way that, in my view, will lead only to the division of Iraq. Indeed, it is already nearly divided. We all have to be very careful to ensure that this does not become permanent. The British have always been against division. They saw what happened in India with Partition – which was demanded by the Muslims, not the British. I lived in India for years and years, and know the mentality of the people. Sudan may also be divided soon. The British left Sudan as a united country – the largest country in Africa – with nine or ten states within its borders. The Americans have not learned or understood how to rule. It is possible to divide and rule within a legal unity.

That is why the role of Britain is potentially so influential, especially working with the support of a country like Egypt. I admit that the role of Egypt has temporarily diminished in the region. It is not as powerful as it was a few decades ago for several reasons. The heroes and stars of mid-twentieth-century politics are no longer around, not only in the Middle East but also on the world stage. This is not the era of Charles de Gaulle, Winston Churchill, Gamal Abdel Nasser or Nehru. We have what I call average leaders everywhere and the game has to be played by different rules. We need and we invite the British to be with us in trying to be more understanding of affairs in Iraq, in Palestine and in Darfur, in particular. But, as I noted above, I sometimes feel that the British are trying to do the minimum.

There are two envoys dealing with Sudanese affairs – one from the USA and one from Britain – apart from the United Nations representative. The British envoy is my good friend Alan Goulty, who was number two in the Egyptian embassy in Cairo and has been British ambassador in Khartoum. I have said to him several times (and seen at first hand) that the interest of Britain in solving the crisis in Sudan is sincere and strong. I have told him frankly that the main problem in Sudan is the behaviour of the Khartoum government itself. It is not keen to maintain the unity of the Sudanese state.

It may prefer a northern independent Islamic state to a completely democratic secular Sudanese state. The dilemma facing us all is that we have to deal with the legitimate and ruling regime as we do with all countries whether or not we agree or disagree with their policies. This is a problem that both the British and the Egyptians face in dealing with Sudan.

One of the major issues of our time is the relationship between the West and Islam. I want Egypt once again to be the centre of moderate Islam as it was in the days of Imam Mohammed Abdu and other religious and social reformers. I want al-Azhar to reactivate its role to offer genuine Islam to the Muslim world. Britain is known in the Christian world for being tolerant on religious issues. The Church of England, especially, if compared with the Catholic and Orthodox churches, is more flexible, more understanding and readier to deal with others. I recall that many statements by the Archbishop of Canterbury have been welcomed in the Islamic world because he knows what to say, and when. That is why Britain and Egypt can together play a role in helping to bring about reconciliation and improving relations between the West and Islam. In addition, British experience of living in and dealing with India, Pakistan and other Muslim countries east of Suez as well as Egypt, Sudan and large parts of Africa has brought them into contact over centuries with the Islamic phenomenon. They know how to deal with it better than others. Al-Azhar itself needs to adapt to the modern world. The Ulama need to learn foreign languages to communicate with others. They need to understand the mentality of those who speak against Islam. They need to learn how to represent moderate Islam in the modern world. If we can send our imams and sheikhs abroad to a country like Britain then I am sure we will have another Mohammed Abdu – a man who used to exchange letters with Tolstoy at the beginning of the twentieth century. Al-Azhar was then active and effective in the world. A moderate al-Azhar can again represent genuine moderate Islam.

Al-Azhar can cooperate with a country like Britain to improve the image of the Islamic world in the West. In the process of doing so they will join in the fight against worldwide terrorism. We in Egypt suffer from terrorism, as have the British, Americans and many others. I need only recall the Luxor massacre of 1997. We Egyptians pay the price twice for such acts: from terrorism in our territory and by the blackening of our image abroad. We are turned back at all airports and we are refused visas in consular sections because of the so-called Islamic terror. Islam has nothing whatsoever to do with terrorism. Islam is a religion of tolerance. The prophet was once sitting with his followers. A funeral passed in front of him, and he stood up as a mark of respect. His followers asked him, 'Why should you do that, prophet? The dead person is a Jew.' He answered, 'Isn't he a human being?' If we understand genuine Islam through examples like this, we will be able to have better cooperation between nations. Britain and Egypt can show the way.

In conclusion, I would like to recall the many statements by Britain in favour of true Islam and good relations between Christianity, Muslims and Jews. I refer in particular to the famous lecture by Prince Charles at Oxford University in 1993. His main points drew on the advice of the late, great Imam Zaki Badawi, an Egyptian Azharite with a broad Islamic vision. However, it is Prince Charles who is trying to play a role in narrowing the gap between civilisations and improving the relations between Muslims and Christians in particular. I had the honour of receiving him at the British University in Egypt in my capacity as its president in March 2006. The United Kingdom has its economic and social role in Egypt and the Middle East but I feel that any advice from the British will be received carefully and respectfully in my country. The son of the president in particular, Gamal Mubarak, in developing his ideas, has been studying the democratic example of Britain. He may be more attached to the New Labour groups but that is not something we are against. It shows that cooperation is not limited to a few areas. We feel that the support of Britain is essential to the democratic transformation of Egypt. We are used to listening to the British. We are ready to listen to them because they are wise, objective and know us better than others.

I was delighted to take part in the conference that has inspired this book. It took place at SOAS and revived and refreshed my memories of a place from which I received my doctorate thirty years ago on 'Copts in Egyptian Politics'. Those were my golden days which cannot be relived but remain in my memory.

MOHAMMED SHAKER

Egypt and Britain Working Together: Dealing with WMD in the Middle East

In my very first days in the Egyptian Foreign Ministry in 1956, shortly after Egypt had nationalised the Suez Canal, the Director of the UN Department, in response to a naive question on my part as a young inexperienced diplomat, told me that the international consequences of the nationalisation would be grave and would last for a very long time. He was obviously right. However, by the time I came to London as ambassador in 1988 there had been a dramatic recovery in relations between Egypt and the UK. Soon after my arrival the late Sir Michael Weir, who had recently retired after more than five years as the British Ambassador in Egypt, suggested the formation of the British Egyptian Society. I readily agreed and had the great pleasure of working with Sir Michael in turning his idea into reality. The conference held in November 2006, and this book, demonstrate the effectiveness of the Society and the close relationship and friendship between Egypt and Britain fifty years after Suez.

A fundamental part of any bilateral diplomatic relationship is the ability of two countries to work together on major global issues. This can be done most effectively when the countries share a common vision and a common interest in the outcome. It involves them working closely together on the issue, and with a host of other countries directly and through the United Nations and other international organisations. I have chosen in this chapter to discuss the proliferation of weapons of mass destruction (WMD) and terrorism including WMD terrorism, with special emphasis on the Middle East. Both issues are of great concern to the UK and the West as well as to Egypt and the countries of the Middle East. They will remain at the top of the international agenda for many years to come.

On the day President Mubarak put forward his initiative for the establishment of a zone free of WMD in the Middle East in 1990, I accompanied Dr Mamdouh El Beltagi, then Director of the State Information Organisation and later Minister of Information, Tourism and Youth, to meet the Right Honourable Douglas Hogg (Lord Hogg), the then Minister of State for Foreign Affairs. Dr Beltagi was the first Egyptian official to inform the UK government of President Mubarak's initiative.

A statement issued by the Foreign and Commonwealth Office later that day merely took note of the initiative. There was no substantive reaction to President Mubarak's visionary proposal on how deal with the threat of WMD.

President Mubarak's initiative of 1990 coincided with several worrying reports that Iraq was trying to acquire equipment and material that could be used in a programme for the development of WMD. In the aftermath of the 1991 operation to free Kuwait from Iraqi occupation, dramatic revelations about Iraq's WMD helped focus the attention of the world on the problem and led to the adoption of UN Security Council Resolution (UNSCR) 687 of 1991. This ordered the dismantling of WMD in Iraq. The process for monitoring and inspecting WMD in Iraq continued until March 2003 when the United States, the United Kingdom and their coalition partners invaded Iraq. The pretext for the war was the need for further searches for WMD. None was found. A key segment of UNSCR 687 indicated that the dismantling of WMD in Iraq could lead to the beginning of the establishment of a WMD-free zone in the Middle East.

The 1990 initiative was preceded a few years earlier by the Egyptian–Iranian proposal of 1974 to establish a zone free of nuclear weapons in the Middle East. In almost every year since then Egypt has put this same proposal to the UN General Assembly, which invariably supports it. A consensus on this initiative was first achieved in 1980.[1] It was one of the factors that encouraged Egypt in 1981 to ratify the Nuclear Non-Proliferation Treaty (NPT). Egypt had previously signed the NPT on the day it was opened for signature on 1 July 1968.[2] Egypt's instruments of ratification of the NPT were deposited with the three Depository Governments of the treaty, namely the USA, Russia and the UK.

The main consideration in Egypt's decision to ratify the NPT in 1981 was its plan to build up to eight nuclear power plants as part of a programme to expand on a large scale its electric power generation. It could not have implemented this plan without ratifying the NPT. If Egypt had continued with its previous policy of linking ratification to the adherence of Israel to the NPT it would, in effect, have handed to others the power to veto the development and promotion of peaceful programmes that were seen as essential to the future prosperity and well-being of its people.[3] Unfortunately, as a result of the Chernobyl accident in the Ukraine in 1986, Egypt decided to shelve its nuclear power project, even though it was on the verge of developing the first power plant in Dabaa, west of Alamein on the north coast of the country.

Egypt has recently revived its nuclear power project in the context of exploring alternative sources of energy. It is not my intention go into that project. However, in the course of Egypt's negotiation of nuclear cooperation agreements with a number of leading supplier countries in the West, in which I participated, I recall that before Egypt's signing of the Memorandum of Understanding Concerning Cooperation in the Peaceful Uses of Nuclear Energy with the UK on 2 November 1981, our British counterparts gave us some good advice.[4] This was that Egypt should take on board the experience of similar developing countries, as South Korea, for example, was doing in those days, in order to avoid the pitfalls they had encountered in their programmes. I hope today our authorities will seriously consider such advice before reactivating our programme.

Let me now return to the proposal that there should be a zone free of WMD in the Middle East. President Mubarak emphasised the following:

> All weapons of mass destruction, without exception, should be prohibited in the Middle East – that is, nuclear, chemical and biological.
>
> All states of the region, without exception, should make equal and reciprocal commitment in this regard.
>
> Verification measures and modalities should be established to ascertain full compliance by all states of the region with the full scope of the prohibitions without exception.[5]

Following the adoption of UNSCR 687, the then Minister of Foreign Affairs in Egypt, Amre Moussa, forwarded a letter to the UN Security Council in which he pointed out that recent events in the Middle East had induced many states to endorse Egypt's latest initiative. The Minister spoke of according priority to ridding the region of WMD. In order to accelerate the establishment of the Middle East WMD-free zone, Mr Moussa put forward a number of proposals. These were:

> Egypt calls on the major arms-producing states – and particularly the permanent members of the Security Council – as well as Israel, Iran and the Arab states to deposit undertakings with the Security Council in which they clearly and unconditionally endorse the declarations of the Middle East as a region free of weapons of mass destruction and commit themselves not to take any steps or measures which would run counter to or impede the attainment of that objective.

Egypt calls on the arms-producing states and the parties to the Treaty on the Non-Proliferation of Nuclear Weapons to step up their efforts to ensure that all Middle East nations which have not yet done so adhere to the Treaty, in recognition of the fact that this is a step of the utmost importance and urgency.

Egypt calls on the nations of the Middle East region which have not yet done so to declare their commitment:

- Not to use nuclear, chemical or biological weapons;
- Not to produce or acquire any nuclear weapons;
- Not to produce or acquire any nuclear materials susceptible to military use and to dispose of any existing stock of such materials;
- To accept the International Atomic Energy Agency safeguards regime whereby all their nuclear facilities become subject to international inspection;
- Egypt calls on those nations of the region which have not yet done so to declare their commitment to adhere to the Treaty on the Non-Proliferation of Nuclear Weapons, as well as to the Convention concerning the prohibition of biological weapons of 1972, no later than the conclusion of the negotiations on the prohibition of chemical weapons being conducted by the Conference on Disarmament in Geneva;
- Egypt calls on Middle East states to declare their commitment actively and fairly to address measures relating to all forms of delivery systems for weapons of mass destruction;
- Egypt calls on nations of the region to approve the assignment to an organ of the United Nations or another international organization of a role, to be agreed upon at a future date, in the verification of these nations' compliance with such agreements on arms reduction and disarmament as may be concluded between them.[6]

Egypt has been pursuing the 1974 and 1990 initiatives simultaneously. The 1990 initiative has not affected the yearly submission by Egypt of a resolution on the creation of a zone free of nuclear weapons to the UN General Assembly. Egypt's priority and main concern is nuclear weapons and, more particularly, Israeli nuclear weapon capabilities.

In 1991 the Madrid Conference on the Middle East convened. Under its umbrella, bilateral Arab–Israeli negotiations took place and multilateral tracks were initiated. Among these was the establishment of a working group on Arms Control and Regional Security (ACRS). The work of ACRS came to a dead end in 1994 as a result of a sharp divergence of views between the Arabs and the Israelis. The Arabs wanted to pursue the nuclear issue and to impress upon the Israelis to open up on it. The Israelis wished to concentrate solely on confidence-building measures, on which some progress had been made in the group. Israel's objections to dealing with the nuclear issue have long been based on its refusal to forgo the element of ambiguity in its policy, arguing that a discussion of this matter would lead Israel down a slippery slope.[7]

The Chemical Weapons Convention was opened for signature on 13 January 1993 and came into force on 29 April 1997. Egypt and a few Arab countries abstained from adhering to the convention in the absence of Israel's commitment to the NPT. This led to speculation that Middle Eastern countries had or might acquire capabilities in waging chemical warfare that would be used to deter Israel from ever using its nuclear weapons capabilities and to give the Arabs some bargaining power in future negotiations.

In 1995, when the NPT was extended indefinitely, a key resolution on the Middle East, which was closely linked with the three decisions adopted by the NPT Review and Extension Conference, called for the creation of a zone free of WMD in the Middle East.[8] There would have been no consensus on any of the three decisions including that on the indefinite extension of the Treaty without the Middle East Resolution. However, the implementation of the resolution has been slow and is still facing difficulties. It should be noted that the resolution was sponsored by the Depository Governments designated by the NPT, i.e., Russia, the UK and the United States. The three states, therefore, bear the main responsibility for implementing this resolution in concert with the states of the region. The UK can play a leading role in this.

The League of Arab States is actively contributing to efforts towards establishing a zone free of WMD in the Middle East. A special committee within the League opted for the setting up of such a zone instead of a nuclear-weapons-free zone and it was entrusted to negotiate a draft treaty. The committee has made great progress but there are still many issues to be settled. These include verification mechanisms within the zone involving the IAEA and possibly the Organisation for the Prevention of Chemical Weapons (OPCW). The geographic boundaries of the zone need to be defined.

At the Arab annual summit meeting in Tunisia in May 2004 a statement was issued calling for the convening of an international conference under the auspices of the United Nations for the establishment of a WMD-free zone in the Middle East. The meeting called for action within the United Nations to follow this up. It was suggested that it should be put on the agenda of the next meeting of the UN General Assembly or that there should be added to an existing agenda item a call for an international conference on the subject: It was agreed that these matters should be carefully prepared and implemented.

The idea of an international conference under the auspices of the United Nations on WMD in the Middle East is not completely new. President Mubarak soon after making his proposal of 1990 hinted at the possibility of convening an international conference for the elimination of all WMD worldwide. This was well before the conclusion of the Chemical Weapons Convention of 1993 and the recent attempts to improve the verification procedures of the Biological Weapons Convention of 1972.

The call for an international conference on WMD in the Middle East reflects a genuine need on the part of the Arab countries for international involvement. They feel that the countries of the Middle East cannot do it alone. There has been international involvement in the creation of other zones even though the initiative for setting these up has come from countries within a specific region. One example of this is the Treaty of Tlatelolco in Latin America and the Caribbean. The parties to that treaty secured nuclear guarantees from the five nuclear-weapon states (including the UK), as defined in the NPT, not to use or threaten to use nuclear weapons against countries in the zone.

The UN so far has failed to convene a further special session on disarmament at which the concept of a Middle East WMD-free zone could have been further elaborated. The possibility of the UN convening a conference on disarmament and arms control similar to the UN conferences on population, women, environment and the like seems far-fetched. There has been more interest in a conference only on WMD in the Middle East. If such a conference were to take place, it would have to be linked in one way or another with the disarmament process in general. This was felt to be important to the NGOs concerned with disarmament. The NPT Review Conference of 2000 prescribed thirteen practical steps on disarmament, and more particularly nuclear disarmament, with the approval of the five nuclear-weapon states. Unfortunately they have not done much to comply with the recommendations of the conference.[9] It should also be recalled that at that conference Israel was mentioned for the first time by name as the only state in the Middle East not party to the NPT. It was called upon to adhere to it.

It would not be an exaggeration to say that the idea of a WMD-free zone in the Middle East has helped to get the international community to consider putting WMD together in one basket rather than in separate categories – nuclear, chemical and biological. One example is UNSCR 1540 of 28 April 2004 on WMD terrorism and the Proliferation Security Initiative (PSI). The major objective of this resolution is to impede and stop the flow of WMD by interdicting potential shipments of proliferation-linked material being transported by sea, air or land. There have also been several studies on WMD as a whole. Foremost among them is the WMD Commission report on *Weapons of Terror*, a report that should prove beneficial in combating WMD proliferation.[10]

The Middle East has greatly suffered from terrorism from state and non-state actors. No discussion on eliminating WMD in the Middle East would be complete without taking into account the terrorist factor. UNSCR 1540, a Chapter VII Resolution, sought to contain, respond to and counter potential WMD terrorism. This is clearly justifiable but there are some reservations about whether it is right for the UN Security Council to try to legislate on matters that should be dealt with by governments through treaties and conventions. It is thus important that there should be a call for an international conference on terrorism that would have the opportunity to tackle, among other issues, WMD terrorism. It could recommend what further action and negotiations were required to bring about international agreements. Egypt has repeatedly renewed its call for an international conference on terrorism. This is yet another initiative that Egypt is keen to see through to implementation. The December 2004 report of the high-level panel designated by the UN Secretary-General on Threats, Challenges and Change, entitled 'A More Secure World: Our Share of Responsibility' has come up with substantive elements of a definition of terrorism. This may clear the way to convene an international conference on terrorism, which, for years, has proved difficult because of controversy over the definition of terrorism.[11]

One of the major issues in this respect is the distinction between terrorism and legitimate resistance against occupation, an issue that has unjustifiably blurred the case of Palestinian resistance against Israeli occupation. The UK and Egypt should attend to this issue in fairness and justice. It is essential to take into account the root causes of terrorism as well as methods of countering it.

Finally, the recent terrorist attacks in London shocked us all in Egypt. I happened to be in London at the time and felt personally their impact on the British people. I felt that I myself could have been a victim of such attacks. We in Egypt and in the UK have to strive together and in cooperation with other states, to face up to this scourge. Terrorism knows neither religion nor nationality and can hit us all anywhere, any time. In this chapter I have sought to describe the ways in which Egypt, the UK and the international community have worked together – not always successfully – to control the spread of WMD with special reference to the Middle East. There is much still to be done. Egypt and the UK will need to work closely together over the next few years to deal with the issues raised here.

Notes

1. Arab Republic of Egypt, Ministry of Foreign Affairs, in Mohammed Shaker, *Egypt and the Treaty on the Non-Proliferation of Nuclear Weapons*, Cairo, 1981, pp. 74–5.
2. For the history of the NPT negotiations, analysis and early implementation, see Mohammed I. Shaker, *The Nuclear Non-Proliferation Treaty: Origins and Implementation*, 3 vols, Dobbs Ferry, New York, 1980.
3. See statement made by the Deputy Prime Minister and Minister of Foreign Affairs of Egypt in the Shura Assembly (the upper house) in Shaker, *Egypt and the NPT*, p. 76.
4. For the text of the Memorandum, see Arab Republic of Egypt, *Egypt and Peaceful Uses of Nuclear Energy*, Cairo, 1984, pp. 131–7.
5. UN Docs. A/45/219 and 5/21252, 18 April 1990.
6. UN Docs. A/46/329 and 5/22855, 30 July 1991.
7. See Nabil Fahmy, 'Reflections on Arms Control and Regional Security in the Middle East', in James Brown, ed., *New Horizons and New Strategies in Arms Control*, Albuquerque, 1999, pp. 173–89.
8. 1995 Review and Extension Conference of the Parties to Treaty on the Non-Proliferation of Nuclear Weapons, *Final Document Part I : Organization and Work of the Conference*, New York, 1995, NPT /Con.1995/32/Part I.
9. See Tanya Ogilvie White, Ben Sanders and John Simpson, *Putting the Final Document into Practice: Possible Ways to Implement the Results of the 2000 Review Conference. A PPNN Study.* Southampton, UK, 2002, pp. 6–20.
10. *Weapons of Terror: Freeing the World of Nuclear, Biological and Chemical Arms*, Stockholm, 2006.
11. UN Doc. A/59/565, 2, December 2004, pp. 48–9.

MUSTAPHA KAMEL AL-SAYYID

The UK and the Question of Democracy Promotion in Egypt

Fifty years have passed since the Suez war and it is amazing that, reflecting on UK–Egyptian relations, one is bound to conclude that the negative impact of what Egyptians call the 'Tripartite Aggression' on the relationship between their country and its former occupying power is only a memory of the past. The two countries which fought each other, with France and Israel playing supporting roles to the UK, have moved from open military confrontation to cooperation and friendly relations, with Tony Blair, the former Labour prime minister, spending his Christmas holidays at Sharm El-Sheikh on the Red Sea coast of Egypt. What explains such a radical transformation of the relationship between the two countries? That question is the major focus of this chapter. It illustrates this transformation by focusing on the espousal by the UK government of a policy of democracy promotion in Egypt as well as other Middle East countries, without much protest from Egyptians who could in the past have considered such a policy as a flagrant interference in the domestic affairs of their country. This chapter argues that such a radical transformation of the relationship is the result of three developments: changes of leadership, UK withdrawal from areas east of Suez and shifts in the regional and international balance of power that have reduced the relative position of each country in its sphere of influence.

The two countries went to war in 1956, apparently over the question of Gamal Abdel Nasser's nationalisation of the Suez Canal Company. However, as historians of the Suez war have rightly pointed out, Nasser's nationalisation of the Canal was only the last straw that pushed the two countries to a situation of armed conflict. The UK and France were frustrated because of Egypt's support of liberation movements in territories they then occupied. Israel took advantage of tensions between them and the largest and, at the time, the most influential Arab country to nip in the bud what it considered a potential threat to its military dominance in the Middle East. Fifty years later, Egypt and Britain have close diplomatic ties with frequent exchanges of visits by their most senior officials. Great Britain is now the largest non-Arab foreign investor in Egypt. British firms enjoy leading positions in the critical sectors of petroleum and natural gas exploration, telecommunications and pharmaceuticals, among others.

A very good example of an issue over which the two countries hold definitely divergent views, but which they have tacitly agreed to manage through dialogue, is the question of democracy promotion in the Arab world. This has become a declared objective of the G8, including Britain, in the region since the Sea Island Summit in the US in July 2004.

The study of the question of democracy promotion in the context of Egyptian–British relations is also very interesting for another reason: it points to one area, at least, in which UK diplomacy deviates from its well-known alignment with the US. The Tony Blair government has aligned itself with US diplomacy on major questions related to the Arab world: the war on Iraq, the war on terror and UN Security Council Resolutions 1559 and 1701 on Lebanon and 1707 on Darfur. Even the Palestinian question, over which British diplomacy usually took a position markedly different from that of Israel and the US, has ceased to be an issue of contention between the two major Western powers. On the question of democracy promotion, the UK tended to adopt a low-key approach, in contrast to the louder carrot-and-stick diplomacy of the Bush administration.

There is no doubt that the UK government, particularly under Tony Blair, is quite sympathetic to the cause of democracy promotion in the Arab world, not necessarily out of the naive belief that democracy promotion is the best defence against terrorism. 'Terrorist' groups were quite active in countries with apparently democratic governments such as those of Germany, Italy and Japan in the 1970s or even Colombia in Latin America since the late 1950s and Northern Ireland from 1968 until recently. Mr Blair's sympathy for the idea of democracy promotion was due to a broader commitment to the cause of human rights worldwide and not exclusively in the Arab world. Unlike the French president, Tony Blair did not declare openly any disagreement with the final communiqué of leaders of the G8 at the Sea Island Summit, at which they adopted democracy promotion as a goal of their foreign policies in the Arab world and also detailed measures to be taken by them in their relations with Arab countries.[1] These measures were to cover many areas of interaction between the G8, on one hand, and the so-called broader Middle East countries on the other, including diplomatic representation, economic assistance, contributions towards improving education, enhancing the status of women and increasing exchanges of visits by members of parliaments, media people and businessmen. The UK participated in meetings of the Forum for the Future, which brought together ministers of foreign affairs and other ministers, business people and civil society representatives to discuss issues of democracy promotion. That Forum has met in Casablanca (2004), Bahrain (2005) and Amman (2006). The UK, as a member of the EU, is also committed to pursuing the goals of the EU Neighbourhood Policy, as well as the Barcelona Declaration, which called for respect of human rights and the promotion of civil society in countries of the southern Mediterranean. The website of the Foreign and Commonwealth Office (FCO) outlined the strategic objectives of the UK in Egypt including promoting economic and political reform, working with the Egyptian government to ensure fair elections, support of secular opposition and promotion of free media and full political participation by all citizens.

Divergences of approach by the UK and the US with respect to democracy promotion in Arab countries including Egypt can be seen in three areas: the relative importance of democracy promotion compared to other goals of the Arab policies of the two countries as reflected in their policy statements; the resources devoted to democracy promotion activities; and the specific activities that are carried out in pursuit of this goal.

It seemed for a time, particularly in 2003–5, that democracy promotion in the Arab world was the major goal for the US in the region. That was announced loudly and clearly by President Bush in his State of the Union address in 2004 and in several other major speeches. Dr Condoleezza Rice took it upon herself to deliver the message right in the centre of Cairo in a famous speech that she gave at the American University in Cairo in the summer of 2005. Violations of human rights in Egypt were criticised at the highest level in the US by the President himself and the Secretary of State. The US government in 2003 went as far as denying the Egyptian government additional aid that it sought to help the country deal with the negative economic consequences of the war on terror. The reason was declared to be the Egyptian government's imprisonment of the outspoken American University of Cairo Professor Sa'd El-Din Ibrahim. US senators and congressmen called upon the US government to halt economic and military assistance to Egypt as a way of penalising its government for human rights violations, particularly the imprisonment on 'flimsy' charges of prominent liberal opposition figures such as the leader of the al-Ghad (Tomorrow) Party and Professor Sa'd El-Din Ibrahim. US media launched campaigns against the Egyptian government for its negative record on human rights.

On all these matters the UK government has adopted a much quieter approach. It is very difficult to find one speech by the British prime minister devoted entirely to the question of democracy promotion in the Arab world. His references to democracy in the Arab world, or the absence of it, have mostly come in press conferences and in replies to questioning by journalists. His statements, as well as those of other British officials, were quite balanced, emphasising steps taken to promote political reform in countries such as Egypt and Saudi Arabia. In his reply to an al-Jazeera correspondent in one of his press conferences, Mr Blair denied that his government stood by authoritarian regimes in the Arab world, particularly those of Egypt and Saudi Arabia. He found it encouraging that the Egyptian president asked for an amendment of the constitution to allow multi-candidate presidential elections in 2005 and praised measures introduced in Saudi Arabia to engage in national dialogue over important issues. In the same spirit Dr Kim Howell, Minister of State at the FCO, delivered a speech at the British Egyptian Business Association on 25 October 2005, in which he expressed his appreciation of the way Egypt had embraced economic change and modernisation since the Nazif government came into office. He also stated that Egypt had taken bold steps to open up its political system by holding its first multi-candidate presidential election. He expressed the hope that the parliamentary elections, which were going to take place a few weeks later, would build on 'progress made towards greater transparency, equal access to the media and access for independent election observers'. The speech was not exclusively devoted to the question of political reform. The Minister talked also about trade, governance, education, terrorism and the regional perspective.

Critical remarks on the Egyptian government's record on human rights were rarely made publicly by senior officials of the British government or made exclusively on behalf of the British government. An example of such critical remarks is a statement by the EU expressing concern about the conviction of Ayman Nour, leader of the al-Ghad Party, who was the runner-up in Egypt's presidential election and who was imprisoned and tried after the election, allegedly for the forgery of documents necessary for the establishment of his party.

The UK joined other members of the EU in issuing a statement on 27 December 2005 arguing that the conviction and sentencing of Ayman Nour to five years in prison 'sends negative signals about democratic political reform in Egypt'. The statement added that the EU expected that any appeal application by Mr Nour would be looked at fairly by the Egyptian courts. The EU raised the matter with the Egyptian Foreign Ministry on 15 February 2005. Mr Nour's appeal was rejected and he was condemned to five years in prison.

According to British diplomats in Cairo, Mrs Margaret Beckett, the British Foreign Secretary, raised the question of political reform in the country in her meeting with President Hosny Mubarak during her visit to Egypt in September 2006. The FCO also issued statements disapproving of the way the Egyptian government ran the elections for the People's Assembly in the autumn of 2005 and its treatment of the Club of Judges in the spring of 2006. The FCO website gave a negative assessment of some aspects of the human rights situation in Egypt, particularly what it described as some discrimination against Copts and the arrest of Ayman Nour.

Another indicator of the relative importance of democracy promotion in both US and UK policies towards Egypt is the volume of resources directly allocated for this purpose. The US allocated $48 million for such activities for 2006 – almost eight times what the UK devoted for similar activities. That sum constituted 10 per cent of total US economic assistance to Egypt for that year. UK democracy promotion programmes in Egypt probably did not cost more than £100,000 sterling, amounting perhaps to 2.5 per cent of total UK aid to Egypt. UK aid for democracy promotion is being phased out in 2007 whilst that of the US will continue until at least 2009. A relatively large number of US government agencies as well as NGOs are involved in democracy promotion, whereas the number of UK government agencies and NGOs carrying out similar activities in Egypt is far smaller. They include, on the government side, the British Council, the British Embassy in Cairo, the Westminster Foundation for Democracy, the Global Opportunities Fund and the Minority

Rights Group. Some of this aid to democracy promotion is channelled through multilateral bodies including the EU and UNDP.[2]

As for specific activities, the US programmes are more varied. They have included no less than eight programmes, namely:

1. Promote and support credible electoral process;
2. Establish and ensure media freedom and freedom of association;
3. Strengthen civil society;
4. Strengthen democratic political parties;
5. Strengthen justice sector;
6. Support democratic local government and decentralisation;
7. Promote and support anti-corruption reform;
8. Protect human rights.

Specific projects supported by the British government agencies in Egypt pursue the same goals but with fewer resources and staff. Prominent among these projects are those related to encouraging credible electoral processes, support of human rights organisations, strengthening the justice sector and ensuring media freedom. However, British aid efforts went beyond the eight programmes supported by USAID. Promotion of women's rights and encouraging so-called 'dialogue among civilisations' figured prominently among the activities of democracy promotion carried out by British government agencies.

Such activities included visits by the Electoral Reform International Service, which observed parliamentary elections in Egypt in late 2005, held informal meetings with judges and went to several polling stations. In order to strengthen the justice sector, the British Embassy offered a grant of £25,000 to the Arab Centre for the Independence of the Judiciary. The British Council has in the past supported international conferences organised by the Supreme Constitutional Court. Support for human rights was demonstrated through a grant of £10,000 to the Egyptian Human

Rights Organisation. The London-based Global Opportunities Fund supported the Ombudsman Office at the National Council for Women for three years. This fund also supported other women's groups. One was the Alliance of Arab Women, which carried out a project in the New Valley in order to promote political awareness among women there and to increase their registration as voters. In order to facilitate the so-called 'dialogue among civilisations', the British Embassy supported exchanges of visits between al-Azhar officials and representatives of the Anglican Church. Some Chevening Fellowships were offered to young Egyptians working on research projects focusing on relationships between Islam and democracy as well as issues of political reform. A few other projects targeted young people in the country. Finally, the Westminster Democracy Foundation is about to start activities focusing on two areas. The first will include projects that will contribute to the empowerment of women. The second will involve the training of parliamentary staff and familiarising members of parliament with British parliamentary practices. [3]

Such activities in support of democracy promotion in Egypt have sometimes caused friction between the two governments. The Secretary General of the Egyptian Human Rights Organization (EHRO) was accused by the Egyptian government of receiving money from the British government to issue a report on the Kush'h incident in 1998, in which twenty Copts were killed. It alleged that the report accused the Egyptian government of persecuting Copts. When it was revealed that the UK grant was used mainly to help handicapped people and women, the charges were dropped – but only after a lengthy press campaign denouncing the EHRO for accepting foreign money to tarnish the image of Egypt abroad. In fact, the report of the EHRO on the Kush'h incident was one of its most objective, factual and courageous actions in defence of human rights. Egyptian newspapers, on the other hand, published news stories wondering why the British government was providing political asylum to Egyptian Islamists accused of involvement in terrorist actions in Egypt. The British government replied that there was no evidence that such charges were well founded.

In assessing UK democracy promotion efforts in Egypt, the most relevant issues are those of credibility and effectiveness. As for credibility, UK involvement in Iraq and the practices of its troops there, silence over human rights violations in Libya and the withholding of aid to the Palestinian government led by Hamas have cast doubt on the depth of UK government commitment to democracy or human rights. In the case of Egypt, the programme of democracy promotion offers support only to secular opposition groups. It deliberately excludes Islamists who are not only the most popular political force in the country but are also the target of repressive measures by the government. The UK programme can be seen only as an exercise in public relations that lacks any credibility.

Human rights in Egypt have not shown signs of improvement over the last two years and have continued to worsen in some respects, particularly regarding freedom of association and of peaceful assembly. There is no doubt that democracy promotion by the UK or the US has not been effective in the case of Egypt. When asked to comment on the effectiveness of this programme, a British Embassy official in Cairo declared that it was difficult to assess its success. She cited the Ombudsman project with the National Council for Women as the most successful because it was easier to quantify, as thousands of women used this service to air their complaints. Such a project, in the view of the author, is only marginally related to democracy promotion.

The lack of effectiveness of UK democracy promotion activities in Egypt is not merely due to the limited resources allocated to them. US activities, which enjoy far larger resources, are no more successful. The major weakness lies in the basic assumption on which they are founded: that using carrots to persuade an authoritarian government suffering from a shortage of legitimacy will induce it to open up the political system and pave the way for the establishment of genuine democratic institutions. The experience of both the US and the UK with the Egyptian government eloquently demonstrates that neither carrots nor sticks can work with a regime determined not to take the risk of conducting fair and free elections.

More importantly, both the UK and the US acted under the naive assumption that free elections would bring into the government people supportive of their other policies in the Middle East. Free elections in Palestinian territories and one phase of relatively fair polling in Egypt led to the Hamas government in Palestine and to a fivefold increase in the Muslim Brotherhood's presence in Egypt's People's Assembly. Both Hamas and the Muslim Brotherhood are hostile to the pro-Israeli policies of the governments led by Tony Blair and George W. Bush. While one may argue that the British government, in particular, does not call the Muslim Brothers 'terrorists', it did not feel happy about Islamists' electoral victories. It joined – as did other EU governments – the US government in withholding economic assistance to the Hamas government. Its failure to condemn repressive measures against the Muslim Brothers in Egypt reflects perhaps a resigned acceptance that a cooperative authoritarian government is better than a potentially less cooperative opposition, at least in so far as foreign policies of the British government are concerned. Terrorist attacks in London in the summer of 2005 weakened the UK appetite, if it ever had one, for a policy that would bring Islamists to government in any country, notwithstanding the academic distinction between Islamist terrorists and Islamists who pursue a peaceful path to political power.

One may finally add a political culture explanation. The British tend to adopt a value-relativist position on the question of other countries' political systems, viewing these systems to be mainly an expression of each country's political culture. Unlike the French colonialists, who tried to disseminate their own culture to their colonies from belief in their *mission civiliatrice*, or the Americans, who believe in the supremacy of the 'American way of life', the British did not try to impose their system of government on peoples they colonised. In fact their colonial rulers felt very much at home with traditional chiefs in Africa and India and distrusted the educated elites in these countries, who were mostly fascinated by British liberal traditions at home.[4] One may suspect, therefore, that the British government's enthusiasm for democracy promotion was mostly lip service to a goal that was loudly proclaimed by the American partner in the 'special relationship'. When the first difficulties were encountered on the road to democracy promotion, it became preferable to abandon it completely except in gestures and diplomatic ceremonial.

Causes of the transformation

The shift from military confrontation in the Suez Canal area or by proxy in former British colonies in Arabia to mutual understanding and cooperation was the outcome of important domestic, regional and international changes.

A change of top leadership in the UK and Egypt facilitated turning the page of confrontation to one of cooperation. Undoubtedly the death of Nasser removed from the political scene an Arab leader associated with active anti-colonialist positions in the Middle East and beyond. The resignation of Anthony Eden, the Conservative British prime minister, who had an almost visceral hatred of Nasser, helped his Conservative and Labour successors to forget the bitter memory of the political defeat of the Empire in 1956 and start a new relationship with Egypt. Under Eden's immediate successor, Harold Macmillan, diplomatic relations were restored at the chargé d'affaires level in 1958 and elevated to full diplomatic relations in 1959. They were broken again in 1965 over differences on Southern Rhodesia, but were re-established under the Labour government of Harold Wilson in 1967. Nasser's successors in Egypt, both the late President Anwar El-Sadat and President Hosny Mubarak, were determined for diplomatic, strategic and economic reasons to improve Egypt's relations with Western countries, notably the US and Great Britain. But more important than a change of leaders was a change of policies by the governments of the two countries. The UK finally decided in the late 1960s to evacuate its military bases east of Suez, which took away some of the causes of tension between the two countries. Following defeat in the June 1967 war, Egyptian troops left Yemen and Egypt became less capable of influencing events in Southern Arabia. Such influence had given rise to feelings of hostility towards Egypt in UK diplomatic, intelligence and military circles. This change of policies facilitated the search for a new relationship between the two countries. A visit by Nasser's close friend and adviser Mohammed Hassanein Heikal to London in 1964 to meet the late Harold Wilson, British prime minister at the time, led to the second resumption of full diplomatic relations between the two countries. Though the June war of 1967 cast its shadow over this relationship and diplomatic relations were broken for a third time, they were re-established definitively in 1969. Since then they have been maintained at the level of ambassador.[5]

This is not to say that the two countries have agreed, following the re-establishment of their full diplomatic relations in the 1960s, on all important bilateral, regional and international issues. It is true that UK is an advanced post-industrial country while Egypt is a developing country which has not yet made it to the status of the newly-industrialised. Old-fashioned dependency theorists would expect complete alignment of policies by Egypt, a dependent country in their view, with those of the UK, a country of the centre. However, even under British military occupation, several Egyptian governments, particularly those of the Wafd, dared to take domestic and foreign policy positions not to the liking of British authorities. Even in more recent times the governments of the two countries have not seen eye to eye on several issues. The Egyptian government did not like the presence in Great Britain of a number of Islamist militants who used to organise meetings and demonstrations expressing their opposition to the Egyptian government's 'repressive' actions against their fellow militants in Egypt. The Egyptian government did not endorse the idea of sending a UN peacekeeping force to Darfur. President Hosny Mubarak did not like the whole idea of democracy promotion in the Middle East, proclaimed by the G8 countries. Nevertheless the two governments managed to continue close cooperation on several issues. They seek to manage their differences even if they cannot resolve them through diplomatic channels or learn to live with them simply as facts of life. Each government was fully aware of the other's position and of the limits of flexibility in its policy. British diplomats and senior officials had no illusions about the willingness of the Egyptian government to undertake genuine democratic reforms. So they would go through the motions of talking to their Egyptian counterparts about such issues whilst not expecting much response. Egyptian officials, being extremely polite, would listen carefully to what was being said, knowing full well that no pressure would be exerted over them if they ignored such advice. This kind of reciprocal complicity allowed bilateral relations to develop despite divergent viewpoints on matters of mutual concern.

The decline in the relative status of the two countries in their respective spheres of influence has made it easy for their governments not to exaggerate the consequences of such divergences. Egypt has lost its status of the 1950s and the 1960s as leader of the Arab world. Britain fell during the post-Suez situation to the rank of a middle power.[6] The Egyptian leadership since the 1970s could not have mobilised Arab masses against Britain over any contentious issue, even had they wished to do so. They also knew that Western policies in the region were largely shaped by US administrations and that Britain could not initiate on her own any decisive action in the Middle East, be it political, economic or military, without prior understanding and consent from the US.[7] An important sign of British loss of influence in the region came later in 1966 when the British Labour government started debating a withdrawal from the east of Suez.[8] It was made glaringly clear when Tony Blair would voice, for example, original ideas such as the holding of an international conference on the Palestinian–Israeli dispute, but would later drop them because of US and Israeli objections. Governments of the two countries knew full well who set the tone in Middle East diplomacy. They found no reason therefore to exaggerate the gravity of their differences on issues over which they had little control.[9]

This way of carrying out democracy promotion in Egypt demonstrates also that, thanks to the UK's approach on this issue, British–Egypt relations are excellent, but not to the benefit of human rights in Egypt.

Notes

1. On European approaches to democracy assistance see Richard Youngs, 'European Approaches to Democracy Assistance: Learning the Right Lessons?' in *Third World Quarterly*, vol. 24, no. 1, 2003, pp. 127–38.

2. A prominent example of relevant activities carried out by the UNDP through UK support is a programme of human rights training that catered for policemen, judges and media people.

3. This section is based on information obtained from the British Council in Cairo.

4. On different approaches towards the colonies, see Michael Stewart, *The British Approach to Politics*, 11th edn, London, 1960, pp. 243–86; Christopher Clapham, *Third World Politics. An Introduction*, London & Sydney, 1985, pp. 12–25.

5. On the history of diplomatic relations between the two countries, see John Marlowe, *Arab Nationalism and British Imperialism, A Study in Power Politics*, London, 1961, p. 198; Peter Hahn, *The United Statess Great Britain and Egypt, 1945–1956: Strategy and Diplomacy in the Early Cold War*, Chapel Hill, 1991, p. 156.

6. On the impact of the Suez war on the international status of Britain as a great power, see Anthony Gorst and Lewis Johnman, *The Suez Crisis*, London, 1997, pp. 147–65.

7. On UK loss of influence in the Middle East, see Ritchie Ovendale, *Britain, the United States and the Transfer of Power in the Middle East, 1945–1996*, London and New York, 1996, pp. 178–217.

8. On this point see also Phillip Darby, *British Defence Policy East of Suez, 1947–1968*, London, 1973, pp. 309–33.

9. Keith Kyle, *Suez, Britain's End of Empire in the Middle East*, London & New York, 2003, pp. 549–86.

HUGH ROBERTS

Islamism and Political Reform in British–Egyptian Relations

I propose to address two elements in contemporary British–Egyptian relations and the nature of the connection between them. Cast in the most general terms, we could call these elements 'Islamism' on one hand and 'political reform' on the other. However, for reasons which will become clear, I shall in fact be talking much more specifically about the Muslim Brothers and the importance of parliaments.

Islamism has become an especially prominent issue in British domestic politics since the terrorist bombings in London on 7 July 2005, but it is by no means clear that the British political class has been on a learning curve since then. It has long been an issue in Egyptian internal politics, of course, but it has become problematical in a new way since the legislative elections of November–December 2005.

Two key questions arise from this. Can the British political class as a whole arrive at an adequate understanding of what it is facing and trying to deal with? And can the Egyptian political class move out of the routine it has operated for some years now and begin to deal imaginatively with what it mostly understands very well?

British misunderstandings of Islamism

A defining feature of the public debate on Islamism that occurred in Britain in the wake of the London bombings on 7 July 2005 was the way in which informed views were almost entirely drowned out and marginalised by the clichés relentlessly recycled by the authorised shapers of mass opinion. The characteristic feature of these clichés was the way they confused the diverse trends within contemporary Islamism by reducing them all to one thing. The proliferation of alternative labels – 'Islamic fundamentalism', 'political Islam', 'radical Islamism', 'reactionary Islamism', 'Islamic militancy', 'extremism' or 'evil ideology' – should not mislead us. These did not indicate different things, but amounted to no more than different ways of branding the same thing, which remained largely unstudied by and unknown to the branders.

This inability or reluctance to distinguish between different kinds of Islamist thought and activism (and thus the tendency to tarnish one by association with another) underlay a particular line of criticism of the British government's foreign policy, which emerged in 2006. Instead of attacking the government's controversial support for and involvement in military action in the Muslim world (Iraq, Afghanistan, etc) and its failure to secure progress towards a resolution of, for example, the Palestine question, the target of this criticism was the government's general inclination to work with what it considered to be 'moderate' or 'mainstream' figures and, in particular, the Foreign Office's project of 'engaging with the Islamic world', which involves 'engaging' with Islamists as well as with Muslims to whom the label would not apply.[1]

The central element of this attack, as developed most prominently by the journalist Martin Bright, was the charge that the Foreign Office 'is following a policy of appeasement towards radical Islam'.[2] A large part of the empirical basis of this charge concerned the Foreign Office's dealings with, or at least its view of, and attitude to, the Egyptian Muslim Brothers. Fundamental to Bright's objection to this attitude was the argument that there should be no dialogue or 'engaging' with the Muslim Brothers because they are – or should be – politically and ideologically beyond the pale. This argument relied heavily on adjectives. The Brothers were variously referred to as 'Egypt's radical Islamic opposition movement'[3] and 'a reactionary, authoritarian brand of Islam',[4] and its leading lights accused of 'medieval'[5] views and endorsing terrorism.[6] In short, they were clearly not, as the French might say, *fréquentables*.

Thus the question of how we are to appraise the Muslim Brothers in Egypt has become an issue in domestic British debate on Islamism in general and government policy towards it in particular. Two aspects of Bright's depiction of the Muslim Brothers call for comment. The first is that it happens – no doubt through coincidence – to chime rather well with the official discourse of the Egyptian government, which is permanently concerned to justify its refusal to legalise the Brothers and is not above resorting to the 'terrorist' smear when it judges it needs to. The second and far more important aspect is that it exemplifies the British intelligentsia's inability or reluctance to come to terms with the complexities that characterise contemporary Islamism in the Sunni Muslim world.

Recognising Islamisms

Four months before the London bombings, the International Crisis Group (ICG) published a report on contemporary Islamism, which drew attention to the extremely important process of differentiation that had been occurring over the previous decade or more.[7] ICG pointed out that Sunni Islamic activism had crystallised into three main currents – political, missionary and jihadi – and that this development had rendered obsolete generalisations about 'radicalism' and 'fundamentalism' and the simplistic distinction between 'radicals' and 'moderates' that has been at the centre of Western discourse.

This is because the three currents do not occupy or constitute different points on a single spectrum of belief and conviction. The differences between them are of another nature entirely. They are premised on different diagnoses of the Muslim predicament, they offer different prescriptions of the appropriate remedy and they operate in accordance with distinct and often competing – if not frankly opposed – strategies of action. As ICG put it:

> Political Islamists make an issue of Muslim misgovernment and social injustice and give priority to political reform to be achieved by political action (advocating new policies, contesting elections etc.). Missionary Islamists make an issue of the corruption of Islamic values (*al-qiyam al-islamiyya*) and the weakening of faith (*al-iman*) and give priority to a form of moral and spiritual rearmament that champions individual virtue as the condition of good government as well as of collective salvation. Jihadi Islamists make an issue of the oppressive weight of non-Muslim political and military power in the Islamic world and give priority to armed resistance.[8]

This analysis and its implications remain to be taken on board by the political and media mainstream in the West in general and in the United Kingdom in particular.

The Egyptian case and the Muslim Brothers

Egypt has been the source of the main form of political Islamism, the Muslim Brothers, which has offshoots in numerous countries, including Algeria, Jordan, Kuwait, Palestine and Syria as well as in Europe. But Egypt has also been the source of the original form or prototype of contemporary jihadi Islamism, the group known as *Tanzim al-Jihad* (the Jihad Organisation), which assassinated President Sadat in 1981 and whose eventual leader, Ayman al-Zawahiri, has been Osama Bin Laden's principal lieutenant in al-Qa'ida over the last decade.

The outlook of political Islamism, as exemplified by the Muslim Brothers, is very different today from what it was when Hassan al-Banna founded the movement in 1928. The notion that, *qua* 'political Islam', they are by definition radical if not revolutionary, fundamentalist, hostile to nationalism and intrinsically and essentially anti-democratic, is badly out of date.

The Muslim Brothers today are not radical. They long ago distanced themselves from the radicalism of Sayyid Qutb's critique of the Free Officers' regime and explicitly rejected the thesis of the *takfiri* fringe groups which condemned the Egyptian state as un-Islamic and infidel;[9] on the contrary, the Brothers accept and endorse the Islamic credentials of the state and even of the government[10] and base their critique of the political *status quo* on other grounds – the absence of freedom and justice and the problem of widespread corruption.

The Muslim Brothers are not fundamentalist. In calling for Egypt to be governed in accordance with and on the basis of Islamic law, the *shari'a*, they are calling for the existing Egyptian constitution, which already defines the *shari'a* as the principal source of law, to be taken seriously. And their attitude to the *shari'a* is far removed from that of fundamentalists properly so-called. It is not based on literalist readings of scripture. Instead, the Brothers insist on the importance of *ijtihad*, the intellectual effort of interpretation of scripture in the light of changing circumstances and social conditions and guided by a conception of the general interest of the society. In taking this position, the Brothers have in fact reverted to the progressive outlook of the Egyptian reformer Mohammed Abduh (1849–1905). Far from fundamentalist and backward-looking, it is in fact properly described as Islamic-modernist.[11]

The Muslim Brothers are not anti-national. Whereas in the past many, if not most, Islamists were ambivalent about, or even hostile to the concept of the nation and the nation state, and tended to counterpose to this the Islamic conception of the *umma* (the supra-national community of believers), today the Muslim Brothers and their offshoots in other countries have all come to terms with the national idea (which they find they can reconcile with the *umma*)[12] and not only accept the nation state but also accept and respect the principle of national sovereignty.

A natural corollary of this evolution in their outlook is that the Muslim Brothers are not revolutionary. They accept the constitution of the state as the framework within which they must act, call for and propose reform of the state not its overthrow, and have clearly been pursuing a gradualist strategy.[13] This strategy has been reminiscent of nothing so much as that of the Fabian Socialists in late nineteenth -early twentieth-century Britain in its combination of two different but congruent ideas: first, the prudent precept (on which the Brothers have very clearly been acting for years) that they must avoid being drawn into any decisive confrontation with the state and, second, the belief that the ideals and principles they advocate will come into their own above all through a process of permeation of the society, a belief which the appreciable re-Islamisation of Egypt over the last three and a half decades clearly vindicates.

Finally, it is no longer possible to stigmatise the ideology of the Muslim Brothers as anti-democratic. Their original outlook, as defined by al-Banna, counterposed the Islamic concept of *shura* – consultation – to democracy, which was rejected as a Western and therefore un-Islamic idea. This position has long since been abandoned, both by the Egyptian Brothers and by their offshoots elsewhere. When the new Supreme Guide of the Brothers, Mohammed Mahdi Akef, assumed the leadership in early 2004, one of his first moves was to proclaim the Brothers' support for a revision of the constitution to make the Egyptian state a 'parliamentary republic';[14] in this way the Brothers outflanked the entire spectrum of 'democratic' opposition parties in Egypt in their critiques of the present presidential regime. And the eighty-eight Muslim Brothers elected to the National Assembly in 2005 have been vigorously demonstrating that they take parliament and their duties as its members extremely seriously, acutely embarrassing the MPs of the other parties in doing so.[15]

Thus the Muslim Brothers in Egypt are neither radical nor revolutionary nor fundamentalist nor anti-national nor anticonstitutional nor anti-democratic. But they are nonetheless illegal. Their status as a banned organisation has numerous problematical implications. Not the least of these is that it constitutes a problem for Western governments, especially those such as the British government, which are concerned to come to terms in some way or another with contemporary Islamism and consider that a necessary element of this endeavour must be some form of active 'engagement' with Islamist organisations. From this point of view, the illegal status of the Muslim Brothers in Egypt constitutes a constraint.

There can be little doubt that Western governments would be well advised to accept this constraint on their diplomatic activity in Egypt. The political cost of being seen to flout Egyptian law could be high. Moreover, the Muslim Brothers have made it clear that they do not intend to be lured into meetings with Western governments behind the backs of the Egyptian authorities. The constraint is qualified, however, by the fact that it is normal for Western diplomats to meet members of the Egyptian parliament and the Egyptian authorities cannot easily object to their meeting certain Muslim Brothers on this basis.

At the same time, Western governments should beware of entertaining unrealistic notions of what they may achieve through 'engaging' with Islamist movements. In particular, they should not expect to change the outlook of the Muslim Brothers in any significant degree merely by talking to them. This outlook has been developed steadily over many years and is the fruit of a long and often painful experience both of internal Egyptian politics and of wider events and processes, including Western – and notably British – policies and actions, in the Middle East as a whole. Neither sweet-talking nor brow-beating can realistically be expected to alter it.

In short, the serious objection to an aspect of the Foreign Office's 'engaging with the Islamic world' project, in so far as it includes engaging with political Islamists in countries such as Egypt, is not that these Islamists are to be considered ideologically beyond the pale but that this kind of engagement is liable to be perceived as a form of interference in these countries' internal affairs by the national governments and unlikely to make much impression on the Islamists themselves.

Egyptian handling of political Islamism

The status of the Muslim Brothers in Egypt is a singular one. It is a banned and therefore illegal organisation there, unlike its offshoots in Algeria[16] or Jordan,[17] not to mention its counterparts in Turkey and Morocco.[18] Moreover, it is not simply that it is not licensed as a political party; it is explicitly criminalised, and members are frequently arrested and imprisoned for belonging to a banned organisation. At the same time, the Muslim Brothers are informally tolerated by the authorities. Their wide range of social (educational and charitable) activities are not seriously interfered with, they play a major role in the country's professional organisations, the Syndicates, and they are also allowed to put up candidates in elections on condition that these stand for office as Independents. In addition, they are consciously employed by the regime to act as a safety-valve on international issues; striking examples of this occurred in February and March 2003, when public anger in Egypt over the British–American invasion of Iraq was intense; the largest demonstrations of this anger were organised by opposition parties and especially the Brothers, with the agreement of the authorities.[19]

As a result, the Muslim Brothers have been able to establish and preserve a virtual monopoly of the opposition presence in society. That this is the case was very clearly demonstrated in the course of 2005, when the Brothers' monopoly was challenged by a new unofficial protest movement, the 'Egyptian Movement for Change', popularly known by its slogan, *Kefaya* (Enough!).

Kefaya attracted a lot of media attention by daring to transgress the provisions of the Emergency Law banning street demonstrations and by the vehemence of its protests against President Mubarak's concentration of power and his rumoured intention to bequeath the presidency to his son, Gamal Mubarak. But Kefaya turned out to be not much more than a nine-month wonder, a flash in the pan. Unable to join any clear positive proposal or demand to its essentially negative discourse on the regime, and so unable to expand its audience beyond a narrow stratum of dissident intellectuals, Kefaya increasingly came to rely on support from the Muslim Brothers to swell its demonstrations, and never looked remotely capable of rivalling or making serious inroads into the Brothers' popular following.[20] As for the legal political parties, hampered by the terms of the Emergency Law, they have been denied any real chance to compete for a popular audience and are effectively confined for the most part to the political salons of Cairo and the editorial offices of their respective, small-circulation newspapers.

This state of affairs has reached an impasse.[21]

Why are the Muslim Brothers illegal? Why is it that the Egyptian government insists on maintaining them as a banned organisation when other Arab governments have had no problem about legalising their local equivalents? The official rationale is that the state refuses, on principle, to allow any 'religious parties', a position proclaimed by President Sadat in 1976 and since written into the constitution. This explanation cannot be dismissed and is supported by elements of the Egyptian elite.

A significant minority of Egyptians, perhaps as many as 10 per cent, are Christians (mostly Copts, plus a few Catholics, Protestants and Orthodox). Although the Muslim Brothers do not express a sectarian hostility towards Christians, there is no doubt that Egypt's Copts are generally apprehensive about the growth of the Brothers' influence. For the government to legalise the Muslim Brothers, therefore, could be to stimulate the emergence by reflex reaction of a specifically Christian or Coptic party and thus the onset of confessional or sectarian politics.

But it is by no means the whole story.[22] In theory, such a development could be offset by other measures. Were the ruling National Democratic Party, for example, to make it its business to woo and represent the Copts and offer avenues of political advancement to Copts, there would be no serious danger of Coptic sectarian politics developing. Quite apart from considerations of this nature, the regime has undoubtedly been concerned that the legalisation of the Muslim Brothers would destabilise the political system in one or both of two ways.

The first way concerns what the regime perceives as the external danger, namely the risk of instrumentalisation of the Muslim Brothers by foreign powers. This is an entirely reasonable apprehension and is likely only to be heightened by the advertised ambition of Western governments, such as the British government, to 'engage' with the Brothers. In this light, it is possible that the regime has an interest in keeping the Brothers illegal precisely in order to impede Western governments from 'engaging' with them, a possibility that carries the implication that Western governments are in fact contributing by their actions to the continued denial of legal status to the Brothers.

The second way concerns the internal danger, the risk that the other legal political parties, the NDP included, could not withstand the electoral challenge from the Muslim Brothers on a level playing field; that is, if they were allowed to play on the same terms as the others, as a licensed political party. The results of the 2005 legislative elections, which saw the Brothers' total of seats won (technically as 'Independents') soar from seventeen to eighty-eight, amply bear out this concern.[23]

In addition, the regime has what one might call a structural problem with the Muslim Brothers. This is a problem of legitimacy, or rather, relative legitimacy, and it arises in Egypt to an unusual degree. The ruling NDP is an evolution of the earlier Arab Socialist Union, itself an evolution of the Liberation Rally set up by the Free Officers after their seizure of power in 1952. As such, the NDP's connection with the 1952 revolution is a rather indirect and tenuous one.[24] Moreover, the NDP is not really a proper political party in the Western sense, but rather a facade for the executive branch of the state, a role that limits its capacity to tap any kind of political idealism and attract political activists. By comparison, the Muslim Brothers, founded in 1928 and so long antedating the Revolution, rooted in Islam but also in most classes of Egyptian society, can lay claim to legitimacy and mobilise enthusiasm in several different registers at once. These features make the Brothers a potential rival to the NDP of formidable dimensions, and one the regime cannot really begin to handle creatively for as long as it identifies its survival with the formal dominance of the NDP.

The first political consequence of this is that Egypt has a system of government without opposition. The legal parties are too small and weak to amount to a serious challenge to or effective curb on the government. There is accordingly a lack of political accountability and the resulting failure to check corruption gives considerable point to the Muslim Brothers' moralistic discourse. The second political consequence is the immobilisation of political life. The third consequence, closely connected to the second, is the increasing depoliticisation of Egyptian society. Even official figures claim no more than 20 to 26 per cent turnouts in elections and referenda.

A way forward

The only answer to the conundrum posed by the Muslim Brothers in Egypt that can allow for positive evolution within the existing constitutional framework is that the regime must foster the legal parties in order to enable itself eventually to legalise the Brothers without grave risk of destabilisation. If the legal parties – the Wafd, Tagammu, the Liberals etc. – can recover a real social presence[25] and thereby end the Brothers' virtual monopoly of social activism, the regime could then afford to integrate the Brothers into the political system in a manner that would strengthen this system instead of jeopardising it.

But this fostering of the legal parties is much easier said than done. At present, the regime appears to be set on doing something superficially of this kind by means of changes in the electoral law –

altering the rules to favour the parties in order to reduce the prospects of independent candidates, and thus cut the Brothers down to size in the electoral sphere. This will do little to enable the legal parties to recover real social influence.

The key precondition of any recovery of social influence by the legal political parties is the revitalisation of the legislative branch of the state, that is, the empowering of the Egyptian national parliament, so that it becomes a genuine locus of political decision-making. Such a development would require more from the parties than they are currently required to do. It would increase their responsibilities and thus their political and representative capacities. And what applies to the legal parties in general would and should apply to the NDP in particular. Were parliament to acquire increased powers of decision, this would, or at least could, stimulate if not oblige the NDP to raise its political game and equip itself with political capacities which, at present, it lacks. Such a line of development could at last enable the NDP to contemplate competing politically with the Muslim Brothers instead of relying on controversial laws and police measures to deal with them.

It is entirely possible, indeed probable, that this line of development will not occur. While the recent constitutional changes include a slight increase in parliament's prerogatives, undoubtedly a (small) step in the right direction, the other measures that the Egyptian authorities are now taking do not correspond to this perspective at all. Rewriting the electoral rules while maintaining the ban on the Brothers may buy the regime some time. But given the depth of the accumulating problems that now beset Egyptian political life, a short-term strategy will only delay the ultimate resolution and make this harder to effect within the framework of constitutional continuity.

However, it needs to be said that the Egyptian government has by no means a monopoly of the responsibility for this depressing state of affairs.

A shared responsibility

The Muslim Brothers apart, the Egyptian opposition parties have not been putting the regime under any real pressure on the issue of empowering the legislature at all, nor did the Kefaya protest movement raise it clearly, despite its condemnation of the 'monopoly of power' it perceived as the corollary of Egypt's emphatic form of presidential rule. This crucial lacuna in the outlook of opposition currents of thought in Egypt, as elsewhere, has reflected an identical lacuna in Western thinking, on which these currents have been intellectually dependent to a self-defeating degree.

The notion that political reform in Egypt or, indeed, elsewhere in the Middle East and North Africa, requires as one of its first steps, if not *the* first step, a shift in power *within* the state from the executive to the legislative branch, has been conspicuous in its absence from Western discourse on reform in the Arab and Muslim world ever since this discourse got under way in the late 1980s. Despite all the disappointing experiences across the region since then, there has been no evidence whatever that Western governments and non-governmental reform advocates have been on a learning curve in this respect.

Moreover, Western governments have hardly been setting a powerful example in this matter in recent years. Were an Egyptian analyst to focus on the problem of Islamism (and, for that matter, other forms of identity politics) in contemporary Western democracies, including the United Kingdom, he or she might well note that a feature of the context in which these issues have become more and more politically septic, if not explosive, has been the relative decline of the role of the legislature in the forms of government of contemporary Western states and of Britain as much as anywhere,[26] and the concomitant decline of the role of political parties in structuring public opinion and offering electorates a real choice in the ballot booth.

Conclusion

So: can Egypt, *Umm al-Dunya*, the Mother of the World, learn from the Mother of Parliaments? That is to say, can the British and the Egyptian political classes raise their respective games, progress up their respective learning curves by learning from one another, and so extend and enrich their respective political repertoires? The answer is that this is unlikely unless certain conditions are fulfilled.

One condition that can be identified is that, if the Egyptian government is to feel able to embark on a new, more imaginative, approach to political reform in general and its handling of political Islamism in particular, it must feel under less pressure from external actors. It follows that Western governments should not presume to interfere in internal Egyptian political life, but should be available to assist if requested to do so.

More generally, it is possible, if not probable, that a necessary condition of genuine political progress in Egypt is that the Western democracies revitalise a crucial element of their own democratic traditions, the indispensable role of strong legislatures – as curbs on executive power, as guarantors of the independence of the judiciary, and as the framework within which vigorous party politics can occur. Unless this happens, it is unlikely that democratic ideas will gain ground in Egypt or anywhere else. The recent signs of a reassertion of the prerogatives and role of the legislative branch in the USA may give grounds for hope, in so far as this example is followed in Britain as well as elsewhere.

But it would be entirely appropriate if the United Kingdom, with its historic parliamentary tradition, were to take the lead and set an example in this. For it to do so, however, the British political class would have to act decisively to reverse the recent trends in Britain itself, which have unquestionably involved the bypassing of Parliament and the diminution, indeed, the belittling, of its constitutional role and gravely undermined Britain's capacity to be a source of useful imitation for other countries.

Notes

1. Ewen MacAskill, 'UK to Build Ties with Banned Islamist Group', *Guardian*, 17 February 2006.
2. Martin Bright, *When Progressives Treat with Reactionaries: The British State's Flirtation with Radical Islamism*, London, Policy Exchange, July 2006, p. 12.
3. Bright, ibid.
4. Ibid.
5. Bright (quoting with approval Michael Gove), ibid., p. 21.
6. Bright, ibid., pp. 20–1.
7. International Crisis Group, Middle East/North Africa Report, no. 37, *Understanding Islamism*, Cairo/Brussels, 2 March 2005.
8. ICG, ibid., p. ii.
9. *Takfir* – frequently mistranslated into English as 'excommunication' – is the act of defining and condemning something or someone as infidel, un-Islamic. As such, it constitutes a judgement and presupposes that the person or persons engaging in *takfir* possess – or have usurped – the authority of judges. This outlook was explicitly rejected by the Muslim Brothers as long ago as 1969, when the Brothers' Supreme Guide, Hassan al-Hodeibi, published a text entitled *Du'ah, Lâ Qudah* (Missionaries, Not Judges) which defined the outlook of the Muslim Brothers and dissociated them from *takfiri* views in general and Qutb's radicalism in particular. For a detailed discussion of Qutb and the Muslim Brothers' relation to his thought, see ICG Middle East & North Africa Briefings, *Islamism in North Africa I: The Legacies of History* and *Islamism in North Africa II: Egypt's Opportunity*, Cairo/Brussels, 20 April 2004.
10. ICG, *Islamism in North Africa II: Egypt's Opportunity*, p. 11.
11. ICG, *Understanding Islamism*, p. 7. For a discussion of the way in which the importance of *ijtihad* is now recognised by derivatives of the Muslim Brothers outside Egypt, see ICG, Middle East & North Africa Report, no. 29, *Islamism, Violence and Reform in Algeria: Turning the Page*, Cairo/Brussels, 30 July 2004, pp. 19–22.
12. ICG, *Understanding Islamism*, p. 6; ICG, *Islamism, Violence and Reform in Algeria*, p. 20.
13. See ICG, *Islamism in North Africa II: Egypt's Opportunity*, chapter IV, section B: 'The travails of Islamic gradualism.'
14. See Gamal Essam al-Din, 'Brotherhood Steps into the Fray', and Amr El-Choubaki, 'Brotherly Gesture?', *Al-Ahram Weekly*, 11–17 March 2004.
15. For an excellent account, see Samer Shehata and Joshua Stacher, 'The Brotherhood Goes to Parliament', *Middle East Report*, 240, Fall 2006.
16. That is, the Movement of Society for Peace (*Mouvement de la Société pour la Paix*, MSP; *Harakat al-Mujtama' al-Silm*, HMS) which has been legal and indeed a junior partner in coalition governments since 1996; two other

Islamist parties, the Renaissance Movement (*Mouvement de la Nahda*, MN; *Harakat al-Nahda*) and the National Reform Movement (*Mouvement de la Réforme Nationale*, MRN; *Harakat al-Islah al-Watani*), which derive from the general tradition of the Muslim Brothers, are also legal and represented in the Algerian parliament.

17. The Islamic Action Front (*Jabhat al-'amal al-Islami*), which won twenty seats in the 2003 legislative elections.

18. These share the name of the Justice and Development Party – *Adalet ve Kalkinma Partisi* (AKP) in Turkey and *Parti pour la Justice et le Développement* (PJD) in Morocco – and are not offshoots of the Muslim Brothers' tradition but home-grown forms of political Islamism.

19. On 27 February 2003, 140,000 people filled Cairo Stadium in a public meeting of opposition to the war; the Supreme Guide of the Muslim Brothers was among the platform speakers, and the Brothers played a large part in organising the meeting, in cooperation with the state security services. On 28 March, the Brothers were once again authorised to lead a 10,000 strong demonstration of protest against the war.

20. For a critical analysis of Kefaya, see ICG, Middle East & North Africa Report, no. 46, *Reforming Egypt: In Search of a Strategy*, 4 October 2005.

21. For detailed analyses of the logic of this impasse, see ICG, *Islamism in North Africa II: Egypt's Opportunity*, pp. 14–16 and ICG, *Reforming Egypt*, pp. 17–23.

22. For a discussion of this debate, see ICG, *Reforming Egypt*, pp. 20–3.

23. The Brothers contested only 35 per cent of the seats in the election, fielding 159 candidates. They would have won well over 100 seats had not rigging in some constituencies and the blatant mobilisation of security forces to prevent people from voting in the later stages of the elections prevented this. Even with 88 seats, their strike rate (88 out of 159) of 55.34 per cent was higher than that of all the other parties, including the NDP (which got only 145 of its 432 official candidates elected, and relied on party renegades running as Independents to make up its overall majority). In other words, the Brothers' demonstrated mobilisation capacity was second to none.

24. In this respect, the NDP contrasts very unfavourably with a party which resembles it closely in other respects, namely Algeria's FLN Party, since the latter can claim a measure of continuity in its leading personnel as well as its name with the historic FLN which fought the revolutionary war of independence. For a detailed discussion of the Egypt–Algeria comparison, see Hugh Roberts, *Demilitarizing Algeria*, Carnegie Endowment for International Peace, Middle East Program, Paper No. 86, May 2007.

25. For this to happen it may well be necessary for the legal parties to unite in a new party with a new profile and agenda, something the regime currently seems disinclined to allow, let alone promote.

26. See Henry Porter, 'How We Move ever Closer to Becoming a Totalitarian State', *Observer*, 5 March 2006, and 'Less a servant of the people, more a hammer of Parliament', *Observer*, 25 February 2007.

AHMED EL-MOKADEM

Egypt, Britain and the USA

Pivotal Power, Great Power and Superpower

In this article I want to examine the impact of the Suez Crisis and subsequent developments in the Middle East on the triangular relationship between Egypt, Britain and the United States. This is a contribution to a model that I am developing for publication elsewhere in which I analyse how a great power (the UK), a pivotal power (Egypt) and a superpower (the US) can influence one another in the handling of events, using events in the Middle East over the last fifty years to test the model. In developing my ideas I have looked in particular at Iraq and how three crises there have been dealt with: they are the Iraqi threat to invade Kuwait in 1961, the Iraqi invasion of Kuwait in 1990 and the US-led invasion of Iraq in 2003. In the first there was a coincidence of interests between Britain and Egypt that helped resolve the crisis. In the second all three states worked together to force Saddam Hussein out of Kuwait. In 2003 the US and the UK acted without the support of Egypt. The consequences are visible every day on our television screens. Whilst I will assert that my ideas work well in this context, I believe that they can also be adapted to analyse how the triangular relationship between the USA, the UK and Egypt has worked more broadly and can be made to work better. The first step is to define terms and look at the historical background, with the Suez Crisis serving as the starting point.

The great power: Great Britain

It is unnecessary, in the context of this article, to engage in a long debate on what is meant by the term 'great power'. The term was coined in 1814 and was used to represent the most important powers in Europe at the end of the Napoleonic War. Recognising the large shifts in power which have occurred since then, most notably in World War I and World War II, 'a great power is a nation or state that, through its great economic, political and military strength, is able to exert power over world diplomacy. Its opinions are strongly taken into account by other nations before taking diplomatic or military action. Characteristically, they have the ability to intervene militarily anywhere, and they also have soft cultural power'. But, significantly, 'One of the hallmarks of contemporary great power status is permanent membership on the United Nations Security Council'.[1]

For the purpose of this chapter, there are two aspects relating to Britain as a great power that have been, and remain, of considerable relevance to an effective role in the Middle East. One is Britain's unmatched, deep, sensitive knowledge of the Middle East and its past and present problems. This knowledge covers the full spectrum – cultural, social, historical, economic and political. Historically, for example, Britain drew borders to create new states, to remove others and to create monarchies and new governing orders. It used its historical knowledge to create new histories. It provided support to preserve cultures and heritages and to educate new generations. Egyptians may not have agreed with colonialism, but many acknowledge that British colonialism was not all bad, at least when compared with the way other colonial powers deliberately eliminated cultures, heritage and even languages. The second aspect, which is discussed below, is that Britain's unique relationship with both the US and Europe gives it a special influence.

Egypt as a pivotal state

Historically, this concept of a pivotal state is not new. It goes as far back as the British geographer Sir Halford Mackinder in the early 1900s. Following the end of World War II, the concept re-emerged in the form of the domino theory. Dominos were seen from the standpoint of American strategic interests as states that required assistance in the face of a security threat from an enemy, and were potentially at risk of internal disorder or collapse. US strategists and policy-makers placed the highest priority on strategic relations with other great powers while attempting to preserve the status quo. They became quite selective in deciding on which other states to enter into obligations with. They could thus focus on those states that were important – the pivotal states.

Robert Chase has pointed out that:

> A pivotal state strategy offered a means to reshape the enduring and somewhat sterile debate between those who regarded traditional military (or 'old security') issues as the greatest threats to US security interests and those who viewed the 'new security' issues – including environmental degradation, overpopulation and underdevelopment – as the biggest dangers.[2]

Chase argued that neither the old nor the new approach is sufficient. In contrast, a pivotal state strategy will 'encourage integration of new security issues into a traditional, state-centred framework and lend greater clarity to the making of foreign policy. This integration may make some long-term consequences of the new security threats more tangible and manageable, and it would confirm the importance of working chiefly through state governments to ensure stability while addressing the new security issues that make these states pivotal.'
I accept this approach, given the centrality of the US as the only superpower since the late 1980s. However, what criteria should be used to select a pivotal state? According to Chase, while factors such

as a large population, an important geographical location, economic potential and physical size are necessary, they are not sufficient.

> What really defines a pivotal state is its capacity to affect regional and international stability. A pivotal state is so important regionally that its collapse would spell trans-boundary mayhem: migration, communal violence, pollution, disease and so on. A pivotal state's steady economic progress and stability, on the other hand, would bolster its region's economic vitality and political soundness and benefit American trade and industry.

Based on the above definition, both Robert Chase and Roger Owen (1996 and 1999) argue, most strongly and eloquently, for selecting Egypt as the 'pivotal state' in the Middle East region, in both its positive and negative aspects. According to Owen:

> It – Egypt – is well placed to play a number of regional roles, whether as a potential leader of the Arab World, an ally of the U.S. ..., or an essential component of the burgeoning Euro-Mediterranean partnership. It also has critical interests in demography, land, and water use and the environment, many of which can best be promoted in a regional or international context. By much the same token, it would be a matter of enormous significance if Egypt were to experience a radical change ... that led either to a sharp reduction in the present limited democracy or to a major shift in its international alignment.[3]

Superpower

It is widely accepted that there is now only one superpower. The bipolar world of the cold war – the eras of Nasser and Sadat in Egypt – has gone, leaving the US dominant with the unmatched magnitude of its utilised and still under-utilised resources and its economic and military might. However, being the only superpower, as Huntington notes, does not mean that the world is uni-polar, with one superpower that can effectively resolve important international issues alone, no combination of other states having the power to prevent it from doing so. Huntington comments: 'The settlement of key international issues requires action by the single superpower, but always with some combinations of other major states', on one hand, but, 'The single superpower can, however, veto action on key issues by combinations of other states', on the other hand.[4] There are several examples of this – the US invasion of Iraq being the most recent and clear.

Interactions: bilateral

US–UK

As Roger Owen and others have pointed out in this book, one of the lessons of Suez for the UK was that it should always place the relationship with the US at the centre of its foreign policy interests.

> As far as both Britain and France were concerned the major lessons drawn from the Suez Crisis became clear within a very short period of time. For Harold Macmillan, who succeeded Anthony Eden as prime minister in January 1957, and his cabinet, the most pressing issue was how to re-establish a close relationship with the United States, something Macmillan was able to achieve within a few months. They were also of the strong opinion that Britain should never again endanger this relationship by embarking on a major military adventure without American support, a position to which succeeding governments have adhered up to the present day.[5]

A cursory examination of Middle East history since Suez suggests that the UK has always placed its relationship with the USA at the centre of its concerns. A constructive example was the proactive cooperation between the two countries in the formidable coalition that liberated Kuwait in 1990–1. Another less constructive example is the total endorsement by the British government of the US invasion of Iraq in 2003. Although the 'special relationship' in defence and intelligence has been one between unequal parties and favourable to the US, politically it was not always one-sided. There are many examples up to the mid-1990s where the parties did not see eye-to-eye on key foreign policy issues. Eisenhower's firm stand during the Suez Crisis forced Britain to withdraw from Egypt. Prime Minister Harold Wilson adamantly rejected President Johnson's attempts to involve Britain in the Vietnam War. Under Margaret Thatcher, Britain frequently voted for resolutions concerning the Middle East which were vetoed by the US. In contrast, the UK more recently has been abstaining on Middle East resolutions out of loyalty to the US, not out of conviction or support for Israel.

Great Britain today is an active member of the European Union, which gives it the opportunity to work with fellow members of the EU to pursue policies that may be different from those of the USA. One of the great debates within the UK in recent years has been the relative weight that should be given to its relationships with the USA and the EU. Britain has also seen itself – and is sometimes seen by others – as a power that can bring Europe and America closer together. But it has to be kept in mind that France, another great power, as a result of Suez sought to create defence and foreign policies independent of those of the USA. There are thus two different views in Europe of the priority that should be attached to the relationship with the US. Of course, there are clear benefits to Egypt from the UK working with both the EU and the US as well as independently of both. Egypt can potentially gain (and lose) by association with the US. London's ability to influence Washington is a factor in its relationship with Egypt. As Egypt has had an association agreement with the EU and is an active participant in many of the fora that bring Mediterranean countries closer together, the EU is a major source of investment for Egypt and a large market for its exports. As Egypt's importance as a gas producer grows, its significance to Europe will also increase.

There are signs that British leaders are reconsidering how the special relationship with the US should be handled. As one analyst has put it, 'If Ireland, or Jamaica, or Chile, or New Zealand, can pursue an independent foreign policy, and bargain with Washington, then why should the United Kingdom be the old mistress, always waiting and available, but with no claim on American generosity?'[6]

A properly reconstructed 'special relationship' does not have to conflict with an independent foreign policy toward the Middle East; nor does it prevent Britain from having a strong relationship with many countries in the world, including, but not limited to, India, China and Japan. In my view, Britain, with its unmatched and profound knowledge of the Middle East, should be in a position to contribute significantly to the solution of the chronic problems of the Middle East, but only if – and it is a big if – constructive, proactive and permanent cooperation is established with Egypt as a pivotal state, on a long-term basis.

US–Egypt

The relationship between Egypt and the US has loomed large from the early days of the revolution. It was the US decision to offer and then withdraw assistance for the construction of the High Dam that pushed Egypt into actions that led to the Suez Crisis and reinforced its relationship with the Soviet Union in the then bipolar world. President Sadat dramatically shifted policy when he expelled the Soviet advisers, launched the 1973 war and then made peace with Israel. This marked the start of the close relationship between Washington and Cairo, expressed in large inflows of military and economic assistance and political cooperation. Though the relationship has evolved, it remains of critical importance to Cairo. Egypt, it can be argued, has played its hand well. It has stuck by its objectives whilst calibrating the support it offered to the US on a case by case basis, depending on how US action affected its interests in the region and public opinion in Egypt and the wider Arab world. It is not a one-sided relationship. Egypt will criticise US policies and it can reject US demands over reform. Cairo recognises US diplomatic clout in the region, but points out that it only appears to use this to serve the interests of Israel. Egypt appears to calculate that the US needs Egyptian support in the region. Without Egypt there would be no peace process. There are special reasons at the moment why Egypt is playing a passive role in the region compared with Saudi Arabia, but Egypt's weight will inevitably bring it back to the centre of the regional stage.

It is a relationship from which both sides clearly benefit and in Cairo, at least, the government would seem entitled to feel that it has handled the relationship well and served Egypt's strategic and economic interests in doing so.

Egypt and the UK: the interaction at work at Suez

In introducing the opening session of the Suez conference, I used an unscientific paradigm for examining the relationship between the three powers in the mid-1950s. I described Egypt at the time of Suez as the heart, Britain as the brain and the USA as the brawn or muscle. I suggested that only when the heart and the brain are in synchrony, peace and harmony prevail. In the run-up to Suez the brain was receiving unusual signals from the heart, which were interpreted as symptoms caused by the withdrawal of British troops from the Suez Canal Zone. But at the same time the muscle reacted almost in spasm to Egyptian moves towards the Soviet Union by cutting off funding to the Aswan High Dam. This provoked the heart – operated by a valve in the form of the charismatic leader of Egypt, Gamal Abdul Nasser – to react by nationalising the Suez Canal Company. The brain reacted impulsively. There was the invasion and the subsequent application of muscle to the brain. Britain was humiliated and forced to withdraw from Suez. It assumed the role of the muscle in an action that was tantamount to heart surgery.

These events have been described in more detail in other chapters of this book. However, some tentative conclusions can be drawn. First, it was a crisis that occurred in an atmosphere influenced by cold war considerations, with the Soviet Union going through a period of significant change following the Twentieth Congress of the Communist Party. It was also a period of great importance for Nasser's regime, as he was trying to strengthen his authority, after a period of intensive internal struggle, within the group of the so-called Free Officers, who carried out the 1952 coup d'état. At the same time, Prime Minister Eden was trying to place his own stamp on the British government and the Conservative Party, after spending long, frustrating years living in the shadow of Winston Churchill and waiting, sometimes patiently and sometimes impatiently, for his turn to lead.

Secondly, this was a crisis between, on the face of it, one great power and a pivotal power that was emerging as the most influential state in the Arab world and, beyond that, in the Non-aligned Movement. Despite the fact that the dispute was limited and simple, at least in the narrow legal sense, and concerned the ownership and management of a 'company' – namely the Suez Canal Company – the short-and long-term ramifications appeared to be grave within the context of the cold war. London feared Nasser's ambitions, and either failed or refused to admit that the days of the Empire were over.

Thirdly, and surprisingly, despite the fact that the crisis started with the unilateral American withdrawal of finance for the High Dam, the US government took a back seat, at least publicly, following Nasser's nationalisation of the Suez Canal. It was only after the tripartite attack on Egypt that the US government reappeared on the world political scene, with its decisive political and economic measures.

Finally, the manner in which the British government (or rather Eden personally, as documents released later showed) conducted the public and secret political campaign was strange. There was a theatrical finesse to the build-up, followed by a theatrically-managed military campaign. No convincing explanation, or even admission, has until now been provided. The question remains as to why Britain should take such high-risk action on a matter that could have been resolved without Britain signing a military secret alliance with Israel, or embroiling itself through a military alliance with France in the Algerian War of Liberation.

Thus, instead of trying to solve the one problem of the Suez Canal, Britain seemed willingly to have decided to engage itself in two other issues: the Arab–Israel Conflict and the Algerian War of Liberation. Moreover, all this was done behind the back of a superpower with whom Britain was supposed to have a special relationship. We should note that the triple alliance may have inspired the US to use similar arrangements later on in planning military action in the Middle East.

Broader considerations

There is not enough space to examine in detail the problems of the Middle East, but they are an important influence on the way that the US, the UK and Egypt interact today. There is the whole question of Arab–Israeli relations and the potential for war and instability created by this relationship and the failure to resolve the rights of the Palestinians. There is a virtual civil war in Iraq and the question of how long the superpower aided by the great power can sustain its presence there. Iran – potentially, of course, another pivotal state – is approaching confrontation with the US and Europe over its nuclear ambitions. Egypt and other Arab states are suspicious of Iranian aims in Iraq, Lebanon and Syria and in the Shi'i communities of the region. There is Darfur; in the Middle East and beyond there are potentially unstable states with apparently stable regimes. Many states are dominated by ageing leaders who have not established acceptable methods for arranging their succession. There is little democracy and much potential for social alienation. There are economic and social problems. There are extremism and terrorism. The Middle East is volcanic – there are small eruptions most of the time and a big one could come along at any time.

Such a situation poses immense problems for the superpower, the great power and the pivotal power. But it poses particular problems for Egypt, which lives in the shadow of that volcano. What are the implications, particularly at a time when Egypt is often accused of not wishing to use its weight in the region?

In recent years Egypt has been focusing on internal change and reform. It has, perhaps, in the process given less attention to foreign affairs. A great deal has been achieved, but Egypt will need to do much more. The dismantling of the Nasserist state needs to be completed, but in a way that does not disrupt the lives of people working in government departments and state-owned industries. The privatisation process must be continued and directed at ensuring that it is to the benefit of the public at large and not a few of the elite. The financial service sector must be genuinely freed, linking the Egyptian economy with the world economy, and acting, as it should, as the driver of the domestic economy with strict compliance with acceptable international standards. Similarly, a healthy and buoyant tourist industry, based on international standards, must be supported. Privatisations of the three national newspapers and other sectors of the media are necessary. The public sector needs to be reduced and private initiative should replace welfare handouts where possible. There is also a case for merging and reforming the security agencies.[7] Egypt has only to look at the transformation of Britain in the 1980s to see what can be done. Such moves would enable Egypt to recapture some of the zeal of the 1919 revolution and allow it to give greater priority to its external relations. Egypt could then resume in full the pivotal role that started in the modern age with Napoleon's entry into Egypt in 1798. It would also have the opportunity to boost its position in world affairs. Egypt should open up strategically and proactively to the surrounding world. Extreme obsession with Arab politics is unproductive. One needs to remember Mohamed Ali's foreign policies in the 1800s and, in particular, the opening up to Europe, which enabled Egypt to become a significant power in a region stretching from Central Asia through Southern Europe and to the Arabian peninsula. Cairo again needs to broaden its horizons.

In doing so it will both enhance its pivotal role and give the superpower and great power even stronger motives for working with Egypt. It can also boost its bargaining power and afford to get tougher with the US. Egypt should recognise that it is of critical importance to the US in maintaining stability in the region. It should show the US that a strong, dignified Egypt cannot accept Israel's monopoly of nuclear arms capability, and Israel's continuing refusal to sign the Nuclear Non-Proliferation Treaty since 1995. There is a case for the Camp David Accord to be renegotiated. Circumstances have changed since it was signed, and some provisions of Egyptian rights over Sinai are no longer acceptable, particularly in view of recent terrorist activities. One should bear in mind that an accord is not real peace. Permanent, lasting peace is one between equals.

It is in the interests of the US and the UK to see Egypt emerge as a greater regional power. Egypt has shown over much of the last fifty years that it is able to exert a major influence in the region. Given the nature of the problems in the region referred to above it is vital that there should be located in the heart of it a stable and strong Egypt which shares the interests, objectives and values of London and Washington. I suggest that in looking at how they conduct relations in the future they might look back at some of the lessons of the Suez Crisis.

The first is that Suez showed that there is a need for serious consultation between a great power and a superpower, particularly when there are so many links between them through what the UK likes to call the 'special relationship'. If nothing else, both were members of the NATO strategic alliance in what was then the world of the cold war. Such consultation becomes necessary when the great power is facing a significant challenge, not only to its vital interests, but also to those of its friendly superpower, its Western allies and other powers – not excluding in this case the Soviet Union. The decision to act alone proved rash. Britain has learned the lesson and has been assiduous – some might say too assiduous – in applying it to events since then.

Secondly, force alone cannot resolve a dispute between a great power – not even a superpower, as events later proved – and an important regional or pivotal power. Much more can be achieved through calm, rational, calculated and consultative diplomacy than through armed force, though, of course, they are not mutually exclusive. This lesson is as valid in the Middle East of the early twenty-first century as it was in the mid-twentieth century.

Finally, there is the critical responsibility of the superpower in crisis management. In the case of Suez, and despite the many interpretations or misinterpretations, there is no doubt that the far-sighted leadership of President Eisenhower, with the assistance of a very aggressive Secretary of State, John Foster Dulles, prevented a long-term disaster for Western interests. Such leadership has not always been apparent in recent years.

Conclusion

The model that I am developing elsewhere is based on the idea that when the superpower, great power and pivotal power work in harmony, they can act for the good of their own interests and those of others in the Middle East. When they are not in harmony, there are problems. It is important for each to understand the triangular nature of the relationship and adjust policies to make it as harmonious as possible. I recognise that these three countries are not the only ones involved. There are other great powers in Europe and new ones are emerging. There are other pivotal states. The USA, the UK and Egypt will operate in several such relationships simultaneously and will need to keep some sense of balance. But I hope I have demonstrated by looking at the US–UK–Egypt example that there is some merit in the model and that it is relevant to the analysis of relationships between states. I also hope that I have demonstrated that the lessons learned at the time of Suez are highly relevant to today's world.

Notes

1. Wikipedia, the online encyclopaedia: *Great Powers*.
2. Robert Chase, Emily Hill and Paul Kennedy, eds, *The Pivotal States: A New Framework for US Policy in the Developing World*, London and New York, 1999, p. 5.
3. Roger Owen, 'Egypt', in Robert Chase, Emily Hill and Paul Kennedy, eds, *The Pivotal States: A New Framework for US Policy in the Developing World*, London and New York, 1999, pp. 120–43.
4. Samuel P. Huntington, 'The Lonely Superpower', *Foreign Affairs*, March/April 1999, p. 3.
5. See Chapter 2: Roger Owen and W. Roger Louis, eds, *Suez 1956: The Crisis and its Consequences*, Oxford: Oxford University Press, 1989.
6. Ian Williams, 'British–USA Special Relationship? Whither the Special Relationship? Bush, Blair and Britain's future', January 2004, www.spectrezine.org/europe/Williams.htm.
7. A. M. El-Mokadem, 'The Politics of Decline: Lessons from the Thatcherite Model', a lecture delivered to the Association of Graduates of British Universities, Cairo 1990, and reproduced in 'Essays on the Security and Stability of the State of Kuwait: Real Fears, Conditional Hopes and the Roles of Independent Great Britain and Independent, Democratic Egypt and Thatcherite Kuwait'. Unpublished, 2001.

HEBA HANDOUSSA

Egypt's New Social Contract for Growth with Equity

The purpose of this chapter is to provide a brief overview of the social dimension to Egypt's transition to a liberal, private-sector-led economy. It also introduces some of the major elements of an emerging new 'social contract' between the state and civil society as proposed by the UNDP Egypt Human Development Report (EHDR) in 2005. The government of Egypt has adopted most of the programmes presented in this vision document – which proposes essentially a policy of pro-poor growth with equity – and a 'Social Contract Centre' has, since late 2006, been specifically created at the Information and Decision Support Centre for the Cabinet in order to coordinate and monitor the implementation of the proposed programmes.

This chapter will be divided into three main sections. The first gives evidence of the need to revise Egypt's social policies in the light of new economic and political realities. The second section spells out the principles behind an emerging new social and economic vision, and the third describes the generous and pro-poor programmes being introduced by the state as part of the new social contract.

The need to revise Egypt's social contract

Soon after the Suez war in the latter part of the 1950s, Nasser inaugurated a socialist-oriented ideology with mass appeal in Egypt and neighbouring Arab countries. This new corporatist model was highly centralised and introduced, in addition to land reform, nationalisation and state ownership of financial and productive enterprises, central planning, an industrialisation drive and guaranteed employment in the civil service for all graduates. However, Egypt's socialist 'social contract' between the state and the people was strongly biased towards the urban middle classes. The poorest of the poor were left behind, especially the rural landless.

In fact, between 1952 and 1972, real wages in agriculture increased by only 1 per cent. This was because the government was taxing agriculture in order to promote industrialisation. It was only with the oil boom of the mid-1970s that outward migration to oil-rich neighbours and remittances from migrants boosted incomes; also wages rose sharply in response to labour shortages in rural Egypt. Another manifestation of the bias towards the urban middle classes was the imbalance in the education budget. Almost half of the budget was allocated to university education, when the share in enrolment of students from the ranks of the poor did not exceed 2 per cent. Yet the most persistent and fiscally distorting example of bias favouring the urban middle classes was the system of automatic recruitment of young graduates of secondary and higher education into lifelong employment in the civil service. In the meantime, more than half of Egypt's working population remained illiterate, occupying unskilled jobs in agriculture and informal micro-enterprise activities.

The transition process towards liberalisation was launched as early as 1973 with Sadat's *Infitah* (open door) policy, but the Nasser legacy of a centrally-planned, state-dominated economy has taken more than thirty years to dismantle. Macro-reforms started seriously in the 1990s with the Structural Adjustment Programme (SAP). These reforms included devaluation and better coordination of fiscal and monetary policy. The reforms of the new millennium helped to speed up economic recovery. However, the SAP reforms also demanded that concurrent changes in social policies take place. These have been somewhat neglected so that under Mubarak, the process of reform – economic, social and political – has continued, but at a cautious pace.

The question therefore arises as to why Egypt has taken such a slow and gradual approach to reform. There are a number of reasons for this. A main concern has been social stability. Eliminating guaranteed jobs in the vast state bureaucracy would add to unemployment, as would the privatisation of state-owned industry and assets. The removal of subsidies was likely to create hardship for large sectors of the population. The removal of tariffs and hence protection of national industries would be unpopular with the productive sector. On the other hand, the state could afford to be gradual in reforming its economy because of its strategic position *vis-à-vis* international financial institutions and donors. Thus, although the transition to an open and liberalised system was accepted as necessary, there was a perceived need to cushion the shocks.

Today, the process of economic reform is almost complete, but, as foreseen, has carried a high cost in terms of social equity. Macro-economic reforms have proceeded well ahead of social reforms, and there is much evidence of an increase in poverty as a result of the SAP. Additionally, reform of the political framework is still in its early stages, creating delays in the delivery of the rewards of democracy expected from liberalisation. This suggests the need for a new social contract and a redefinition of the roles the state, the private sector and civil society have to play in providing new opportunities for the people of Egypt. The state has finally accepted the need to address poverty. What is envisaged in this dramatic shift in paradigm? There is recognition that the poor need to be at the forefront of any future strategy. The state has increasingly recognised that there is a need to integrate social and economic policy in order for Egypt to continue on its current growth trajectory.

Can Egypt afford a welfare state?

One of the key principles behind the new social contract is a recognition of 'capability poverty', which prevents the poor from having equal access to quality public goods (education, health care, social insurance) and hence to equal opportunity in the marketplace in terms of jobs and incomes. This rights-based approach leads to the design of policies and programmes for actions that can correct the elements of access and quality so as to fulfill all citizens' constitutional rights. Under the new social contract, the poor are not only recipients and beneficiaries of subsidies, aid transfers and services, but also participants in a new social contract between the Egyptian state and its citizens.

The second key principle of the new social contract is to empower the poor to help themselves. In the new social contract, the state encourages further political, social and economic participation from civil society. This occurs through extending and integrating institutions that promote democratic practices, improving accountability of these institutions, raising the quality of public goods and their delivery and developing policies that encourage private sector participation in development without adverse distributional effects. The vision is for equitable and efficient service provision associated with a welfare state – as envisaged in Egypt's constitution. The idea is to retain the spirit of justice and equal opportunity that is enshrined in the Egyptian constitution.

A third key principle is that of 'equity for growth', in the sense that growth itself is fuelled by the enhancement of human capital and by applying the principles of equitable distribution. Under this new paradigm, the less privileged half of the people become dynamic new players as producers, consumers and savers, by activating and modernising those sectors in which they mostly reside – namely the small and medium enterprise (SME) sector, rural off-farm agro-industry and farm mechanisation.

The new social contract thereby adopts a pro-poor vision of

growth by identifying key sectors of the economy that can incorporate the poor and also serve as important drivers of the economy. These sectors also include two modern high-growth sectors – tourism, and information and communications technology. Growth engines will directly empower the poor as owners of projects and assets that will encourage upward and downward linkages in the national economy. Other important areas of employment are in the care and social service sector. There is a significant need for more teachers, nurses, social workers and pre-school teachers in geographically disadvantaged areas. These sectors will create employment opportunities and at the same time improve the quality of social services to the poor.

Supporting these engines of growth would occur within a complete structural change of the economy that would lead to increased demand for labour across all regions and sectors of the economy. Support for small and medium enterprises (SMEs) is especially important as these new enterprises are critical for creating off-farm jobs in rural areas of Egypt. The EHDR of 2005 has proposed the setting up of business resource centres, extension services and credit programmes to support the creation and development of these enterprises. Support for the housing market is a public service deliverable but also a potential driver for growth through the creation of numerous employment opportunities in this sector. The activation of the mortgage market would trigger growth in this sector by providing financing opportunities for the poor and the young. These mechanisms would drive the economy in a context of pro-poor growth because each of the engines of growth depends on the active economic participation of the poor as both consumers and producers. As such, the poor would also be the primary beneficiaries of such a growth trajectory.

The EHDR of 2005 proposed a total of fifty-five programmes under the new social contract. The report also developed a detailed budget that calculates the number of beneficiaries as well as the amount of resources that are needed to implement each of these programmes over the next ten years.

The cost of this additional EHDR budget for the new social vision has been calculated using a macro-model, such that it is fiscally consistent with a best-case growth scenario of 7.3 per cent over ten years. In other words, there are sufficient revenues in the estimated ten-year budget to implement the proposed fifty-five social welfare programmes. The reallocation of budget resources to prioritise the disadvantaged segments of society has very positive implications in reducing unemployment while maintaining fiscal stability. The main vehicle that improves macroeconomic performance over the decade to 2015 is savings, which is projected to rise from 20 per cent to a sustainable 30 per cent. The savings instrument is activated via SME credit, social insurance, health insurance and housing mortgages. These financial markets have hardly been tapped in Egypt in the case of microcredit and mortgages and are still at less than half their potential for pensions and health care.

The increase in savings will be a consequence of the activation of the financial sector through the pension system, universal health and social insurance and the mortgage market. Economic growth will be stimulated by leveraging this increase in savings through lending and credit programmes.

Decentralisation is another important mechanism that will enhance good governance, transparency, accountability and public participation in the delivery of quality public services. By virtue of physical proximity to local communities and their better understanding of local demands and needs, decentralised administrative bodies and NGOs, as well as civil society leaders, are best suited to develop and implement programmes aimed at increasing participation, enhancing capabilities and reducing poverty.

There is clear evidence of the political will for the implementation of the new social contract. The National Democratic Party (NDP) supports a number of these proposed programmes. During his re-election campaign in 2005, President Mubarak proposed a Ten Point Plan that adopts many of the programmes in the EHDR proposed budget. The cabinet has approved most of the programmes of this additional budget and the prime minister has established a 'Social Contract Centre' which is in charge of coordinating the implementation of these programmes.

Egypt now has a cabinet that is cohesive, young, extremely well-educated and actively working in a well-orchestrated manner. This bodes well for the continued high-growth trajectory of the economy and for coordinated support of the new social contract and social vision. Moreover, the rise of the Islamist movement can act as a positive competitive pressure on the state to deliver better quality services and allow more participation.

However, a major obstacle to the realisation of the new social contract is the very low credibility of the state across all classes of the population. There is little trust among the citizens in the government and its programmes (a legacy of the 'old social contract'). A special survey was conducted for the EHDR of 2005 in order to gain a better understanding of people's experiences, expectations and perceptions of public goods and services. The results include:

1. Services are viewed as entitlements with no expectations of quality. For the social contract to make a breakthrough, it must elevate people's expectations for quality public services;

2. Willingness to participate in improving the quality of services is modest. Perhaps because public goods and services are perceived as the obligation of the state, few people are willing to consider participation in committees, associations or consumer groups. The low propensity to believe that participation can improve services puts a responsibility on the state to lead by example and to integrate the role of the communities in oversight, accountability and decision making in the structure of services and of public spending;

3. The state is sometimes unable to communicate with its citizens. People are not aware of the extent and

magnitude of subsidies and the difficulty of sustaining them;

4. There is low willingness to pay for better public services. Even the better off are not willing to share in the cost of public services in order to raise quality despite their willingness to buy services in the parallel private market.

There is therefore a need to educate and build awareness of the new concept of the social contract and to let people know that they have a vital role to play in its implementation, especially in ensuring accountability in service delivery by public and private sector providers. The challenge is to change the ingrained perceptions and attitudes of citizens.

Major elements of the new social contract

The EHDR of 2005 recommends two mechanisms for the implementation of the new social contract and the development of Egypt. The first mechanism is a set of social public goods that provide high quality services in the areas of health, education, social protection and citizenship rights. It will ensure equal access to quality public services by the poor half of Egypt's population. The other mechanism – as described earlier – entails a number of growth engines that directly empower the poor as owners of projects and assets that will drive economic growth through encouraging rapid structural change in the national economy.

The proposed new social contract will reinforce the legitimacy of the welfare state through the equitable and efficient provision of higher quality public goods and services that are better targeted to those in need. The vision focuses on five deliverables that address the constitutional right of individuals to equal opportunity in a system of public goods based on social justice. The five proposed deliverables are: an integrated package of income transfers and service access for families in extreme poverty; provision of quality education for all; universal health insurance; state contributions to social security and social insurance; and the rapid introduction of urban planning, housing and sanitation measures. Mubarak's Ten Point Plan includes most of these social protection measures, and they have been adopted by Egypt's current cabinet.

The first deliverable is an integrated package of income transfers and service access for the poorest families in Egypt. This programme targets the one million poorest families in Egypt and is based on the successful implementation of the Solidario Programme in Chile. The programme aims to engage the participation of families living in extreme poverty in a two-year process that enables them to access improved living conditions and public social service networks. The families are given guaranteed subsidies, counselling and preferred access to social promotion programmes if they abide by the 'Solidario Agreement', which commits them to meeting a number of registration, work, income, health, education and housing conditions. Families will be selected to participate in the programme based on a composite index that evaluates the 'capability poverty' of families based on thirteen variables grouped in four principal factors: housing, occupation, education and income/assets.

The key to the success of the programme is the creation of an independent, trustworthy and highly professional cadre of social workers. This new leadership role for Egypt will require a substantial budgetary commitment for the screening, recruitment, training and support of the social workers as well as salaries that are commensurate with the new responsibilities of the job. The Ministry of Social Solidarity is currently piloting the 'Million Poorest Families' programme in the governorates of Assiut and Sharqiya. Through this pilot programme, they will develop the specific criteria for eligibility and also pilot the package of deliverables and subsidies for future expansion throughout the entire country. The successful implementation of this programme will create a system of public assistance to the poor that is better targeted and thus more cost efficient and effective.

The second deliverable is the provision of quality education for all, including the introduction of universal pre-school education for all four- and five-year-olds. While Egypt has made major strides in access to primary education with an enrolment rate reaching a level above 90 per cent, equity in and quality of education remain major challenges. Educational reforms require the creation of child-centred schools that develop children's intellectual curiosity, creative and critical thinking, tolerance, problem-solving skills and ability to work in cooperation. A reformed educational system will act as an agent of change by allowing a generation of children to reach their full human potential. It will also create a society that is open to participation and true democratic citizenship by exposing children to the rights-based values of justice, inclusion, equality and participation.

Reforms in the educational system require a new understanding of the processes of education and the rights of the child as well as social recognition of the value of the teaching profession. It will need an improvement in teaching standards. It will further require the reallocation of existing assets and the expansion of resources through community participation and multiple partnerships with government, civil society and the general public. Transparency, accountability, and the participation of children, parents and community members are needed for effective reforms to take place. The EHDR has proposed reforms in the educational system that will streamline its organisation and create new structures to respond efficiently to new educational priorities and guarantee quality assurance. Other proposed reforms include reducing class size, better curriculum development, the provision of learning materials, reform of learner assessment, the provision of maintenance and furniture, as well as activity-based in-service training for teachers, principals, inspectors and educational leaders.

Enrolment in pre-school education is another challenge, as only 15 per cent of children aged four and five are currently enrolled in pre-school, and most pre-schools operate in the private sector. The benefits of early childhood and pre-school education for all children are widely known. Pre-school education sets the course for a lifetime of learning by developing the communication and problem-solving skills and cognitive and analytical thinking of young children at an early age. Less-recognised benefits include the positive impact on breaking the cycle of poverty and increasing social mobility. Enrolment in early education also helps in the monitoring of children's health and nutrition status during this critical stage of development. These benefits are especially important for young girls. Pre-school education allows young girls to start their lives on an equal footing with boys.

There are other benefits. The provision of early childhood education programmes eliminates a common constraint on older girls' enrolment in primary and secondary education. Pre-school education frees older girls from their childcare responsibilities within the home, thus allowing them to attend school. Pre-school education programmes also encourage women to enter the workforce. Increased labour force participation of women can increase overall household income, contributing to the well-being of families as well as national economic growth and development. Increased demand for pre-school education can also lead to the generation of formal jobs for girls and women as pre-school teachers. The EHDR of 2005 estimates that an increase of pre-school enrolment by 30 per cent will create over 100,000 additional jobs in the next decade. Thus, the development of pre-school education programmes has an important impact on national growth and development.

The third deliverable is universal health insurance for all Egyptians, including the very poor, unemployed and the informal or home-based workers. This proposed programme has been fully adopted by Egypt's current leadership. In addition to health insurance for those who are not covered by Egypt's Health Insurance Organization (HIO) or any other system, the EHDR proposes to enhance the health insurance system in schools by providing fortnightly health care within school premises. Despite high spending on health care by both the government and private citizens and the abundance of health facilities and physicians throughout the country, health inequity persists. Health provision remains inadequate with the burden of ill-health disproportionately large among poor families.

Reform in health care provision requires an integrated approach that addresses the many interlinking factors that affect health outcomes, including education, sanitation, nutrition, housing and environmental conditions. Decentralisation of public health provision is also needed to streamline health-related services. This process would involve delegation of authority to the health directorate at the governorate level but also involvement of governors, governorate officials, local councils, beneficiaries, media and community leaders. The decentralisation of the system would make health care provision more accountable to beneficiaries by increasing the effectiveness of accountability mechanisms through community participation and citizens' health charters.

The fourth deliverable is social security for all employees. The EHDR proposes a system by which the government pays a part of the employers' contribution to social insurance for new workers and employees of micro-enterprises, while the Mubarak plan proposed universal social insurance for all Egyptians. Under the current system, all employees working in the government and public sector enterprises are socially insured, while about 30 per cent of private sector enterprises do not pay contributions for their employees and 40 per cent contribute only a percentage of the required contribution. The EHDR programme is based on the premise that a major barrier to formal job creation in the private SME sector is the high cost of insuring workers. Implementing a system of social security that covers a wider scope of private sector employees would help in redirecting the flow of young job-seekers from government employment to the private sector. Government contributions to social security for employees of small and medium enterprises will also encourage the registration and formalisation of these enterprises.

The fifth deliverable is a series of urban planning, housing and sanitation measures. The EHDR has proposed programmes that would provide sanitation facilities and water connections for households and provide infrastructure and credit for the construction of two million houses for low-income families. Other proposed programmes include measures to improve conditions in the slums, the covering of canals and the protection of the banks of the River Nile. Improvements in sanitation and housing would disproportionately benefit the poor because they are most likely to live in substandard housing and in polluted environments that adversely affect their health.

Implementing the vision

These key components of an ambitious vision for pro-poor growth in Egypt reflect a revised understanding of the roles and responsibilities of the many actors that together constitute the reality that is Egypt today. A new understanding of these relationships is based on the premise that an integrated programme of economic, social and political action and partnerships between state and civil society will fire growth by enhancing human capital through the application of equitable distribution. The new social contract will depend upon many factors including administrative reform, budget reallocations and fiscal decentralisation and an increase in domestic savings. It will need the dynamic participation of the private sector and civil society. Most importantly, perhaps, it will require political will. The paradigm shift of a new social contract is indeed a challenge. It is now being taken up by the state – evident in the creation of Egypt's new 'Social Contract Centre' as mentioned above.

FIONA MOFFITT

Egypt's Economic Reform Programme

Rising Growth and Major Challenges

The purpose of this chapter is to give a brief overview of the performance of the Egyptian economy since the start of the economic reform programme in 1991; to discuss the much-improved situation today, following the appointment of a reformist economic team in July 2004; and broadly to consider the major challenges now facing economic policymakers.

Background

The Egyptian economy is going though a period of rapid change after years of stagnation. Today, there is a feeling of optimism about Egypt's economic prospects following the success of recent reform measures in significantly improving economic performance.

This confidence has not always been apparent. In the late 1980s the economy was in a parlous state. Mismanagement added to a sharp drop in international oil prices had combined to produce huge deficits in the fiscal and current accounts, and Egypt was forced to borrow heavily from abroad. By 1987 external debt had peaked to $44.1 billion or 183 per cent of GDP. However, the twin incentives of large-scale debt relief – including the write-off of $7 billion from Arab states and $7.1 billion from the US – and major donor finance following Egypt's pivotal role opposing the 1990 Iraqi invasion of Kuwait, persuaded Cairo in 1991 to implement its first comprehensive economic reform and structural adjustment programme, a three-year arrangement regulated by the International Monetary Fund (IMF).

There was an initial successful stabilisation of the macroeconomy. Higher capital inflows were attracted by a more stable and more freely convertible pound and higher interest rates (although the latter deterred investment), while the budget deficit declined in response to subsidy cuts. Structural reforms remained modest, notably in the crucial sectors of public and financial sector reform, privatisation and trade and investment restrictions. Of note is Egypt's pledge, in its October 1996 two-year IMF stand-by arrangement, to privatise one public sector commercial bank and one state insurance company by the end of 1998 and to completely remove the state's implicit subsidy on petroleum products by July 1999. These are controversial issues the government is still grappling with today, although 80 per cent of the smallest state commercial bank, the Bank of Alexandria, was sold in October 2006 to Italy's Sanpaolo IMI Group for US$1.6 billion.

By 1988, the reform drive had slowed. In part this was a result of external shocks, notably the 1997–8 Asian crisis, but also heavy state investment in costly and large-scale infrastructure projects (Toshka, the massive land reclamation scheme in the desert southwest of Aswan aiming to increase Egypt's habitable land from 4 per cent to 25 per cent, was initially budgeted at LE300 billion over twenty years), hasty and unwise credit allocation by banks and sluggish structural reform. Moreover, Egypt's primary sources of hard currency – oil, workers' remittances, tourism and the Suez Canal – were adversely affected by the fall in oil prices, the resultant depression in Gulf economies, the sharp drop in tourists in the aftermath of the November 1997 Luxor massacre and the downturn in world trade. These were hit again by the fallout from 9/11.

Increasingly, monetary policy became of particular concern. After the marked rise in the current account deficit in 1998, government policy was increasingly directed towards keeping the Egyptian pound stable against the US dollar at around LE3.4:$1. Central Bank dollar sales extracted pounds from the system and led to a decline in money supply growth, which had a beneficial effect on inflation but allowed foreign exchange reserves to fall and interbank interest rates to rise to a peak of 17 per cent in early 2000. With credit just too costly, the local private sector failed to invest. Faced with a rapid decline in foreign exchange reserves, a chronic shortage of US dollars and poor Egyptian pound liquidity, the government removed the pound's ten-year peg to the US dollar in May 2000. But after a number of attempts at a managed peg regime, which failed to smash the black market (which had become the channel for the majority of foreign exchange transactions as it offered values some 7 to 10 per cent above the official rate), the government floated the pound in January 2003. The subsequent devaluation (25 per cent between January and July 2003) helped non-oil exports and tourism but stoked inflation; while investment, both local and international, remained low. The latter reflected a lack of confidence in the sluggish economy and in particular the widespread assumption that the government lacked the ability and political will to tackle the fundamental issues.

It is only since the appointment in July 2004 of an energetic and capable economic team, strongly committed to liberalisation, privatisation and deregulation, that the economy has begun to turn around. The aim is to create strong private-sector-led growth, which will allow the economy to be both more efficient and globally competitive, under the slogan 'Egypt: Open for Business'. Finance Minister Youssef Boutros Ghali has recently noted: 'Egypt is a rich country that has not been run very well.'[1]

Key reforms implemented since mid-2004 include an overhaul of Egypt's customs regime (Egypt's weighted average tariff has been lowered to 6.9 per cent from 14.6 per cent in mid-2004) and moves to simplify and standardise procedures according to WTO norms. Egypt's notoriously opaque tax regime has been reformed with a Unified Tax Law that has reduced corporate tax from 42 per cent to 20 per cent (although petroleum companies remain at 40.55 per cent) and personal income tax from 40 per cent to 20 per cent. Egypt has passed its anti-trust and consumer protection laws. Reforms in the financial sector include a five-year restructuring plan for the banking sector, to reduce the number of banks to around twenty-five by end-2007 from fifty-six at the end of 2004; clearing the major problem of non-performing loans (NPLs), estimated by IMF in 2005–06 to be at least 25 per cent of total bank loans; the sale of state stakes in joint venture banks; the restructuring of the four major state-owned insurance companies; and the launch of an ambitious programme of improved management of state assets including evaluation, restructuring and sales.

The latter, that has included the December 2005 privatisation of 20 per cent of the state-owned Telecom Egypt for LE5.1 billion along with 80 per cent of the Bank of Alexandria, has proved highly controversial. The government's challenge now is to try to explain the benefits of privatisation to an unconvinced public. The key economic ministers admit that the concept that privatisation is essentially improving the lot of the underprivileged – by generating funds, or freeing up state funds, so basic services can be improved – is not understood. Nevertheless, privatisation proceeds rose to LE15.2 billion in the last financial year, 2005–6, and have reached LE13 billion by end-March in 2006–7 (ending 30 June), compared with LE543 million in 2003–4, prior to the reformist economic team taking power. Public enterprise companies made a profit of LE2.28 billion in 2005–6 compared with LE91 million in 2003–4, while public enterprise debt has been reduced to LE9.8 billion from LE31.2 billion.

Improved macroeconomic picture

Since mid-2004, economic growth has been on the rise, underpinned by key structural reforms, strong foreign earnings and rapidly growing foreign direct investment. Admittedly, the government has also benefited from fortuitous timing in that the economic reform process has coincided with the sharp rise in global trade and tourism growth, a strong Euro (some 70 per cent of Egypt's tourists come from Europe), huge Arab Gulf liquidity as a result of the major hike in oil prices, and the post 9/11 wish by Gulf investors to diversify their investment portfolio away from the West and towards regional projects.

Real GDP growth rose to its highest rate in over fifteen years, at 6.8 per cent in 2005–6, up from 4.5 per cent in 2004–5 and 4.1 per cent in 2003–4. GDP grew by 7.1 per cent in the second quarter of 2006–7 (October–December 2006) and is projected by the government to reach 7.4 per cent for the whole of 2006–7. Growth has been boosted by the surge in foreign investment, high oil and gas prices – Egypt's first liquefied natural gas (LNG) exports began in January 2005 and Egypt is now the world's sixth largest LNG exporter – and strong private consumption. Growth has been particularly high in the natural gas, construction, communication and Suez Canal sectors (reaching over 12 per cent in the first quarter of 2006–7) and manufacturing and tourism sectors (7.2 per cent and 6.8 per cent respectively). Officials note that in the past Egypt has posted growth of around 5–6 per cent but this has been very dependent on budgetary and public sector spending. Today, growth is mainly coming from private spending, and is therefore built into the economy, an important structural change. According to the Ministry of Finance, between 2003–4 and 2005–6 the private sector has contributed around two thirds of the GDP growth rate.

Moreover, the balance of payments is in surplus (at 3 per cent of GDP in 2005–6) and the current account in shrinking surplus (1.6 per cent of GDP in 2005–6 compared with 3.2 per cent and 4.3 per cent in 2004–5 and 2003–4 respectively) due to the surge in imports more than offsetting strong growth in exports and invisible revenues. But over 50 per cent of Egypt's imports are capital and intermediate goods, which should then lead to further growth. On the capital account, there has been a notable rise in foreign direct investment (FDI) inflows, which reflects the success of the new privatisation strategy and greater investor confidence in the Egyptian economy. FDI jumped to US$6.1 billion in 2005–6, a 51 per cent rise on the previous year, and a major leap from the US$407 million received in 2003–4. Egypt's FDI is also becoming increasingly diversified. In 2005–6 the oil and gas sector accounted for some 30 per cent of FDI, down from 66 per cent the previous year. Recently Arab investment has been particularly strong, directed towards a number of large-scale tourism, real estate and communication projects. But at present the majority of Egypt's FDI is resource-seeking and market-seeking. The challenge is to attract more efficiency-seeking investment that would then allow Egypt to become a manufacturing platform for the rest of the world.

Meanwhile, there is a strongly-led Central Bank that has managed to eliminate the parallel market for foreign exchange, stabilise the pound and implement an inflation targeting monetary policy. There is a dollar surplus, compared with the chronic dollar shortage that plagued Egypt until 2004, and steadily rising foreign exchange reserves. By the end of March 2007 the latter had risen to $26.3 billion, nearly 17 per cent higher than a year earlier and sufficient to cover Egypt's import bill for ten months. External debt is also on the decline, as of 30 September 2006 standing at $28.9 billion or 27 per cent of GDP, with only some 5.6 per cent of short-term maturity.

Nevertheless, the size of the fiscal deficit remains of concern despite a series of structural budget reforms including the 2005 reclassification according to the IMF GFS standard (modified to cash principles), in line with international best practices. The cash budget deficit fell from 9.4 per cent of GDP in 2004–5 to 8.9 per cent of GDP in 2005–6. But much of the fall was due to two large one-off payments: the proceeds from Telecom Egypt's IPO worth 0.8 per cent of GDP, and a transfer of 1.2 per cent of GDP from the Egyptian General Petroleum Corporation (EGPC) to settle tax arrears. According to the Minister of Finance, the revenues from the sale of the Bank of Alexandria and the July sale of Egypt's third GSM licence to UAE-based Etisalat for $2.9 billion will lower the

2006–7 budget deficit to 5.5 per cent of GDP, although without these singular revenues the deficit is projected to rise to 6.5 per cent of GDP the following year. Public debt therefore continues to be problematic. Net and gross domestic debt rose to a high of 40.4 per cent and 88.5 per cent of GDP respectively in June 2005 (the end of the 2004–5 financial year) compared with 31.5 per cent and 63.8 per cent in June 2001. The Ministry of Finance has pledged to reduce the budget deficit by 1.0–1.4 per cent annually over the next four years, but it admits that possible sources of pressure on the budget in the coming years include energy price adjustments, pension reforms and bank restructuring. Moreover, the government has highly ambitious spending plans to improve infrastructure and the provision of basic services, including an urgent LE8.5 billion upgrade of Egypt's dilapidated railway system, while subsidies, wages and interest payments account for some 75 per cent of total expenditure, leaving little flexibility. A major problem for policymakers is the massive system of state subsidies – including the social security network, food items, energy, transportation and goods and services offered to the public by state companies and authorities at artificially low prices – but here reformers run into social stability concerns. According to Prime Minister Ahmed Nazif, subsidies, both direct and indirect, cost the government LE100 billion a year, including over LE40 billion on energy alone. Some 50 per cent of the fuel sold on to the public at subsidised prices has been purchased by the government on the international markets. To put this in perspective, the government spends LE30 billion a year on education and health combined. Yet despite a yearly increase in budgeted state spending on subsidies, the latest UN Human Development Report (2006) estimates that 44 per cent of the Egyptian population – about thirty-five million people – are poor (living on less than $2 per day or LE342 per month). Local analysts note that recent high inflation rates mean that this number could be greater.

Inflation has continued to rise, with obvious concerns for the mass of the lower income population. Latest official figures from the state statistics agency, CAPMAS, show year-on-year consumer price inflation rose to 12.8 per cent in March, its highest level in over two years, compared with 3.7 per cent in March 2006. The latest Wholesale Price Index figures reveal year-on-year inflation at 16.4 per cent in February, its highest level since May 2004, compared with 1.3 per cent in February 2006. Inflation has been climbing steadily since April 2006 due in part to economic growth and tax reforms – the latter freed up extra income and thereby increased aggregate demand – but also to a number of supply shocks that led to increases in food prices: notably the avian flu epidemic and cattle disease, a rise in utility prices and the pass-through effect caused by a reduction in the energy subsidy in July when petrol prices were hiked by 30 per cent and natural gas by 25 per cent. The government has refuted charges that the economy is overheating and explains the rise in inflation as effectively self-inflicted, a transitional cost necessary as part of the adjustment to a market-driven economy. But nevertheless the price rises have been hard for the general public and have made decisions on further subsidy reductions, particularly on energy, that much more difficult.

Challenges

Despite the impressive progress made by the government's economic team, a number of substantial and long-term challenges need to be addressed if Egypt's economic revival is to translate into sustained strong private-sector-led economic growth. Here it is important to stress that these are areas the government has listed as a priority in the coming years, but they do pose a major threat to Egypt's development.

First and foremost, there is the challenge of job creation. There are 700,000 to 800,000 new entrants into the job market annually. This huge increase stems from Egypt's population explosion. According to the preliminary results of the 2006 population census, released in early April, the number of Egyptians has doubled in thirty years, and increased by some 22 per cent since the last census ten years ago, to 72.5 million residents and 3.9 million Egyptians living abroad. Despite a revived economy, labour force growth still exceeded employment growth in 2005: by 6 per cent annually compared with 4.5 per cent. According to the latest census, unemployment stands at 9.3 per cent of the workforce, up from 8.95 per cent in 1996. Critically, it is estimated that some 60 per cent of Egypt's unemployed are males under twenty-five years of age. Underemployment is also rife. Moreover, there is tension in the labour market, a pool of the not only unemployed but unemployable, who do not possess the skills the labour market demands. There is a critical need to reform the educational system, because unemployment remains high amongst educated youth, who need to be retrained. Tourism Minister Zoheir Garana maintains that what is holding back Egypt's tourism industry today is not lack of facilities or the threat of terrorism but the need to upgrade workers to international standards. Meanwhile, there remains a brain drain as those with the ability to find jobs leave Egypt for the Gulf or the West in search of higher salaries and living standards.

The extent of Egypt's informal economy, which the government admits employs over one third of the labour force, makes accurate assessments difficult, but the social and security implications of such high unemployment are clear. It is estimated that real and consistent GDP growth of at least 6 per cent annually is the minimum required to absorb the new job seekers. Real growth needs to be in the 7–9 per cent range and broad-based before it will start to make some dent in the current unemployment rate – a major task. But as the local investment rate stands at around 19 per cent and the country needs around 25 per cent for 6 per cent growth, it is crucial for Egypt to attract much higher levels of FDI if it is to progress. Moreover, it is preferable to attract the right sort of FDI – the type that creates jobs. There are, for example, many jobs in tourism, far fewer in a petrochemicals plant. According to Minister Garana, the tourism industry feeds into seventy other industries while a million new tourists create 200,000 new jobs. Egypt received nine million tourists in 2006. The government is aiming to raise this to fourteen million by 2011.

There is an urgent need to improve the lot of the mass of the Egyptian population, who have yet to feel the trickle-down benefits of the economic reform programme and have found their living standards hit by high inflation. Again, there are social stability concerns. The government has made it a major priority in 2006–7 to improve the provision of basic services – health, education, utilities and transportation – that have long suffered from low investment and poor quality control. But in order not to derail budgetary reforms, the aim is to tackle the problem through non-traditional solutions, in particular by employing Public–Private Partnerships (PPPs), wherein finance and expertise are provided by the private sector. But credible PPP projects demand predictability, transparency, accountability and rule of law, while the scale of the undertaking is immense. An estimated 15–17 million Egyptians live in shanty towns, according to the Ministry of Housing and the National Institute of Planning. The UNDP Egypt Human Development Report for 2005 notes that some 35 per cent of the population cannot read or write, putting Egypt in the top nine countries in terms of illiteracy. Of the 17 million Egyptian students, only a minority finish secondary school and only 8 per cent will become university graduates. The CAPMAS 2006 census found that only half the country has access to a proper sewage system, compared with over 99 per cent having access to electricity. If transportation is to be improved, then organisations like the Egyptian Railway Authority need to be upgraded, with skills and salaries considerably raised. It employs some 70,000 people.

The government has started to address the significant challenges that need to be overcome to enhance the business environment. Progress has been made, but the World Bank's 'Doing Business in 2007' report ranked Egypt only 165 out of 175 countries surveyed, and Egypt dropped eleven places in the 2006–7 World Economic Forum Global Competitiveness Index (to sixty-third out of 125 countries covered). In the World Economic Forum's Business Competitiveness

Index, Egypt ranked twenty-three among twenty-six emerging economies, only ahead of Russia, Venezuela and Mexico.

These low rankings have much to do with bureaucracy. Egypt has some 5.6 million civil servants, 800,000 in the Ministry of Agriculture alone. There is a strong commitment to reform at the higher level, but the question is whether it filters down to lower levels of management. The major problem facing reformist ministers is that of changing the mindset: how to convince a civil servant that he or she has an interest in simplifying regulations, that he or she is there to attract investment and no longer to protect the state against the investor. Changing ingrained habits takes time.

Dispute settlement procedures and lengthy judicial processes are a major impediment to investment. Egypt's legal system is slow and therefore can be expensive. Courts are overloaded and judges often lack the necessary expertise for commercial cases. According to the IMF, the average length of a commercial court case is six years with the record so far at fifteen years, but this will be broken by cases pending. However, a law introducing a new system of special economic courts was being drafted in mid-2007, which is designed to improve the speed and expertise of rulings in commercial cases.

There is a shortage of land for investment projects, which the government is trying to solve through the sale of unused land held by state companies. There is also the issue of access to finance. Both policy makers and the public and private sector banks are only just waking up to the crucial need not just to deal with the major Egyptian companies but to take notice of small and medium enterprises (SMEs). A 2006 study found that 0.2 per cent of clients were responsible for 52 per cent of bank credit to the private sector and only 17 per cent of all companies have access to bank credit facilities. The Ministry of Finance estimates that only 10 per cent of SMEs have access to formal credit, yet 97 per cent of Egypt's enterprises are small and 80 per cent of employment in the private sector is in SMEs. In part this weak credit growth reflects the greater caution of banks in lending to the private sector after the unwise loans of the 1990s and subsequent preference to go for safer investment from interest income earned on government debt instruments. But while there are recent signs that credit to the private sector is growing, the concern remains that government financing of its large budget deficit through local borrowing can crowd out the private sector.

Is reform sustainable?

Finally, the question remains as to whether Egypt's economic reform process is sustainable. The privatisation programme in particular has led to a high level of public debate, sometimes acrimonious, about the economic reform programme. On the positive side, the issues have come out into the open and are being discussed. The government is now explaining the cost of not reforming. But although there has been a huge debate on issues such as the details, price and pace of reform, there has been no real argument about the need for reform. There is no strong, coherent ideology against economic reform in Egypt today and this can only prove positive for the sustainability of the programme. However, a number of hard decisions will have to be made, with both social and political consequences, in areas such as the privatisation of labour-intensive industries and the reduction of state subsidies, and these will prove controversial. Ultimately, success will rest on the presence of a strong political will and commitment to reform.

Note

1. Interview with Dow Jones Newswires, 21 July 2007.

DAVID LUBIN

Dollar Shortages, Dollar Surpluses and Egyptian Economic Policy

What is the relationship between the strength of a developing country's balance of payments and the quality of its economic policymaking? One line of thought characterises the relationship in the following way. When a country's balance of payments is weak there is, by definition, a shortage of foreign exchange. That shortage puts policymakers in a situation where they are dependent on an inflow of capital to finance the gap between domestic investment and domestic saving. This dependence requires policymakers to pursue policies likely to attract capital inflows. This in turn leads to a policy framework which emphasises strengthening the country's national balance sheet – through fiscal discipline and privatisation – as well as enhancing the environment for private sector economic activity. Perhaps the strongest example of this kind of relationship was seen among developing countries in the early 1990s when, in the aftermath of the 1980s debt crisis, countries found it necessary to improve their policy frameworks in order to attract capital inflows.

At the same time, this conventional line of thinking suggests that countries with strong balances of payments can afford to pursue policies which pay less attention to the need to please international capital markets: since these countries do not have any dependence on external financing, they are freer to do what they like without fear of

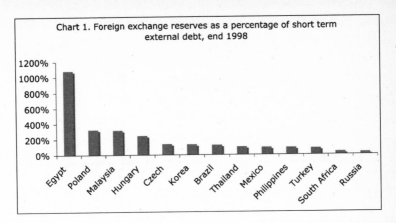

Source: Institute of International Finance

being 'punished' by an outflow of capital. The classic example of this relationship is the commodity-exporting developing country: when commodity prices are high the incentive to pursue market-friendly economic policy diminishes since capital inflows are unnecessary. The financial histories of Venezuela or Nigeria typically come to mind. In sum, the conventional view is that the quality of economic policymaking is negatively correlated with the balance of payments: the bigger the dollar shortage, the stronger the incentive to promote 'good' economic policy, and vice versa.

The history of economic policymaking in Egypt during the past ten years does not easily fit into this view of things. In fact, there seems to be a good argument to suggest that Egyptian economic policymaking gets worse when the balance of payments does and better when the balance of payments improves.

The story behind this argument begins in 1997–8, when international investor confidence in developing countries was shaken by the succession of emerging markets' financial crises, culminating in August 1998 with Russia's default. This confidence collapse resulted in a sharp withdrawal of capital, particularly by international banks, from emerging economies. Egypt did not at this time exhibit many of the indicators of vulnerability that were visible in so many countries in the 1990s: it did not have a large stock of short-term external liabilities, and nor did it have a very large current account deficit. Egypt's current account deficit was less than 3 per cent of GDP in 1998 – hardly an indicator of crisis. Moreover, Egypt had one of the strongest balance sheets among developing countries. Chart 1 shows the ratio of foreign exchange reserves to short term external debt, a very common indicator of vulnerability based on the idea that financial weakness increases if a country has insufficient foreign exchange assets (i.e. reserves) to pay for its short-term foreign exchange liabilities (i.e. short-term debt). On this basis alone, there appeared to be no reason why Egypt should have experienced any capital outflow at all.

Nonetheless, the crisis atmosphere that characterised the relationship between developing countries and international capital markets during the late 1990s proved to be particularly painful for Egypt's financial health. International banks reporting to the Bank for International Settlements took a total of some US$12.5 billion out of Egypt between 1994 and 2001. In 1994, international commercial banks reported net cross-border assets in Egypt of some US$25 billion. By 2001, the net asset position had fallen to US$12.5 billion. Since Egyptian gross domestic product was some US$85 billion in 1998, the scale of this capital outflow was considerable.

In principle the Egyptian authorities could respond in either of two ways to this capital outflow: they could let the exchange rate absorb the shock of the outflow, by allowing the currency to depreciate; or they could finance the outflow by selling the central bank's reserves. As things turned out, both these mechanisms became inevitable, but what is important for this discussion is the relative priority that the Egyptian authorities gave to these two mechanisms. First and foremost, the authorities attempted to deal with the outflow by selling foreign exchange reserves, to the extent that Egypt's reserves position became very substantially depleted. This is evident from Chart 2, which shows the sum of Egypt's central bank reserves together with the net foreign asset position of the Egyptian

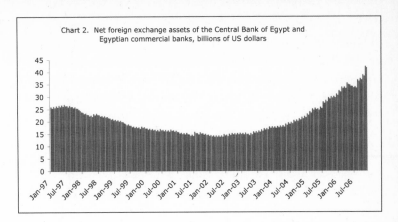

Chart 2. Net foreign exchange assets of the Central Bank of Egypt and Egyptian commercial banks, billions of US dollars

Source: IMF

commercial banking system. Together these reserves fell during the late 1990s from a peak of US$26 billion to a trough in 2001 of some US$14 billion.

This collapse of reserves created the phenomenon known as Egypt's 'dollar shortage', a phrase that would dominate investors' descriptions of the Egyptian economy between 1999 and 2003, and which was the source of a tremendous fall in economic confidence in Egypt. The loss of confidence was reinforced by the sometimes arbitrary way in which the Central Bank supplied dollars to the market, since it introduced what amounted to a regime of *de facto* exchange controls, whereby access to dollars was not necessarily free on demand. Restrictions were imposed on access to letters of credit, for example; and a squeeze on the imports of public sector entities was introduced. Moreover, there was, during the period 1998 to 2004, little evidence of dynamism in the formulation of economic policy as a whole.

The depletion of reserves that led to the 'dollar shortage' in turn made inevitable a series of adjustments to the exchange rate, albeit that these were made belatedly and in a way which consistently attempted to preserve control over the price of foreign exchange. These adjustments can be seen in Chart 3, which shows that the

Central Bank permitted a set of step changes in the exchange rate, culminating in a large devaluation in January 2003. In spite of these devaluations it was consistently clear that the authorities were preventing the exchange rate from adjusting to the extent necessary given the dollar shortage that had been created by the sale of reserves. The evidence for this is the emergence of a parallel market for foreign exchange, in which US dollars could be purchased informally at a premium to the rate quoted by the banking system; if the exchange rate had been allowed to adjust properly, the official foreign exchange market would have balanced supply and demand, thus eliminating the need for a parallel market. In other words, the mere existence of the parallel market suggests that the officially controlled exchange rate left an unsatisfied demand for dollars for which Egyptian firms and households were prepared to pay a premium.

One critical question in all this is why the Egyptian authorities were so reluctant to allow the exchange rate to float, in order to remove the dollar shortage by allowing the dollar to be priced in a way that reflected the underlying supply and demand for it. A related question is why the authorities were so apparently reluctant to introduce the kind of economic reforms that might have helped to stem the capital outflow and increase the world's demand for Egyptian financial assets.

The answer to these questions is complex. To simplify it drastically, two ideas are worth putting forward. The first has to do with the priority that successive Egyptian governments have placed on the concept of 'stability'. The second, related, idea has to do with the possibility that it is difficult for a government – particularly in a country with a delicate social fabric – to take economic risks in an atmosphere of uncertainty.

In principle it is possible to think of a number of reasons why the Egyptian government might have been fearful of a full float of the exchange rate. In the first place, a large one-off change in the exchange rate would have stoked inflationary pressures, and in a society where low-income groups have few means with which to protect themselves

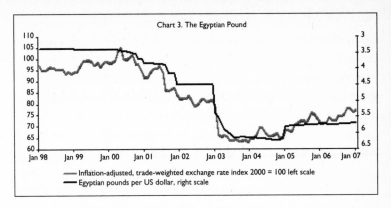

Source: IMF; Institute of International Finance

against rising consumer prices, the social consequences of inflation are arguably to be feared. Indeed, the large devaluation of 2003 did push Egyptian inflation into double digits, suggesting that the authorities were correct to worry about the implications of currency devaluation on the price level.

In addition, there is possibly something to be said for the idea that currency stability is somehow seen to be a reflection of the success of the regime: that there is some equation in the minds of policymakers that links the concept of 'currency stability' with that of 'country stability'. In that sense, it may have been the least bad course of action to postpone the necessary adjustments to the exchange rate during the turn of the century, on the grounds that a depletion of foreign exchange reserves was a less visible way of absorbing the shock of a capital outflow, and therefore politically more desirable. In other words, a policy which allowed the exchange rate to absorb more of the shock would have involved too many risks – that is, too much uncertainty – for Egyptian policymakers.

This preference to avoid risk-taking may also have characterised Egyptian economic policy as a whole during the period of the dollar shortage. In the face of a capital outflow, an orthodox economic policy response would include not only a reliance on a floating exchange rate, but also a broad set of measures to enhance confidence: that is fiscal consolidation, privatisation, measures to boost microeconomic efficiency and an effort to modernise the monetary policy framework. In broad terms, however, none of these policy initiatives were adopted during the period of the dollar shortage. A kind of stasis characterised Egyptian policymaking during this period.

The only truly visible change in economic policy occurred in 2004, when the new government of Ahmed Nazif was appointed by President Mubarak. This government moved very quickly following its appointment to introduce considerable changes to the Egyptian economic policy framework. An ambitious tariff reform was introduced, cutting the average tariff from 14.6 per cent to 9.1 per cent; a tax reform was implemented which cut personal and corporate tax rates, and which also simplified the tax system; and an ambitious privatisation programme was implemented, culminating in the sale in late 2006 of the Bank of Alexandria, the first ever sale of one of Egypt's state-owned commercial banks. And many other reforms were introduced as well, notably the creation in late 2004 of a functioning interbank market for foreign exchange.

To be sure, the policy initiatives introduced by the Nazif government did not come out of the blue, but were the culmination of a process of policy development that had begun in earnest towards the end of 2002, when Gamal Mubarak was appointed as coordinator of policy for the National Democratic Party. Under his auspices a new set of economic policies was developed by a younger generation of Egyptian policymakers, which included Mahmoud Mohieldin (later to be appointed as Investment Minister in the new government) and Rachid Mohamed Rachid, who emerged in 2004 as the Trade and Industry Minister in the new government.

What is particularly noteworthy about the ambitious economic programme of the Nazif government was that it was implemented against a background of an exceptionally strong balance of payments. The data in Chart 2 show clearly that the fall in Egypt's stock of foreign exchange reserves began to go into reverse from the beginning of 2003, from which point foreign assets started to grow impressively. A number of factors were behind this decline in the dollar shortage, including: (i) the strong depreciation of the real Egyptian exchange rate, which fell by over 30 per cent in the years after 1998; (ii) the downward pressure on import demand which resulted from the lack of availability of foreign exchange during the period of dollar-shortage; and (iii) the rise in energy prices from 2002, which helped to catalyse capital inflows from the Gulf and boosted Egypt's revenues on the current account of its balance of payments.

The combination of these factors produced a steady improvement in Egypt's balance of payments, so that by 2002 Egypt was able to boast a current account surplus. This surplus in turn allowed the Central Bank to be more generous in its supply of foreign exchange, helping to ease the dollar shortage and reduce the parallel market premium in the foreign exchange market. By the time the Nazif government was appointed in 2004, the dollar shortage was effectively over.

This brings us back to the link between the balance of payments and the quality of policymaking in Egypt. What seems clear over the past ten years is that the quality of Egyptian policymaking deteriorated at a point when the balance of payments was weak; and improved only when the dollar shortage became a dollar surplus, in 2004. Perhaps this is a coincidence, but it is not the first one: the high quality of Egyptian economic policymaking in the early 1990s was also evident against a background of strong US dollar liquidity. A more reasonable explanation lies in the idea that Egyptian governments find it easier to take the risks necessary to improve economic policymaking when the confidence of households and firms is being supported by a high degree of availability of foreign exchange. When dollars become harder to find, Egyptian governments seem less willing to gamble.

ALI E. HILLAL DESSOUKI

British–Egyptian Relations: The Future Seen through the Eyes of the Past

Few events in contemporary history have impacted upon the Middle East and its global configuration as the Suez Crisis did. The importance of the crisis lies not in what took place some fifty years ago but rather in what it heralded and opened the door to. The significance of the crisis is not in its immediate effect, i.e. the nationalisation of the Suez Canal company and its management, but rather in the larger issue of the relations between Western powers and the newly independent states in Africa and Asia.[1]

The Suez Crisis is remembered for at least three reasons. First, it was a microcosm of the transformation at the top of the world: the gradual erosion of the influence of European states and the steady rise of the two new world powers – the United States and the Soviet Union. Secondly, it was part of a changing world order that saw the emergence of new forces, issues and conflicts. A sequence of events during the period 1955–6 illustrates the change: the Baghdad Pact, the Bandung Conference, Prime Minister Nehru's call for neutrality in foreign relations, Prime Minister Nasser's daring decisions to establish diplomatic relations with communist China and purchase arms from the Soviet Union, President Tito's attempt to chart an independent path of development, and, last but not least, the revolution in Hungary. The Suez Crisis epitomised a changing international environment and gave strong impetus to the process of decolonisation. Thirdly, it was the first major confrontation between the young leaders of Egypt and a number of European countries. At its close Nasser had consolidated his power internally and emerged as an Arab hero and a champion for African and Asian peoples. In sum, the Suez Crisis reflected the contradictions and contractions of a changing international system in the mid-1950s.[2]

Today, we approach history with an eye on the present and the future. We examine events of the past so that we may not repeat its mistakes. Those who misinterpret the events of the past or remain captives of its details and memories are condemned to misread the present and fail to plan for the future. Some of the issues which were at the heart of the Suez Crisis are still with us today, though in different forms and articulations: issues such as international political equality, democracy in international organisations, the intrusion of global influences into domestic politics and societies, the arrogance of power and the double standards of its practitioners. Another issue is the increasing socio-economic inequality, globally, between rich and poor nations, and within each state between rich and poor people.

Culture and religion constitute another important issue. It is most ironic that in our present day global village we observe increasing misunderstandings, and even conflicts, not only between adherents of different religions but also between groups within the same religion. For a while ideas such as a clash of civilisations and cultures attracted much attention. These are battles in which there are no victors; all participants in such battles are doomed to lose. Tolerance and respect for those of different religions and cultures are basic prerequisites of domestic stability within nations as well as of peace and security between nations.

Think of the dilemma of many Egyptian, and indeed Arab or African, intellectuals who are told that there is one path to development, one way of doing it and one train to ride. This is presented as one package: take it or leave it. There are legitimate fears, doubts and anxieties that have to be considered and discussed in an open and transparent manner. For instance, the process of globalisation raises serious questions about maintaining cultural identity and specificity.

What does bring Egypt and Britain together? The two countries are tied by bonds of history, culture and interest. British–Egyptian relations are long-standing and multifaceted. The cultural heritage of ancient Egypt has attracted the attention of British historians and archeologists for a long time. British scientists have had a distinguished role in the development of Egyptology as an academic discipline.

As a result of the growing British interests in India, the opening of the Suez Canal brought the importance of Egypt into sharp focus in the British political mind. Not only that, both the words 'Suez' and 'the canal' captured the imagination of many British writers during the Victorian age.[3] From the other side, the Egyptian elite has long looked at Great Britain as a symbol of science, industry and democracy. Indeed, Egyptian intellectuals have had an ambivalent love–hate view of Great Britain. It represented the colonial power, which has to be resisted and hated. On the other hand, it was the model of progress to be emulated.

I will now address some specific political and economic issues in relations between the two countries. Relations between states are based on shared political visions and mutual economic interests. In appreciating the present and planning for the future we have to bring the visions and interests of Egypt and the United Kingdom closer to each other.

As to politics, most Egyptians appreciate the long-standing traditions of British diplomacy in the region. They expect Britain to do more because of its historic role in the making of the modern Middle East, especially regarding the issue of Palestine and the Arab–Israeli dispute.

Concerning Iraq, events have demonstrated that occupation policies were ill-guided and misinformed. There exists no military solution to the conflict in Iraq. The solution does not lie either in increasing the number of foreign combat troops or in forcing timetables on the Iraqi government. It is time for the allies to reconsider the logic of their thinking, revise their priorities, initiate a political process of negotiations with influential political groups and follow a policy of reconciliation and inclusion.

All agree that the peace process in Palestine should be revived and energised. We believe that delving into more details about the road map is a non-starter. A major diplomatic deficit of the past years has been the emphasis on the process rather than its substance. For a while it appeared that keeping the process alive became an objective in itself. What is needed now is to negotiate the framework of a final settlement and from there to work backward to identify phases and timetables. The solution of the Palestine question is central to peace and stability in the region. The continuity of conflict breeds extremism and anti-Western feelings over the whole region.

As for economics, we have a definite success story. There is significant growth in British–Egyptian relations in investment, trade and technical assistance.[4] The United Kingdom ranks first on the list of non-Arab countries investing in Egypt and British direct investment is twice as much as that of the US. From less than one billion pounds sterling in 2002 and 2003, investment flows increased to £1.1 billion in 2004, £1.8 billion in 2005 and reached £4.2 billion in the first nine months of 2006.[5] British companies operating in Egypt are active in many different sectors such as oil, banking, tourism, telecommunications, pharmaceuticals and textiles. This is a good achievement, but when we remember that total UK foreign direct investment in 2004 was £51.8 billion, of which £41.4 billion went to non-EU countries, we should recognise that Egypt has a great opportunity to attract more British investment.[6] Egypt is attractive for British investors because it has a large and growing market. It can be used as a manufacturing base or a distribution centre for the region. The fundamentals of its economy are sound and it has the advantages of its geographical location and political stability.

The United Kingdom is the second largest non-Arab trade partner with Egypt after the US. Trade relations have increased significantly over the last few years. During the first six months of 2006 total trade value increased by 21 per cent compared with the same period in 2005. Egyptian exports to Britain increased from £232 million to £363 million. Egyptian exports of oil products increased by 140 per cent and of non-oil products by 44 per cent.[7] The growth of trade was accompanied by a similar increase in the volume of tourism. The number of British tourists visiting Egypt in 2006 was twice that of three years earlier.

British technical aid to Egypt covers many areas including illiteracy, curriculum development, young leadership programmes, the training of lawyers, the provision of micro-credits and environmental management. These activities cover many provinces such as work with women in the Siwa Oasis and legal services for women in Aswan. Egypt benefits from British experience in the area of competition and consumer protection. For example, the experience and procedures of the Office of Fair Trading (OFT) were used as models by the Egyptian authorities.

The reasons behind this success story are obvious and we have to promote them: political will, clarity of objectives and collaboration between government and private sectors. Ministerial visits and high-level exchanges were crucial elements of our bilateral relations. Prime Minister Blair visited Egypt twice in 2001. The Defence Secretary made a visit in the same year. Other visitors include the Minister of Arts in 2002, the Minister for Culture, Media and Sport in 2003, the Foreign Secretary (who visited in 2004 and again in 2006), the shadow Foreign Secretary and the Minister of State for the Middle East in 2005.

Visits by Egyptian senior officials to the UK include that of President Hosni Mubarak in 2004, as well as visits by the Prime Minister and numerous visits by the Ministers of Investment, Finance and Foreign Affairs. In June 2006, Mr Rashid M. Rashid, Egypt's Minister of Trade and Industry, concluded a successful visit to the UK, and a return visit from his British counterpart is expected in 2007. The British Egyptian Business Council meets annually. British and Egyptian Federations of Industries are active partners in a process whose objective is for Egypt to become a strong part of the Mediterranean European economy. Naturally, the process is not without difficulties and challenges, for example the lengthy process of decision-making, instances of bureaucratic obstructionism and slow settlement of commercial disputes in Egypt.

The bilateral relations between the two countries have developed over more than 150 years. It is a stable and mature relationship. We have achieved a great deal during the last few years, which we have to build upon.

Notes

1. The event still evokes deep emotions and sentiments. See 'An Affair to Remember – The Suez Crisis', *The Economist*, 27 July 2006, and Herman Arthur, 'A Man, A Plan, A Canal: What Nasser Wrought when he Seized Suez Half a Century Ago', *Weekly Standard*, 31 July 2006.
2. See an analysis of events and personalities in Erskine B. Childers, *The Road to Suez*, London, 1962; Robert Stephens, *Nasser: A Political Biography*, New York, 1971, and Anthony Nutting, *Nasser*, London, 1972. The crisis had its impact on the IMF as well: see James M. Boughton, *Northwest of Suez: The 1956 Crisis and the IMF*, IMF working paper WP/00/192, December 2000.
3. Emily A. Haddad, 'Digging to India: Modernity, Imperialism and the Suez Canal', *Victorian Studies*, vol. 47, no. 3 (Spring 2005), pp. 383–418.
4. Statistics used are taken from numerous reports of Egypt's Ministry of Trade and Industry, Egyptian Commercial Service.
5. Egypt's General Authority for Free Zones and Investment.
6. Office of National Statistics, UK.
7. Trade statistics are from UK Customs.

PART THREE

Cultural Relations

AYMAN EL-DESOUKY

Notes on Political Memory
and Cultural Memory

The crowd gathered in the square would not let him finish. Thousands of people burst into cheers and began shouting patriotic slogans which made us, up on the stand, forget everything except that at this moment the independence of Egypt was being decided and that if the price of nationalizing the Canal was war, or even ten wars, this nation was prepared to sacrifice itself for it, just as it had paid for its construction with the lives of one hundred and twenty thousand of its sons.[1]

Sayyid Mar'i

Our quarrel is not with Egypt, still less with the Arab World, it is with Colonel Nasser. When he gained power in Egypt, we felt no hostility towards him; on the contrary, we made agreements with him, we had hoped that he wanted to improve the conditions of life of his people, and to be friends with his country. He told us that he wished a new spirit in the Anglo-Egyptian relations, we welcomed that, but instead of meeting us with friendship, Colonel Nasser conducted a vicious propaganda campaign against our country. He has shown that he is not a man who can be trusted to keep an agreement.

Sir Anthony Eden

The Egyptian Government considers the proposal for the creation of an international authority is but a mild word for what should be called collective colonialism. This proposal, which was based on misleading statements to the effect of giving the Egyptian Company an international character, makes it clear that the three governments wish to deprive Egypt of one of its inherent and sovereign rights.[2]

President Nasser

This was I suppose one of the most humiliating moments of my life in a way, that we were suddenly being told by the government in London who had no idea what was going on the ground that we would be withdrawn. It was humiliating to have done two-thirds of the job, lost some casualties, because I had got 3 wounded and I knew there had been some more killed ... that it is you suddenly find yourself in this sort of position.[3]

Captain Derek Oakley, 42 Commando

The different acts of reflection on the past fifty years since Suez represented in this volume, while issuing from within diverse personal, professional and cultural world views, reveal two crucial and inhering orientations to our modern world. The first is that aesthetic, economic and political modes of production in society are all equally forms of cultural production and that these cultural forms are very often also equally the products of discursive formations that reveal competing ideologies, which themselves reveal a deeper political structure. The second orientation has to do with the nature of the act of reflection itself, and particularly of historical reflection, whether personal or collective, which is revealed to be political in nature, or at least to have been primarily so since the end of the Second World War, despite the increasing understanding of cultural differences and sharpening of cultural sensibilities. That is, while the political is seemingly but one of the many different forms of cultural production, the understanding of, and approach to, any particular culture and its specific modes of existing, of knowing and of engaging with the other, have become highly politicised.[4]

When it comes to the memory of Suez, one must also inescapably consider the various acts of retrieval from memory, and of subsequent reflection, in the context of the urgencies of our own historical moment, paramount amongst which are the war on Iraq and the equally radically consequential political and cultural dilemmas it has presented. The events surrounding Suez 1956 and their memory, as many have noted, still provide many relevant and illuminating parallels fifty years on![5] While the present volume focuses on British–Egyptian relations, the issues raised are still of particular relevance and urgency to the contemporary world scene and the larger dynamics of international relations.

The two epigraphic statements by Nasser and Eden, representing the two perceived positions and opposed ideologies, are deliberately flanked above by two statements of memory: the first by Sayyid Mar'i, a chief engineer trusted by Nasser and one of the few informed by him of the decision to nationalise the Suez Canal in a private meeting before the famous speech in Alexandria, and the last by Captain Derek Oakley, the oldest surviving officer of 42 Commando, and one of the first to land on the beach in Port Said. The first hints at some of the forces unforeseen by Eden and the second at consequences equally unpredicted. Between event and memory the story of Suez was to unfold, curiously always poised between a strong sense of national pride and an equally strong sense of blunder, but offering an indomitable mutual lesson in the form of a continuing culture of resistance. I shall leave the statements suggestively standing for open reading, as visible gestures toward the larger narrative.

Aside from his contribution to this volume and the sheer value of his personal and professional memories, the argument that Roger Owen makes in an earlier essay over how best to understand the British occupation of Egypt in 1882 is perhaps still of significance to the case of Suez 1956.[6] Owen basically argues that the British occupation of 1882 should not simply be looked at as a case study in imperialism or the result of imperialist economic interests. The event might also be best understood from within the respective social and political histories and realities of the two countries, a simple but radically revisionist insight. Suez 1956 represents a significant juncture in the social and political orders of both Britain and Egypt in the 1950s. Britain was still gripped by the Empire mentality, particularly manifest in the floundering ambitions of Eden, notwithstanding their peculiar personal expression in his statements and policies. Meanwhile, there were new forces emerging that were barely understood, not just in Egypt and the region, but even at home, in Britain, and especially among the young ranks of the emerging New Left – best represented, as far as we are concerned in this section, by the emergent field of Cultural Studies and the attention it brought to focus on the marginalised other (at the time mostly the working classes, but later all kinds of marginalised groups), the play of power dynamics in social realities, and the significance of popular forms of cultural production. In Egypt, on the other hand, revolutionary sensibilities with increasingly powerful vocabulary and institutional formations were beginning to take over, a sense of an 'appointment with destiny', as the Arabic phrase goes, was beginning to crystallise round the figure of Nasser, and, ironically, was fully confirmed as he emerged almost unscathed after the Suez debacle. Moreover, the Egyptian claim over Suez had been a dream that cut across the Egyptian social and ideological spectrum, keen even among those who still belonged to the old regime.

We generally speak of memory in the personal or the collective, and of course in terms of the tension between the two domains over the authenticity of the experience and the veracity of the content of the memory. Acts of retrieval, whether voluntary or involuntary, as consequential in themselves, began to be taken seriously after Freudian psychoanalysis and philosophies of reflection and of process from the nineteenth and early twentieth centuries. It must be said, though, that the attention to history and historiography since the nineteenth century has also added to our understanding of what is at stake in the work of memory, particularly on the collective level.[7] One of the radical turns of history since the Second World War, and in its aftermath during the cold war era, is the foregrounding of the ideological subliminal structures of our acts and belief systems, and not least because of the emergent nationalisms and nation states, their concomitant ideologies of destiny and fulfilment, as Benedict Anderson and others have demonstrated, and the almost haphazardly selective agendas of 'enlightenment'. These emergent orders of reality, ideologically informed and committed, territorial, foundationalist, secular as well as religious, constitute some of the forces at play that Eden had overlooked or underestimated. Eden's statement: 'Our quarrel is not with Egypt, still less with the Arab World, it is with Colonel Nasser', cited above, is quite revealing in this regard. The attitude of personalising challenges, while revealing Eden's own personal prejudices – and the tone is unmistakably personal in this statement – is a clear expression of the lingering colonialist and orientalising world view: the appeal is still not to a modern nation, but to a subject nation, and an oriental one at that, the figure of the despot looming large, as the owner of his lands, and while the aim is to fight him, the summation of his 'country' in his own person is unmistakably present in the rhetoric. And yet this rhetoric still led to official state policy and even to action, despite all the protestations coming from the left and even many conservatives. Indeed, Eden's expressions remarkably echo a similar statement by Lord Cromer (Proconsul in Egypt, 1883–1907) roughly fifty years before: 'We do not govern Egypt, we only govern the governors of Egypt.'[8] From within the urgencies of our present, it should be noted, the parallels with Iraq are quite obvious, and it is the oversight that has proven deadly and demoralising in both cases: the new forces at play in the region, first the movements of independence and Arab nationalism, and now political unrest and the rise of extremist ideological and militant forces in the name of religion to fill the void.

These new orders with their wider, popular base and revolutionary social and political ideals, along with changing economic, social and class conditions, lie behind the indignant outcries over Hungary and Suez in the 1950s, and may in part account for the subsequent culture of resistance in Britain and the awakening into possibilities of political participation among the young leftists. The new orders of reality were given an even stronger impetus after Suez and as a result of it, not only in Egypt but in the rest of the Arab region as well, as Rashid Khalidi has briefly but pointedly demonstrated.[9] The mood of the time in Britain is brilliantly captured in Penelope Lively's evocative brief memoir of her time at Oxford included in this section: 'The Suez Crisis dominated that autumn, as events unfolded. I think that for many of my generation it was the first experience of intense political involvement – of finding yourself with strong feelings about what was going on, about what your own government was doing and might do'. She goes on to express more poignantly, 'The Suez Crisis was a baptism of fire, as a kind of political awakening, a recognition that you could and should quarrel with government, that you could disagree and disapprove'. Lively's testimony is particularly significant; not only has she spent the first twelve years of her life in Cairo, she also represents a long and illustrious line of British writers with strong associations with Egypt, E. M. Forster, Lawrence Durrell, Keith Douglas, Terence Tiller, among others, to whom I would add one of my English professors at the American University in Cairo, Leslie Croxford, who wrote a novel on Alexandria, and who represents a whole class of British writers whose work has yet to receive wider dissemination. Just as the work of a whole generation of Egyptian writers with association to British culture, from playwrights such as Sa'd Wahba to novelists such as Gamal Hassan (who resides in London), has yet to receive similar attention. Lively's memory of a particular place in Cairo, the Gayer-Anderson Museum, previously known as Beit al-Kritiliya and inhabited by Major Gayer-Anderson at the time when Lively visited with her family as personal guests of the Major, offers us a brilliant glimpse of lived experience, imaginatively crossing several boundaries, of a place that is later to stand as an example of one of the most positive aspects of British–Egyptian relations: the work of conservation and preservation of cultural heritage, in this case as undertaken by Nicholas Warner, whose moving but sobering account of the restoration is also included in this section. Together, the two narratives provide an excellent synchronic moment of the work *of* and *on* lived cultural memory.

Collectively, the memory of Suez 1956 is a political memory. Personally, the memory is of intellectual and cultural expansiveness, of personal lives unfolding as trajectories of intellectual resistance, whether in the world of letters, of political activism or of revisionist histories. Political memories, though, still remain strongly within the immediacy of causes. The morning of the massive demonstrations in Trafalgar Square in March 2003 against the war in Iraq inevitably brought forth the memory of the hitherto unprecedented 'Law Not War' demonstrations against the bombing of Cairo in 1956, and British papers featured reports and articles on Suez as the only other instance in living memory in which the left and many other factions in society had so rallied round a single cause.

In Egyptian memory, Suez and the entire Canal Zone has continued to stand as an icon of resistance, perhaps also due to the fact that the Canal Zone has witnessed a series of crucial war episodes, in 1951, 1956, 1967 and 1973, which stamped in the history and popular imagination of Egyptians an image of heroic accounts of resistance and martyrdom, the likes of which Egyptians associate mainly with the Algerian War of Independence and the continuing plight and struggle of the Palestinians. This time it was all on Egyptian soil and featuring ordinary Egyptians in heroic circumstances. On the Egyptian side, the collective memory of Suez 1956, as political memory, is sadly still mostly restricted to personal memoirs, reports and interviews, as no official documents have yet been declassified, and with the memory of nationalisation in July 2006 overshadowed by the more immediate spectacle of the Israeli bombardment of Lebanon. The irony of the two moments involving Israeli military aggression was not lost on many Egyptians though; the myth of invincibility surrounding the Israeli army that had been created by the 1956 war was being shattered exactly fifty years after through their misadventures in Lebanon. The difference in the Egyptians' national sentiment surrounding the two moments was sharply marked. Suez 1956 still offered a strong sense of national pride, to the point of nostalgia, hearkening to that first moment of awakening which the present urgencies of a new historical moment seem to fail to retrieve, or to inspire. Still, a few commemorative events were organised, and special reports and magazine issues appeared in memory of Suez. A handful of memoirs by key figures such as Sayyid Mar'i, Abd al-Latif al-Bughdadi, Abd al-Hamid Abu Bakr, and M. H. Heikal, and a few lengthy interviews with some of the key figures in the main events are still the main available sources.[10] The memoirs reputed to have been written by Engineer Mahmoud Younis, who was placed by Nasser in charge of the take-over on 26 July 1956, have not yet seen the light.

Cultural memory, on the other hand, is engaged in structures of continuity, in collective social, artistic and literary practices. Suez 1956, along with the subsequent Canal wars, has indelibly inscribed the Canal Zone and its inhabitants in the modern Egyptian national imaginary, for the first time since labourers were rounded up from villages all over to serve in digging the Canal itself. This has been achieved not only through the events that transpired there, followed by Egyptians everywhere and covered by writer-journalists such as Gamal al-Ghitani and novelists such as Yusuf al-Qa'id. Perhaps more wide-ranging and powerfully emotive were the new art forms, popular forms born of resistance such as the Children of the Earth Song, the Theatre of the Trenches, the Trenches Cinema and others.[11] More significant still are the musical performative arts such as the *simsimiyya* and national character types with folk legendary dimensions such as Abu al-'Arabi (the subject of a recent Egyptian film bearing his name) and the living legend of resistance, Captain Ghazali of Suez – all disseminated throughout by the Canal refugees in the Delta as well as state-sponsored national festivals. Not to mention, of course, the legendary singer Umm Kolthum's famous song celebrating the Egyptian captain-guides and their success in the first real challenge after the decision to nationalise the Canal, taking over after the foreign captains had been forced to resign all at once, thereby threatening to shut down all navigation through the Canal and proving Egyptians incapable of taking over: the song was entitled 'How sweet you look, you Egyptian at the helm!' (*Mahlak ya masri winta 'ala al-daffa*).

By comparison, few British works have appeared surrounding the events at Suez or their aftermath, the one notable example being John Osborne's *The Entertainer* (1960), first written as a play and then made into a film.[12] Indeed, as Egyptian director Yousry Nasrallah notes in his contribution in this section: 'It is very remarkable, how very little work has been done – on a popular level – to revise, rethink and reanalyse British colonial politics in the Middle East. There is not a single film about the presence of Britain in Palestine, none on the role of Britain in Iraq'. No 'collective anti-colonialist conscience' has been created in intellectual and artistic circles, he sharply notes, as has been the case with the Algerian cause in France. While Nasrallah's observation might hold true, particularly when applied to British cinema, the work has been done more quietly by some British historians, writers and scholars, only more in the spheres of cinema and the novel when it comes to the case of India. The strong relations between cinema and the nationalist question that exist in Egypt, he further notes, do not exist in the same way in Britain. Perhaps it is not in cinema that we may look for comparable symbiotic identity-forming or entrenching cultural practices; the case of the BBC comes to mind, the history of which, particularly in relation to Egypt and the Arab world is offered by Gamon McLellan, former head of the BBC Arabic Service. 'Suez was a critical episode for the BBC and for its credibility, at home and abroad, as a journalistic organisation independent of Government', as McLellan begins his insightful and rather illuminating account. The decision to give the leader of the Labour Opposition, Hugh Gaitskell, the right of reply to a ministerial broadcast by Eden had incurred government disfavour and a partial loss of the BBC's Grant-in-Aid. Moreover, the British government decided in 1956 at the height of the crisis to use the Sharq al-Adna station, which had been set up in Palestine during the Second World

War, and turn it into a propaganda service under a new name. However 'The Voice of Britain' was a short lived enterprise. Similar issues of independence and credibility would also surround the BBC during the Blairite era, over questions of national security.

A newly-emergent and historically better-informed consciousness of the political, economic, educational, scholarly and cultural aspects of the bilateral relations between Egypt and the UK is clearly informing the different contributions and personal and professional points of view in this volume. The challenges to intercultural relations, whose present visions and exigencies are dictated more by urgencies on the political levels, have been subjected to revisionist thoughts and practices rallied from complex cultural forces: historical to be revised, political and ideological to be resisted or transformed, intercultural to be heeded and deployed, power dynamics to be adjusted, regional and interregional to be reconceived and globalising universalities to be invited but held at a suspicious arm's length. Principles for a radical reconception, inevitably on the side of all that has been previously marginalised, with fresh explanatory powers, are seeking to become principles of a new type of action.

The contributions in this volume from the fields of Egyptology, archaeology and conservation by Fekri Hassan, Stephen Quirke and Michael Jones, respectively, offer just such radical visions for new actions, at once transformative of their respective fields and culturally revolutionary. Egyptology, archaeology, and conservation work together offer the longest chapter in the history of British–Egyptian relations, beginning with the handing over of the Rosetta Stone by French officers to the victorious British in 1801. The story of Thomas Young's rivalry with Champollion over decipherment of the Egyptian hieroglyphics is well known, and sets the tone for subsequent rivalries, far-reaching and consequential, that were no less nationalistic in their impulses than those the Egyptians were later to be accused of when it came to their relation to their antiquities and ancient history. Hassan, one of the few noted Egyptian Egyptologists, offers an excellently rounded and well-attuned (to both the British and Egyptian sides) synoptic view of the history of British involvement in Egyptology and archaeology, beginning with another significant event: the campaign by Amelia Edwards to save Egyptian antiquities in 1882 and the subsequent establishment of the Egypt Exploration Fund (later the Egypt Exploration Society). In his rendition of the pivotal social, political and cultural forces at work behind the key moments in this history, Hassan offers radical insights into Egyptian realities and contexts, including the role of Egyptians and the first Egyptian Egyptologists. Hassan's expertise and searching cultural gaze lead him to offer some key suggestions for the enhancement of British–Egyptian relations, and they deserve to be quoted here:

> The way forward to improve British-Egyptian relations, to promote a better understanding of ancient Egypt, to contribute to the advancement of science and knowledge, and to safeguard Egyptian heritage for Egypt and humanity must include bilateral efforts to support (1) a well-designed public education programme to acquaint the public in Egypt with the fruits of archaeological and Egyptological research; (2) the institution of a programme of field restoration and conservation as a major component of archaeological activities in Egypt to complement the current emphasis on restorations of museum specimens; (3) the implementation of a strategy of cultural heritage management through legal and institutional means: (i) to ensure the conservation of Egyptian cultural resources, (ii) to present and interpret appropriately the achievements of Egyptian civilisation in all fields of knowledge and as a dynamic, creative society, and (iii) to provide jobs and improve economic conditions through proper sustainable, economic management of Egypt's archaeological and cultural resources; and, most importantly, (4) allocation of sufficient resources to train Egyptian archaeologists, Egyptologists, restorers, conservators, museologists and heritage managers and the creation of an appropriate managerial, scientific and technical infrastructure as the

only viable and sustainable means to safeguard and valorise
Egyptian heritage.

These insights, Hassan notes, are now shared by many Egyptians and
Egyptologists. A good example is Hassan's colleague and curator at
the Petrie Museum of Egyptian Archaeology at University College
London, Stephen Quirke. Quirke, who is also one of the leading
Egyptologists devoted to the critical study of the literature of
ancient Egypt, offers a radical, alternative version of the history of
archaeology. Away from the prevailing History of Ideas approach
in most histories of archaeology, Quirke offers 'a return to specific
practices and practitioners upon which the great ideas-men of
today and yesterday depend. The men, women and children who
move the mounds of earth for excavation directors, and usually tell
directors where to dig, are not anonymous.' These workers represent
a kind of economy of labour, which Quirke defines as an economy of
absence, and they exist on both sides, so while he cites the Lancashire
mill workers, he offers a list of the Egyptian workers employed by
Flinders Petrie on his famous excavations, having had unique access
to the Petrie archives, and explores some of the unique aspects of the
interpersonal and intercultural relations involved. Quirke concludes
with a series of key questions posed to the predominant archaeological
and museological practices.

In his account of some of the projects for the conservation and
management of Coptic Christian cultural heritage, Michael Jones
offers an excellent articulation of the new hard-won sensibilities
in the field. As Jones puts it, 'Conventional approaches to cultural
heritage preservation have concentrated on the tangible and material
features of culture. This has had the effect of isolating monuments
from their social and historical contexts and then leaving them to
their own devices'. He offers instead a more holistic approach based on
the correct identification of origins and affiliations, material culture
as a significant identity marker in the national imaginary of living
communities. As he strongly notes, the Copts are the inheritors of

an unbroken tradition that began in the first century with the arrival of St Mark. With the new approach, for which he gives the good example of conservation of monasteries, Jones notes that 'the effect goes far beyond the tangible and is perhaps more vitally intangible. Pilgrims, tourists and residents are no longer presented with what looks like a neglected and debased culture and the monks, who are the custodians, understand better how to protect it. Specialists have access to new material and the Coptic faithful practise in enhanced surroundings. All these elements successfully increase heritage valorisation in the Coptic community and beyond'. This kind of effort perfectly exemplifies Hassan's recommendations, as the issues surrounding cultural heritage are of a more immediate significance to living continuities in Egyptians' identity and their sense of themselves. This is especially the case when it comes to one of the oldest churches and richest body of continuous practices involving deep issues of faith and identity.

The implications behind these pioneering views of one of the strongest aspects of British–Egyptian relations have a direct bearing on the field of education, another important aspect of these bilateral relations. Peter Mackenzie Smith offers an illuminating overview of UK–Egyptian relations in the field of education in the past fifty years. Together with Hoda Rashad and Paul Smith, they offer a positive view of the potential for further collaboration. This is especially the case as they all note the significance of the recent phenomenon in both Egypt and the UK of the growth in the role of the private sector in education. This growth involves not only school education but also higher education programmes, many of which are overseen by the British Council in Cairo, which has considerably expanded its operations in recent years, as Paul Smith demonstrates. Peter Mackenzie Smith, Hoda Rashad and Paul Smith all seem to agree on the necessity and vitality of a more rounded vision of education, which, while taking into view respective cultural realities, still offers a more international outlook, one that will at once meet the challenges of globalised economies and hegemonic world views.

The debates articulated here amply illustrate the excellence and significant achievements of many practices on British and Egyptian sides. All agree, however, that there is an even greater potential for collaboration for enhancing cultural relations: in cinema and the performative and visual arts, in government and private initiatives for the creation of much needed fora for cultural and professional collaboration, in the establishment of cultural heritage institutes and cultural studies and translation studies programmes, and perhaps in supporting already-successful examples on the ground, such as *al-Multaqa,* the Egyptian, Arab and British Cultural Forum, organised by Egyptian professional expatriates in London. Modern literary and cultural histories of both countries offer many rich and mutually-illuminating intersections, the pursuit of which is guaranteed to enrich not only key chapters in modern history in general, but also vitally conceived and relevant intercultural insights. It is these insights that are hoped to provide the building blocks of the structures of continuity of cultural memory, over and above the immediate causes and exigencies of political memory.

Notes

1. Statement by Sayyid Mar'i is quoted from excerpts from his *Political Papers,* edited and translated by Moshe Shemesh and included in Selwyn Ilan Troen and Moshe Shemesh, eds, *The Suez-Sinai Crisis 1956: Retrospective and Reappraisal,* London: Frank Cass, 1990, p. 361. Mar'i was one of the few trusted with the decision before its announcement in the speech in Manshiyya Square. He was later to be entrusted with the task of overseeing the evacuation and temporary relocation of the refugees from the Canal Zone throughout the Delta.

2. Statements by Eden and Nasser are transcribed from records in the BBC archival library, online at: http://news.bbc.co.uk/1/hi/uk/6092170.stm.

3. Statement by Captain Derek Oakley is transcribed from records in the BBC archival library cited above, produced by Alison Trowsdale, Samantha Smith and Phil Coomes. Some of the archive images were taken by Derek Oakley.

4. Behind these statements there is a hermeneutic which ultimately puts forth a certain understanding of the nature of historical change, and which Fredric

Jameson has elaborated under the rubric of a 'Political Unconscious'. 'From this perspective', Jameson explains, 'the convenient working distinction between cultural texts that are social and political and those that are not becomes something worse than an error: namely, a symptom and a reinforcement of the reification and privatization of contemporary life ... The assertion of a political unconscious proposes that we undertake just such a final analysis and explore the multiple paths that lead to the unmasking of cultural artefacts as socially symbolic acts', in Fredric Jameson, *The Political Unconscious: Narrative as a Socially Symbolic Act*, London: Routledge, 1983, pp. 4–5.

5. An entire volume recently published in commemoration of Suez is premised on the parallels with the war on Iraq: Martin Woollacott, *After Suez: Adrift in the American Century*, London: I. B. Tauris, 2006.

6. See Roger Owen, 'Egypt and Europe: From French Expedition to British Occupation', in Albert Hourani, Phillip S. Khoury and Mary C. Wilson, eds, *The Modern Middle East: A Reader*, Berkeley: University of California Press, 1993, pp. 111–24.

7. See Paul Ricoeur's recent study, *Memory, History, Forgetting*, trans. Kathleen Blamey and David Pellauer, Chicago: University of Chicago Press, 2004.

8. Quoted in Afaf Lutfi al-Sayyid, *Egypt and Cromer*, New York: Praeger, 1969, p. 68; see also Edward Said, *Culture and Imperialism*, London: Vantage, 1994, p. 239. For a recent biographical and historical investigation into the life of Lord Cromer and his times, see Roger Owen's excellent study, *Lord Cromer: Victorian Imperialist, Edwardian Proconsul*, Oxford: Oxford University Press, 2004.

9. See Rashid Khalidi, 'Consequences of the Suez Crisis in the Arab World', in *The Modern Middle East: A Reader*, pp. 535–50, first published in William Roger Louis and Roger Owen, eds, *Suez 1956: The Crisis and its Consequences*, Oxford: Oxford University Press, 1989, pp. 377–92.

10. Sayyid Mar'i was the engineer in charge of enacting the Agrarian Reforms after the revolution. He became Minister for Agriculture and Agrarian Reform and Deputy Prime Minister for most of the period between 1956 and 1971, and continued to hold high position during Sadat's regime. Abd al-Latif al-Bughdadi was a member of the Egyptian Revolutionary Command Council; he was appointed a Minister of War in 1953 and in 1957 became the elected chairman of the first parliament to be established after the revolution. Excerpts from al-Bughdadi's memoirs were translated by Moshe Shemesh and included in *The Suez-Sinai Crisis 1956*, pp. 333–56. Engineer Abd al-Hamid Abu Bakr was one of the three in charge of carrying out the takeover of the International Company's headquarters during Nasser's famous speech, chosen along with Engineer 'Izzat 'Adil by Mahmoud Younis to help with the mission. M. H. Heikal is the famous journalist and writer who was personal adviser to Nasser and, having amassed massive archives of secret documents, published two volumes on Suez in Arabic, *Malafat al-*

Suwais (Suez Archives), Cairo: Dar al-Shuruq, 2004, and *Cutting the Lion's Tail*, London: Andre Deutsch, 1986.

11. See Muhammad Haykal, *'Ala shatt al-Qanah: Muwatinun ikhtaru al-watan*, Cairo: Dar al-Hilal, 2006, pp. 10–26.

12. Woollacott offers good insights into the relevance of Osborne's *The Entertainer* and argues how it may have unsettled the increasingly growing fiction of the great victory in 1945 in his final chapter 'Magic Carpets', in *After Suez*, pp. 130–2.

Cultural Confusion

In the nineteen-thirties, and into the forties, Cairo was a cauldron of different cultures. It was above all Egyptian – Islamic – but it was also host to many outsiders. British, French, Maltese, Lebanese, Syrian, Turkish, Italian – until the outbreak of the Second World War. I was born and spent my childhood in this cauldron – English, but surrounded by all the signals of other communities, and above all of Islamic culture. My qualification for speaking here today is perhaps as someone who experienced cultural upheaval in youth – who knew herself to be English but identified with Egypt, who felt an alien in her own country when eventually she arrived there at the age of twelve.

My home was outside Cairo, in open country – fields of berseem and sugarcane, the canals, the villages. That area – Boulac el Dakrur – has long since been digested into the urban sprawl of Cairo, but twenty years ago or so the house still survived, somewhat battered, doing duty as a training college. Finding it back then, I recovered at once that sense of home, of the place where I belonged, but that instinctive response had been there from the first moment of my return to Egypt as an adult. A child absorbs a cultural climate, it seems to me, unquestioningly and uncritically. For me, the only known climate had once been that of cosmopolitan, polyglot Cairo and Alexandria, with those extremes of poverty and of prosperity, and the abiding backdrop of Islam, but also the mysterious sense of a place in which everything coexisted – Pharaonic, Greek, Roman, Mameluke – and, for a couple of helter-skelter years, with the distant roar of the Libyan campaign not far off in the western desert. When Rommel's advance looked unstoppable, we left for Palestine, as it then was, with other British families, and my experience of the Middle East expanded and I glimpsed further complexities. But from the child's eye view, that was merely a brief local difficulty, quickly overcome, and we were soon back with the eucalyptus and casuarina trees of Boulac el Dakrur.

Only as an adult did I come to realise to what extent Egypt made me, how profoundly my imaginative landscape had been formed by that place at that time. When I was about seven I went with my parents to visit an archaeological dig somewhere in the desert. I remember being shown a shallow scrape in the sand, in which lay a crouching skeletal outline – the curve of a skull, the fan of ribs, the folded limbs. I don't think I listened much to the explanation given, but I remember that it came to me with a sense of wonder that once, long, long ago, this had been a person. A seminal moment, and one which I am sure sowed the seed of a lifelong concern with the past, with time, with the operation of memory. I now think that what we saw must have been a pre-Dynastic burial site, possibly at the Fayoum. The pyramids were of course a mundane and familiar sight; like any child growing up in the Cairo area I saw a pyramid simply as a normal and expected landscape feature, nothing to get excited about. We visited the pyramids once a week or so, and my interest was focused entirely on the delicate and difficult matter of which donkey to select from the donkey line.

The Beit il Kritiliya was another matter – that wonderful survivor from the Mameluke period, now the Gayer-Anderson Museum. Back then, it was still Major Gayer-Anderson's home – Gayer-Anderson Pasha – and we were sometimes invited to tea. I was a child formed by reading – my education was a home-based affair that centred entirely on reading, and my imaginative life was driven by the stories of Greek mythology and by the *Arabian Nights*. For me the Beit il Kritiliya was the *Arabian Nights* made manifest – the furnishings, the fountain, the mashrabiya windows. I used to go home and enact narratives in which the goings-on of the *Arabian Nights* took place in the Beit il Kritiliya and I was right in there too – wiping out, in the process, the inconvenient figure of the Major and the standard English tea that would have been served.

There's plenty of cultural confusion here – a child whose imaginative world derives from Bronze Age Greece and medieval Arab storytelling, whose native land is an unknown and mysterious place where apparently everyone speaks English and it rains all the time. Britain of the late nineteen-forties was a far cry from the multicultural society of today; to arrive in that pinched post-war place after the vibrancy of Egypt was to experience further cultural shock. The next few years were a grim rite of passage, imbued with nostalgia for what came to seem a lost home. Much later, the conditioning of that childhood – above all a vision of time and memory – would powerfully affect the kind of fiction that I would eventually come to write.

Egypt does that to people. There is a long tradition of writers who succumb to the fascination of the place, the people, the abiding sense of the past, from Flaubert struggling up the Great Pyramid in 1849, back to Herodotus, and the writers of the Second World War period who clustered in Cairo and Alexandria in the nineteen-forties – Keith Douglas, Terence Tiller, G. S. Fraser, and of course Laurence Durrell. Durrell was honing his own maverick view of Alexandrian society at the same time as I was surfing out at Sidi Bishr, aged nine, and hunting for chameleons in a leafy garden in rue Rouchdi Pasha, and sometimes being allowed the treat of an ice-cream at Baudrot's, where, conceivably, our paths may have crossed. But, needless to say, Durrell's vision of Alexandria is almost unrecognizable for me, though occasionally it evokes some physical detail – sand on the slats of Venetian blinds, the glint of tramlines. Keith Douglas's poetry, on the other hand, and his brief memoir, *From Alamein to Zem Zem*, bring back sharply both the place and the time – the desert, the Mediterranean, Cairo in the war, those hordes of very young men, like Douglas himself, who poured through the Middle East during those years. But, above all, I appreciate the thought of being, in a very small way, a part of that succession of writers who have been conditioned by Egypt.

Enough of childhood indoctrination. I want to turn now to what it was like to be a young adult at the time of the Suez Crisis, back here in England. There will not be that many of us who had that experience, and I think it may be worth recalling. I was in Oxford, having taken my degree there a year or so before, and I was working as research secretary to a member of St Anthony's College, then as now a centre of postgraduate Middle Eastern studies. I had just met my future husband, Jack Lively, who had joined the college as a Junior Fellow. The Suez Crisis dominated that autumn, as events unfolded. I think that for many of my generation it was the first experience of intense political involvement – of finding yourself with strong feelings about what was going on, about what your own government was doing and might do. Opinion was polarised, in the university as elsewhere – those violently opposed to Eden's policy, those supportive, and those uncertain what to think or whom to believe. My memory, though, is that opposition was the stance of the majority in Oxford, and Jack, along with a colleague at St Anthony's, set about a campaign to coordinate a response by senior members of the university, immediately after the first bombing raids on Cairo. I remember cycling round from college to college to deliver personal letters summoning sympathisers to the meeting at which a statement was drafted, signed by 355 members of Senior Common Rooms and ten heads of colleges, led by Alan Bullock of St Catherine's. The statement read: 'We consider that this action is morally wrong, that it endangers the solidarity of the Commonwealth, that it constitutes a grave strain on the Atlantic Alliance and that it is a flagrant violation of the principles of the UN Charter.' I couldn't be at the meeting, not being a senior member of the university, but I remember vividly the heightened atmosphere of that time, the urgency of the newspapers, the climate of discussion, of argument, and eventually, for many of us, of outrage. For me, what was happening had a personal dimension – here was my own country dropping bombs on the country that I still thought of as a kind of home. The place was still in my head – the look of it, the feel of it, the familiar homely sound of spoken Arabic. The Suez crisis was a baptism of fire, as a kind of political awakening, a recognition that you could and should quarrel with government; that you could disagree and disapprove. I was fresh from student life, and I think that my generation of students was politically apathetic. There was the Labour Club and the Conservative Club, but they fulfilled a mainly social function. South Africa aroused some strong feelings – there was an anti-apartheid group – but it now seems to me that the vast majority of students were pretty indifferent to both current events and political opinion. Suez changed all that. Such was the heat of argument, and the force of opinions both for and against Eden's policy, that any thinking youth had to be drawn in. The line-up was not exclusively one of left against right; opinion cut across the political spectrum. Families were divided; traditional Tories found themselves unable to accept the government's actions. To be young at that period was to be made suddenly aware that political judgement is a personal matter, that it is not only a right but an obligation to question the policies of those Olympian figures who dictate history.

I am profoundly grateful for the cultural confusions of my upbringing. I don't know that they have provided me with insights, but they gave me a sense of the depth, breadth and otherness of the world, an awareness of variety, of difference. Egypt became an imaginative resource that has served me all my life, in various ways, has fed into the fiction I have written, has provided a particular way of looking at the world, a climate of the mind. The first twelve years of life are the crucial storehouse, for any of us – both memory and conditioning. My adult life has been spent in my own country, but I know that that early identification with an elsewhere has been a profound influence.

GAMON MCLELLAN[1]

Suez and its Aftermath:
The BBC Arabic Service and Egypt

Suez was a critical episode for the BBC and for its credibility, at home and abroad, as a journalistic organisation independent of Government. The BBC was determined to reflect in all its broadcast services – to the home audience as well as to listeners around the world – accurate news of what was happening, but also the full extent to which public opinion in Britain was divided about the British government's actions. This provoked considerable anger within the Government and among prominent Conservative backbenchers in the House of Commons. The particular point that angered the Government was the BBC's reporting of opposition within Britain, which was seen as 'giving comfort to the enemy'.[2] The BBC also irritated the Conservative government by insisting on giving Hugh Gaitskell, the leader of the Labour Opposition, the right of reply to a ministerial broadcast by the prime minister, Sir Anthony Eden. Gaitskell's reply was transmitted in English in both the Home and External Services (as Eden's broadcast had been) and reported in translation by the Arabic Service. At one point, a junior Foreign Office minister summoned the Director-General, Sir Ian Jacob, to tell him of the Government's displeasure with the BBC and to inform him that the Grant-in-Aid[3] for the External Services would be reduced by £1 million.[4]

The BBC was not deflected from its determination to assert its independence from Government. As Gerard Mansell, Managing Director of the BBC's External Services during the seventies, has written in his history of BBC External Broadcasting:

> Future generations of BBC officials would henceforth have before them a precedent which illuminated with stark clarity the precise nature of the BBC's constitutional obligations and of its relationship with the Government. There could have been no more effective demonstration that the External Services were truly as independent as they claimed to be.[5]

The Arabic Service, broadcasting to an outraged Arab world, was at the centre of the row. It was not the first of such confrontations with Government. There had been a major row following the BBC's first Arabic broadcast on 3 January 1938, which at 6.00 PM had included the chimes of Big Ben, followed by a news bulletin. The third story in the bulletin had read as follows:

> Another Arab from Palestine was executed by hanging at Acre this morning by order of a military court. He was arrested during recent riots in the Hebron Mountains and was found to possess a rifle and some ammunition.[6]

In 1938, Britain had considerable interests in the region: Palestine and Iraq were governed by the British under mandate from the League of Nations, and the British had a significant presence in Egypt, Sudan and the Arabian Peninsula. Aden was a Crown colony. A senior Foreign Office figure was appalled at the broadcast of this story; he did not like the idea of straight news, which he referred to as 'a BBC expression'. After a meeting with two senior BBC representatives, a Foreign Office man complained that the whole attitude of BBC officials was entirely contrary to Foreign Office ideas as to how the Arabic broadcasts should be run.[7]

Upsetting the Foreign Office did no damage to the Arabic Service – which has since been recounting with some satisfaction the story of its first clash with Whitehall. Suez, though, had immediate repercussions for the Arabic Service. To broadcast to the Arab world from London in the forties and fifties was to be much more remote from the region than is the case today. By early 1943, the BBC had become concerned to reflect the region more closely in its output, and had set up an office for the Arabic Service in Cairo. By the following year, a quarter of the Arabic Service budget was being spent in Cairo.[8] Programmes and talks started to be produced in Cairo, where a range of speakers and music were more available than in London.

The immediate effect of Suez on the Service was the closure of the Cairo office and the resignation of the Egyptian staff in London. This placed considerable additional pressure on the remaining Arab broadcasters at a critical time.

The BBC Arabic Service was not the only British broadcasting operation in Arabic at the time. During the Second World War, the British had set up a station in Palestine, the Near East Broadcasting Station, Sharq al-Adna. The station broadcast for considerably longer each day than the BBC Arabic Service and was carried on both medium and short wave.

The Arabic Service initially was only broadcast on short wave. After the war, Sharq al-Adna ostensibly became a commercial company and moved its operations to Cyprus. It broadcast news, talks and music, as well as advertisements, while the BBC Arabic Service pursued a more highbrow programming policy aimed at educated listeners in the Arab world.

In 1956, at the height of the Suez Crisis, the British government decided to take over the Sharq al-Adna station and use it for official announcements. The Director of the Station protested and was removed at bayonet point,[9] and most of the staff declined to cooperate with what became a propaganda service called 'The Voice of Britain'. It was not a success. It was described in the House of Lords as 'amateur attempts at propaganda which were absolutely laughable and brought this country into contempt'.[10] The Voice of Britain lasted for a matter of months, and its medium wave transmitter in Cyprus was eventually handed over to the BBC Arabic Service.[11]

The BBC was thus to benefit from the closure of the Voice of Britain – indirectly, that is, from the Suez debacle. The acquisition of a medium wave facility was to increase very considerably the long-term effectiveness of the BBC's broadcasts to the region. Until the arrival of direct broadcasting by satellite, short wave would remain the only way the BBC could reach listeners across the entire Arab world. Without the option of transmitting from within the countries to which it was broadcasting – unthinkable in the fifties and sixties – the BBC, like other international broadcasters, was heavily reliant on short wave transmission. But the aftermath of Suez coincided with the transistor revolution, when cheaper, portable radios became widely available in the Arab world as elsewhere, dramatically increasing radio ownership.

Most domestic and entertainment radio was broadcast on medium wave, and the Arab world was no exception. Audiences who had short wave bands on their radios would tune to them to hear news from London – but to broadcast on medium wave was to broadcast like a local station. In the limited area in which the medium wave signal could be heard, the BBC was received alongside the listeners' own national radio stations and became in effect an alternative domestic station for listeners in the region.

The Sharq al-Adna medium wave transmitter was replaced by a more modern transmitter in 1969, and by the seventies the BBC had three medium wave transmitters in Cyprus with their respective frequencies: one to carry the World Service in English to the eastern Mediterranean region and two carrying Arabic – one directed eastwards, the other transmitting to the south.

Unlike short wave broadcasts, medium wave transmissions are regulated by international agreement, to avoid interference. Frequencies are allocated to particular locations, and the permitted power of the transmitter, the direction in which it is aimed and the hours during which it can broadcast are specified and regulated. Medium wave signals travel horizontally during daylight hours: one of the BBC's two Arabic frequencies from Cyprus thus reaches – during the day – Lebanon, the western areas of Syria and Jordan, as well as the West Bank, Gaza and Israel. The other reaches just beyond Cairo. After dark, however, medium wave signals reach much further, and the BBC's signals from Cyprus can be heard in Iraq, Saudi Arabia, Upper Egypt and in most of Sudan. In 1969, the BBC also acquired medium wave facilities in the Sultanate of Oman, enabling it to provide the Arabic Service on medium wave during the evening to eastern and central Saudi Arabia, the Gulf States and Iran (where there is listening in Arabic as well as in Farsi).

With a much more audible presence in the eastern Arab world, the BBC also started broadcasting for longer each day. In 1957, Arabic Service was increased to nine and a half hours a day, and there was a further expansion to twelve hours in 1959. The Service thus found itself developing from a matter of a few hours' broadcasting each day into a fully-fledged regional radio station for the Arab world, making a particular impact in those regions which it reached on medium wave. It became the only BBC foreign language service to operate as a full radio station, complete with its own continuity announcers and a broader range of programming.

The departure of the Egyptian contingent from the Service in 1956 was a major blow; but Egyptians did return to the BBC after an interval. The original broadcasting staff of the Service in 1938 had been entirely Egyptian, although broadcasters from other Arab nationalities had joined the staff from early on, particularly from the start of the Second World War. It became clear that broadcasting from London did impose certain characteristics on the output of a station – and particularly something of a pan-Arab character. Nevertheless, with the exception of the immediate post-Suez period, Egyptian broadcasters played a major role in the Service throughout most of its history, not least in helping to shape its emerging pan-Arab identity. In 1941, a report suggested the BBC Arabic Service had become a 'microcosm of the Arab world, responsive to the intellectual movements of its various parts'.[12] And that had a political consequence for a Service broadcasting to the Arab world of that particular time. One of the leading figures in the Service wrote at the end of the Second World War:

> To become the 'national programme' of the Arabs was not our conscious aim, but it was in the nature of things that an Arabic Service from London should be metropolitan rather than regional, and thus work in harmony with the Arab urge towards the strengthening of their common nationhood.[13]

Despite this, the BBC had started in 1941 a service not at all pan-Arab in its conception: broadcasts to North Africa in colloquial Maghrebi Arabic. This was an operation kept distinct from the main BBC Arabic Service. It did not survive the Second World War, and the BBC never again attempted to broadcast in any form of the language other than the Modern Standard Arabic that became the norm for news broadcasting across the Arab world.

After Suez, the 'Voice of the Arabs', the Egyptian international broadcasting station, had its heyday, broadcasting Gamal Abdul Nasser's nationalist, anti-colonialist message across the Arab world. The BBC found the radio waves more crowded, but it retained its reputation as a trusted source of news. This was enhanced when the Arab world was again plunged into war in 1967. The news of the defeat of the Arab armies came as a profound shock to Arab listeners – but it enhanced the standing of the BBC, which was judged to have been a reliable source of accurate news. The Voice of the Arabs, putting out a more palatable version of events, was eventually seen to have been misleading.

In 1972, relations between the BBC and the Egyptian government became strained when the Arabic Service broadcast a report of an unsuccessful coup against President Anwar Sadat. For a short period the Arabic Service was jammed. However, despite making threats against Egyptians working for the BBC, the Egyptian authorities did not interfere with the workings of the Cairo office.[14]

By the time of the 1973 war, the BBC had a new competitor on the Arab airwaves. The French semi-commercial station Radio Monte Carlo started broadcasting to the eastern Arab world in 1972. Like the BBC, Monte Carlo (which is now part of Radio France Internationale) broadcast on medium wave from Cyprus, and its attractive mix of news and entertainment has made it a serious competitor for the BBC ever since. The Arab world, however, hungry for reliable news, particularly in times of crisis, turned to all available news outlets. Successive audience research surveys indicated that at such times the same listeners would turn to the BBC, Radio Monte Carlo and also to Kol Israel (the 'Voice of Israel') Arabic Service. Kol Israel provided very detailed information about events in Israel, the West Bank and Gaza.

Increasingly, the BBC Arabic Service built up its radio journalism. The main current affairs programmes following the news bulletins at 13.00 and 18.00 Greenwich Mean Time became required listening across the Arab world. There was greater concentration on competitive journalism after Eric Bowman – who had previously been BBC representative in Beirut during the civil war in Lebanon – became Head of the Service in 1981, particularly after he appointed Benny Ammar as his deputy. Ammar, who had been born in Egypt and had spent his early childhood there, had been a producer and editor in BBC current affairs programmes, initially in the English Service for Africa and later in the World Service in English.

In 1988, Arabic Service journalism was further boosted by the appointment of Bob Jobbins as Head of the Service. Jobbins was an experienced radio journalist who had done two tours as BBC correspondent in Cairo, where his duties also involved running the BBC office. In 1981 he had been present at the parade where President Anwar Sadat was assassinated, and his reporting then had been carried on the Arabic Service.[15] Jobbins realised that, in a world where increasingly television was becoming the dominant medium, the early morning had become the time when radio could still be competitive. The Service mounted two live current affairs programmes in its morning transmission. He also introduced a new structure into the Service, creating four broadcasting units each headed by an editor-manager. Arab editors were brought into the management team of the Service – essential as the output of the Service included ever-increasing amounts of material originally generated in Arabic. Two Jordanians – Sami Haddad and Jamil Azar – took charge of the Current Affairs and the News and Presentation units respectively. Both went on to acquire further fame as presenters on al-Jazeera television. Hasan Muawad took over the Current Affairs unit and developed its journalism dramatically during the expansions of the nineties. In 2001 he joined al-Arabiya television.

The Iraqi invasion of Kuwait in 1990 and the Gulf War of 1991 marked the beginning of dramatic changes in the Arab broadcasting world. The Arabic Service increased its output during the conflict to fourteen hours a day, with intensive news and current affairs coverage of the conflict. After the war, Arabic broadcasts were reduced to ten and a half hours – an increase of one and a half hours on the pre-1990 period. Arab leaders, however, had been impressed by the performance of CNN during the war and started to dream of owning an Arabic CNN. The Saudi ruling family, who already owned two Arabic newspapers published in London and controlled the lucrative advertising business in the region, opened the Middle East Broadcasting Centre in London, which started broadcasting by satellite a mix of television entertainment and news across the Arab world. The news set new standards of production for television news in Arabic. It was still clearly dominated by a Saudi agenda, and no news appeared which was unfavourable to the Saudi authorities, but MBC's television news broadcasts did not include the protocol news that made the news broadcasts of most national broadcasters in the Arab world so unwatchable. MBC became popular – and dish ownership spread across the Arab world.

Another Saudi-owned satellite broadcaster, Orbit Communications, then approached the BBC's commercial division with a request for a news channel. Orbit had a number of channels uplinked from a facility in Rome. They wanted a prestigious news channel to enhance their offer to subscribers, and they signed an exclusive contract with the BBC for the provision of a television news channel in Arabic. Orbit paid for the capital equipment (which would remain their property) and all the revenue costs. Editorial control of the channel would be the exclusive preserve of the BBC, and the channel would be branded as BBC Arabic Television.

BBC Arabic Television started in 1994, and its broadcast journalism was a considerable success – but it was a success which ultimately did not benefit the BBC. Its major impediment – apart from insufficient funding – was that Orbit had invested considerable sums in an encryption system, and the Service was not broadcast in the clear. To watch it, subscribers needed a decoder, which initially cost several thousand US dollars. This made it expensive even for middle-class Saudis, let alone the majority of potential viewers in the Arab world, and the result was that very few people watched it. It had a small number of wealthy viewers in the Gulf region

But its success lay in the fact that it was produced to BBC editorial standards, which for the first time were applied to television news broadcasting in Arabic. The channel ran for two years – two years which coincided with some of the most vociferous activity by various Saudi opposition figures in the West, particularly in London, which was the natural headquarters for a number of Arab opposition and dissident movements. One prominent Saudi critic of the ruling family, Mohammed al-Mas'ari, featured not infrequently in international news. From time to time he made his appearance on various BBC outlets, radio and television, including BBC Arabic TV and Arabic Radio. There is no reason to think that, when they approached the BBC, Orbit's owners had been anything other than sincere in their wish to see an editorially independent news channel within their satellite broadcasting offer, but they had considerable business interests within Saudi Arabia. It soon became clear that coverage on the channel of activities involving criticism of the Saudi regime was not making life very easy for Orbit's owners. After a number of difficult meetings between Orbit and the BBC, matters came to a head in March 1996. The BBC channel regularly broadcast the BBC 1 television programme *Panorama* with an Arabic soundtrack. That week's *Panorama* had been about Saudi Arabia and had upset the Saudi authorities when it was broadcast in English. Considerable pressure was put on the BBC not to put this particular programme out in Arabic. The BBC resisted this pressure, and the programme was duly broadcast. Shortly afterwards, the BBC and Orbit decided to go their separate ways.

The staff was made redundant. The result was considerable hardship for many of them, particularly those who had come to London specifically to work on the BBC television channel, and whose work permits became invalid as soon as they lost their jobs. Paradoxically, though, the impact on Arabic television news broadcasting was positive. The previous year, Shaikh Hamad bin Khalifa al-Thani had taken over as Emir of Qatar. He was a keen listener to the BBC Arabic Service and had been impressed by the BBC Arabic Television channel. Work was already in progress in Doha on a news television service, and a large number of BBC Arabic Television staff moved to Doha, bringing their methods of working and the BBC newsroom system to the new venture. Al-Jazeera went on air later that year, looking very much like a reincarnation of the old BBC Arabic Television. Many of the presenters were the same, and a number of programme titles were very similar to BBC Arabic Television programme titles. There were two crucial differences: al-Jazeera was much better funded than BBC Arabic Television had ever been, and, unlike the BBC channel, it broadcast an unencrypted signal. It established itself remarkably quickly – and evolved its own distinct identity over the following years.

Back in London, the BBC Arabic Service was having to adapt to a much more competitive environment. As well as news and current affairs, the Service concentrated on putting out programmes on controversial themes. Programmes on such subjects as female genital mutilation, not widely discussed in the Arab world, made an impact, as did two educational series on sex education. The Suez issue was covered in detail in special programmes produced by Mohammed Shokeir, an Egyptian producer in the Service, to mark the twenty-fifth anniversary of the death of Gamal Abdul Nasser. The programmes reflected a wide range of views from across the world, including some of the old British Conservative politicians who had supported the Suez operation, and Egyptians and British participants in the fighting. A full range of opinion from across the Arab world was included, and it was followed by a phone-in programme to allow listeners to have their say about Nasser. The Service and the producer received messages of appreciation from listeners in Egypt, as there had been no significant marking of the anniversary there. It is perhaps ironic that a comprehensive analytical tribute to Gamal Abdul Nasser should have been broadcast from the BBC in London.

From 1992 onwards, the management of the Service identified the need to increase broadcasting hours so as to be available to listeners across the Arab world at times they wanted to listen. Priority was given to lengthening morning programming and then to filling the gap between the morning and afternoon transmissions. The Arab world covers five time zones,[16] and to provide essential morning news programming at 07.00 across the Arab world it was imperative to broadcast a continuous five-hour news programme. It took a number of years of steady expansion to increase the broadcast hours – initially without any additional funding. The morning gap between transmissions was eventually filled in the late nineties, and the Service finally started broadcasting twenty-four hours a day in 2001. This proved essential by the time of the invasion of Iraq in 2003: the initial air assault was concentrated during the night.

The other strategic aim was to improve audibility by seeking to broadcast on FM in major urban centres in the Arab world. By the mid-nineties, audiences had come to demand the high standards of radio reception provided by FM broadcasting, particularly when listening in their cars. FM transmission, though, is essentially domestic broadcasting: it almost always requires broadcasting from within the country in which the audience is resident (unless a particular urban concentration is close to an international border). Arab governments traditionally regarded broadcasting as a matter of national sovereignty, and until the nineties were generally reluctant to provide facilities for foreign broadcasters. Developments in international television, however, led some Arab governments to be more flexible in this area.

The BBC's first FM operation, which started in 1996, was in Doha. The Emir of Qatar was clearly keen to open up his country to the foreign media – and in any case that was the year which saw the launch of al-Jazeera. A year or so later, the BBC signed an agreement with Jordanian Radio and Television enabling it to start broadcasting in Amman. Once again, the BBC found itself in fierce competition with Radio Monte Carlo and the Saudi-owned MBC FM to acquire FM facilities in Arab capitals. King Hussein opened the Amman FM transmissions of all three stations in March 1998. The following year saw the BBC open an FM transmitter in Khartoum, with Wad Madani, the capital of Jazeera State, following suit the next year. Availability in these cities doubled the size of the BBC audience in Sudan, already one of the two largest BBC audiences in the Arab world. Two other Sudanese cities have since been added to the BBC FM operation. The BBC now broadcasts on FM in most of the cities in the small Gulf states, and since 2003 has acquired FM transmitters in Baghdad and other centres in Iraq. The success of the BBC in acquiring FM facilities in Arab cities was largely the work of a senior Egyptian member of the Arabic Service management team, Hassan Abu al-Ala, who negotiated the agreements and worked with leading officials and engineers in the respective cities to ensure transmission facilities were properly installed. He also led negotiations that resulted in the BBC Arabic Service being carried on Nilesat and other satellite services covering the Arab world.

So far, Egypt – the Arab world's largest country and traditionally the BBC's largest audience – has not allowed the BBC to broadcast on FM in Arabic. However, the BBC World Service English programme *Newshour* is now broadcast on Egyptian Radio's English Service to audiences in Cairo – which perhaps might suggest that before too long the BBC Arabic Service might follow suit.

The third significant strategic development occurred in 1998. The BBC had already established itself as a significant online news provider with the English-language site now known as bbcnews.com. The BBC had moved into online journalism at the start and now realised it was essential to start a competitive online news service in Arabic. A small-scale operation began in early 1998, and it was relaunched later that year under the direction of Hosam El Sokkari, an Egyptian journalist who had been a programme presenter on the old BBC Arabic Television and was presenting a programme about internet usage on the Arabic Service before he was appointed Editor of bbcarabic.com. The online operation expanded quickly, gaining new consumers for the BBC in the Arabic-speaking world, and winning international prizes in Dubai two years running for its news content. The Arabic Service is streamed live on the site. During the 2003 invasion of Iraq, the Service carried daily live talkback programmes, presented by Hosam El Sokkari and some other colleagues.

Egypt was to prove critical to effective coverage by the BBC Arabic Service during that invasion. It was clear that the Arabic Service would have to make a dramatic increase in its news broadcasting once the fighting started, and it would have been extremely hard to sustain this just from London. With a number of reporters operating in Baghdad, northern Iraq and the surrounding region, additional production facilities were needed to maintain round-the-clock news broadcasting. Hassan Abu al-Ala accordingly went out to Cairo in February 2003 and set up a newsroom and production centre there, employing and training some thirty staff. When the fighting started, the Cairo production centre was able to originate six hours of continuous news broadcasting, releasing the London team and enabling the BBC to sustain a continuous rolling news service twenty-four hours a day for the duration of the conflict. Cairo was the ideal location, as the headquarters of the Arab League and other pan-Arab and international organisations, and Arab voices from across the Arab world – as well as Israeli commentators – were regularly heard on air via the Cairo centre.

Meanwhile Hamdi Faragalla, another colleague originally from Egypt, had started reporting from Kuwait. As the invasion progressed, he moved into Iraq and eventually installed himself in Baghdad, setting up a small production office there, which developed into a third centre of production for the Arabic Service news operation. He also laid claim to FM facilities in Baghdad and elsewhere, and before he returned to London, the BBC was broadcasting on FM in Baghdad. Other cities soon followed.

The continuous rolling news operation of the BBC Arabic Service on radio with a corresponding continuous, integrated online news service, relying on production from two news production centres, with a third coming on stream after the fall of Baghdad, was a complex undertaking. As in any modern broadcast news operation, events were continually developing, and fast decisions had to be taken by presenters, producers and duty editors. Fouad Razek, an experienced Egyptian editor, was in charge of the radio news and current affairs operation. Equally, it was important to ensure consistent coverage across both media. Mostafa Anwar, Deputy Head of the Service, who had earlier led the process of systematically expanding the service to a twenty-four-hour operation during the previous decade, now had the heavy responsibility of ensuring the consistent quality of the output.

Once again, Britain was involved in a war in the Arab world and was widely condemned by Arabs – particularly outside Iraq – for what it was doing. There was no discussion, however, at any stage, about whether or not the BBC should reflect the full range of the debate on the rights and wrongs of the invasion. That debate, both within the United Kingdom and around the world, was fully reported by the Service. Suez had indeed set the precedent for future generations of BBC officials, and none of the editors and managers of the Arabic

Service (or of other Services) had any doubts: it was the BBC's duty fully to reflect the divisions of opinion within the United Kingdom about whether the invasion should have gone ahead.

In 2006, the BBC announced it would be starting in 2007 an Arabic Television Service. This time the Service is to be financed in the same way as the radio – by a Grant-in-Aid from the British Parliament. Like the Arabic Service Radio, it will be staffed by broadcast journalists from across the Arab world. In 2004, I retired from the BBC, and the BBC appointed Hosam El-Sokkari (Editor of bbcarabic.com) to take over as Head of the Arabic Service. He will now have the task of overseeing Arabic output on television, radio and online. Salah Negm, also originally from Egypt, has been appointed to take charge of the Arabic news production operation. He had a major role in setting up the previous BBC Arabic Television newsroom, and was subsequently Head of the al-Jazeera newsroom, head of BBC Arabic Current Affairs, and then Editor of News at al-Arabiya (a Saudi-owned satellite television news service broadcasting from Dubai). They and their teams will have a tough task to take on such stations as al-Jazeera and al-Arabiya. But an integrated television, news and online operation from London should be a considerable force to be reckoned with.

Notes

1. Head of BBC Arabic Service, 1992–2004.
2. Gerard Mansell, *Let Truth Be Told: 50 Years of BBC External Broadcasting*, London, Weidenfeld and Nicholson, 1982, p. 228.
3. The BBC's international radio broadcasts were – and still are – financed by a Grant-in-Aid voted by Parliament as a discrete element of the Foreign Office budget.
4. Mansell, *Let Truth Be Told*, p. 230. The threat was not carried out.
5. Ibid., p. 233.
6. The exchanges between the Foreign Office and the BBC following the first bulletin are described in Peter Partner, *Arab Voices: The BBC Arabic Service 1938–1988*, London, BBC, 1988, pp. 17ff. The book had been commissioned

by Jim Norris, Head of the BBC Arabic Service, 1986–8, to mark the fiftieth anniversary of the Arabic Service. A recording of the BBC's first Arabic broadcast, including the controversial news bulletin, was rebroadcast in January 1998 in a special programme to mark the sixtieth anniversary of the Service.

7. Partner, *Arab Voices*, pp. 19ff.

8. Ibid., p. 52.

9. Mansell, *Let Truth Be Told*, p. 231.

10. Lord Glyn in *Hansard*, HL 10 C5, cols. 1456 ff., quoted in Mansell, *Let Truth Be Told*, p. 285.

11. The British Government followed a similar course during the 1982 Falklands War, when it took over one of the BBC's short wave frequencies from the relay station on Ascension Island to start a radio operation known as Radio Atlantico del Sur (Radio South Atlantic). The aim was to undermine morale in the Argentine garrison on the Falklands.

12. Partner, *Arab Voices*, p. 55.

13. Sigmar Hillelson writing in *The BBC Handbook 1945*, quoted by Partner, *Arab Voices*, p. 55.

14. *The BBC Handbook 1973*, quoted by Partner, *Arab Voices*, p. 128.

15. Bob Jobbins' original dispatch from the scene of the assassination is available as an audio file on the BBC's website at: http://news.bbc.co.uk/1/hi/world/middle_east/790978.stm.

16. Morocco and Mauritania use Greenwich Mean Time. Oman, the United Arab Emirates and (in summer) Iraq are in the GMT+4 time zone. A complicating factor is that Iraq, Syria, Lebanon, Israel and the Palestinian territories, Jordan, Tunisia and Egypt observe daylight saving (i.e. their clocks are put forward one hour in summer). Other countries maintain constant time throughout the year.

YOUSRY NASRALLAH

Egypt, Cinema and the National Imaginary

1896 The first presentation of film in Egypt was made in January 1896 by Brunio (a Lumière photographer) while he was there shooting film for the Lumière Bros. A Lumière camera and film programme were used.

1912 The first film produced in Egypt was *Dans les Rues d'Alexandrie* in 1912. An Italian photographer living in Alexandria, Omberto Doris, built a studio and produced films like *The Bedouin's Honor*, *Poisonous Flowers* and *Towards the Precipice*. These were still not considered pure Egyptian films. That same year, however, Egyptian producer Abdel Rahman Salheya hired foreign technicians to make the first Egyptian short films.

1917 By 1917, Egypt boasted about eighty theatres.

1919 Mohamed Bayyoumi, an Alexandrian film-maker, shot documentaries during the 1919 revolution and documented Saad Zaghloul, leader of the liberal Wafd Party, returning from exile.

The first feature film over one hour was *Koubla fi al-Sahara'* ('A Kiss in the Desert') in 1927. The same year, the first full-length silent movie, *Layla*, was produced.

The first 'talkie' was *Onchoudet el Fouad* ('Hymn of the Heart') in 1932.

Other than Shadi Abdel-Salam's *The Night of Counting the Years*, released in the seventies by Contemporary Films, I do not think that any Egyptian film has had a theatrical release in Britain. In the nineties, Channel Four broadcast a season of Arabic films: Chahine's *Saladin*, *Alexandria ... Why* and *Cairo: Central Station* were among the films selected. Apart from these special events and some sporadic screenings at the London Film Festival, British spectators have hardly ever been exposed to Egyptian films and very few people here are aware of the existence of an Egyptian cinema industry with a history that goes back to the twenties. It is not my aim here to fustigate the British media or the distributors for their lack of interest in Egyptian culture in general and Egyptian cinema in particular, but I do wish to raise a few questions concerning the place of Egypt in the British popular imaginary.

When trying to recall what Egypt could possibly represent to an averagely cultured British mind, and without doing any extensive research, this is what I come up with: E. M. Forster (*Pharos and Pharillon*, *Guide to Alexandria*), Lawrence Durrell (*The Alexandria Quartet*), Agatha Christie (*Death on the Nile*), the Egyptian Collection at the British Museum, Howard Carter, etc. Most of this is related to Pharaonic Egypt, or to the cosmopolitan culture of a mythical Hellenist Alexandria.

Nothing, with the exception of the recent discovery of Naguib Mahfouz (after the Nobel Prize in 1988) is related to a more contemporary Egypt, and nothing at all is related to the British presence in Egypt from 1882 until 1954 or to the Suez war in 1956.

Television series like *Fortunes of War*, films like *Lawrence of Arabia* or *The English Patient*, have some scenes taking place in Egypt, but hardly deal with the country other than as an exotic location where British characters, due to extremely vague circumstances, just happen to live. In *Lawrence of Arabia*, nothing explains what on earth Lord Allenby is doing in Cairo.

India, in contrast, exercises a much more powerful fascination on British minds than Egypt. Egypt has never been a 'Jewel in the Crown' of Britain, probably because seventy-two measly years of 'protectorate' over Egypt can hardly compete with centuries of occupation in India. It is remarkable how very little work has been done – on a popular level – to revise, rethink and reanalyse British colonial politics in the Middle East. There is not a single film about the presence of Britain in Palestine, none on the role of Britain in Iraq. India has films like *Gandhi* or *A Passage to India*, clearly taking sides with the oppressed against the oppressors. In contrast, the history of Britain in the Middle East has inspired very little.

The fact that British policy in the Middle East could be described by some as 'shameful' is hardly a reason why it should be hushed up.

The French occupation of Algeria was probably more disastrous, but intellectuals like Sartre, Camus and political parties in France who have criticised French politics in the colonies have succeeded in creating a kind of collective anti-colonialist conscience in France that has been a source of inspiration for many films, novels, plays and songs. These works have become part of French mainstream culture and are now part of the 'founding myths' of modern France – an integral part of how France wants to perceive itself as a nation, regardless of how truthful or hypocritical this perception really is.

It is very likely that Britain's lack of interest in Egyptian cinema lies in its lack of interest in its own cinema.

In his brilliant book *La Projection nationale – cinéma et nation*, Jean-Michel Frodon analyses the link between nation and cinema.[1] He quotes Benedict Anderson, one of the best modern specialists on that question: 'The nation is an imaginary political community, imagined as intrinsically limited and sovereign.'[2] A century before, Ernest Renan had defined the nation as an 'invention', a fiction just as much as it is a 'taking-into-account' of an objective reality: 'The essence of a nation is that all of its individuals have many things in common, and also that all of them have forgotten many things.'[3]

There exists a common nature between nation and cinema: nation and cinema exist, and can only exist, by one and the same mechanism: that of projection.

In short, a nation invents itself on the basis of a reality reviewed and corrected according to a dramaturgical plan.

So does cinema.

It is striking that the invention of cinema is practically synchronous with the concept of nations that dominated the last third of the nineteenth century and most of the twentieth century. The twentieth century was, without any doubt, the century in which cinema became a pastime of the masses, an artistic activity and a producer of the mythologies of its time.

It is impossible to imagine America without its cinema. Independent Egypt is almost as impossible to imagine without its cinema. But we shall come to that later.

Why is it then, that it is perfectly possible to imagine Britain without its cinema? Tom Nairn (in *The Break-up of Britain*, quoted by Frodon) argues that the reason could possibly be that most nations have tried to condense the experience of constitutionalism, which Britain had taken centuries to elaborate. Most nations were born in a world where the English Revolution had already triumphed. The bourgeois societies that developed later in the world could only repeat that first experience.

Imitating the English Revolution has created something very different. Namely, the modern doctrine of an abstract or impersonal state.

It follows that Great Britain existed before cinema and did not need cinema to perceive itself as a nation. Being less abstract, being an island, hence less inclined to open up to the outside world, Britain is more wary of projection. It has never perceived itself as responsible for the salvation of the world, and is in that respect very different from French and American imperialism.

Britain had the Royal Navy to control the seas. It did not need cinema to impress the world. It had a mega-star: Queen Victoria. The symbolic representation of the British nation is monopolised by the royal family. Stephen Frears' brilliant film, *The Queen*, is probably the best illustration of this. At risk of seeming callous, I could say: Who needs Marilyn Monroe when you have Lady Diana Spencer? It is possible to imagine Britain without its film industry, but almost impossible to imagine it without its royal family!

Egypt's relationship to cinema follows more or less Frodon's analysis of national projection. Talaat Harb, the father of Egypt's independent economy, founded Bank Misr in 1920. This was a direct effect of the 1919 revolution in Egypt, led by the Wafd Party, a revolution that demanded Egypt's independence. Not long afterwards, in 1925, came the creation of the Misr Company for Acting and Cinema, as one of Bank Misr's establishments. The real move forward in the film industry, however, was the establishment of cinema studios: in 1935, Talaat Harb founded Studio Misr. This studio undertook production depending on its existing cinematic facilities and direct financing from the Misr Company for Acting and Cinema. It made these facilities accessible to other producers, just as it distributed films it produced, and other producers' films. Studio Misr and its school became a solid foundation for the cinema industry in Egypt. In his speech at the inaugural ceremony on 12 October 1935, Harb said the studio was one of the industrial economic projects of Bank Misr, aiming to make available all the requirements for making films to all workers in the field.

The studio's policy was to hire foreign experts in the different cinematic specialisations and appoint Egyptian assistants who could learn from them. It also sent Egyptian missions to study cinema abroad even before building the studio itself. The first mission was sent in 1933 and included Ahmad Badrakhan and Morris Kassab, who studied film direction in France, and Mohammad Abdel Azim and Hassan Murad, who studied photography in Germany.

Studio Misr's success was an incentive for other studios to be established. Five were built, and all contributed to the continuation of the cinema industry in Egypt although they were different in both their function and the nature of their production and distribution. They did have one thing in common, though: the idea that making films was a sign that Egypt was part of the modern world. The films that were produced in Egypt were culturally a contribution to the debate about how Egypt wanted to define itself as a nation, with a middle class that was both modern and very deeply attached to and worthy of its independence.

Egyptian films were very popular in the Middle East, and have definitely contributed to the image of Egypt as the leader of the Arab world, an image that Nasser used later to promote the idea of a 'Unified Arab World'.

The characteristics of Egyptian cinema are thus defined by its very close relation to the national question. Historically, it had all it needed to become a major industry. In the forties, it even succeeded in generating more income than the Suez Canal. It had stories, a past, traditional narrative forms and an enlightened, cosmopolitan intelligentsia capable of insuring its evolution. It had authors like Kamal Selim, who directed *al-Azima* ('Willpower') in 1939, Salah Abou Seif, Henri Barakat, Togo Mizrahi, followed by Youssef Chahine, Fateen Abdel Wahab, Ezzeddine Zoulfikar and Shady Abdelsalam. It also had its panoply of stars (Laila Mourad, Farid El Attrach, Oum Kalsoum, Mohamed Abdel Wahab in the forties, followed by Omar Sharif, Faten Hamama, Samia Gamal, Souad Hosny in the fifties).

In the fifties, the real register of Egyptian cinema became obvious. It was not the Egyptian nation per se, but the Arab nation led by Egypt and its charismatic leader Nasser. The destiny of the Egyptian nation and that of Nasser are strangely linked. The great tradition of the Egyptian cinema industry started its decline after the military defeat of 1967, and suffered a definite low in the seventies, after Nasser's death.

Paradoxically, the fact is that some of the finest Egyptian films were produced after the 1967 defeat: Chahine's *Earth*, *The Choice*, *The Sparrow*, *Alexandria ...Why*, Shady Abdel Salam's *The Night of Counting the Years*, to name just two film-makers whose names have some relevance in Britain. These films were direct results of the 1967 defeat. Chahine, still attached to the idea of Arab unity, made films trying to redefine it in a way not related to the figure of the 'Raïs', and Abdel Salam, disillusioned by the defeat of Arab nationalism, tried to find Egypt's soul in its Pharaonic past.

Post-1967 cinema in Egypt is a cinema that reflects on the reasons for the demise of the 'National Project', a cinema that was part of a much vaster range of intellectual and political activity, and centred around trying to regain some semblance of national dignity. The Egyptian portrayed in that cinema was an Everyman attempting to redefine himself as someone who has not been defeated by the defeat of a regime, as someone who is still clinging to the idea that the dream was right, but that the leaders were irresponsible and that there was still hope to make it come true by modifying the repressive nature of the state. Films like Chahine's masterpiece *The Sparrow* (dealing with the defeat), Hussein Kamal's *A Little Bit of Fear* (an allegorical depiction of the illegality of the Nasserite regime), Kamal El Cheikh's *Miramar* (based on Naguib Mahfouz's novel) and Ali Badrakhan's *al-Karnak* (dealing with secret police brutality), are very representative of that trend. The focus of all Egyptian films of that period is the State. The protagonist in those films is a victim of a repressive but modifiable political system. The dominant ideology itself was never questioned. The common Egyptian was the 'real' Nasserite, whereas the system itself had betrayed the ideals of Nasserism.

After the 1973 war began an era that could best be described as the era of disillusionment. All the films dealing with issues like corruption and fundamentalism had and still have one thing in common: nostalgia for a period in which Egypt had a 'National

Project', a refusal to accept that the State had ceased to incarnate the dreams and aspirations of all Egyptians (and in fact all Arabs) and had become a more or less abstract construct while keeping most of the traits of the authoritarian Nasserite system. And the protagonist has become the victim of corrupt businessmen and their associates closely linked to the regime. A victim of economic and political forces, far more powerful than anything else.

Strangely, it is after the 1973 war against Israel, celebrated by everyone in Egypt as a victory, that the actual effects of the 1967 defeat became more than obvious. The main trend in cinema was despair and self-deprecation. The most representative films of that period are Said Marzouk's *The Guilty*, Salah Abou Seif's *The Malatily Bath*, Kamal El Cheik's *Against Whom Should We Point Our Guns*, Ali Badrakhan's *People at the Top*, and most of Adel Imam's non-comedy films.

This trend has stayed dominant until very recently.

I have so far deliberately avoided the use of the word 'individual'. A victim can only be defined in terms of who victimises him. A victim is not accountable. A victim has very little self-esteem. A victim needs a saviour. If the saviour is not a new leader, then it can only be God. A victim is not an individual, and what is worse, a victim has no story to tell, except that of his plight.

There are exceptions, though.

Recent films, like Daoud Abdel Sayed's *Kit Kat* and *Land of Fear*, Cherif Arafa's *Terrorism and Kebab* and *The Headmaster*, Oussama Fawzi's *Asphalt Kings* and *I Love Cinema*, Hany Khalifa's *Sleepless Nights*, Kamla Abou Zikri's *On Love and Passion*, Mohamed Moustapha's *Leisure Time*, and my own films, are starting to give more space to the individual who defines himself as someone other than a mere victim of forces bigger than himself. These films emerge from a political spirit of resistance against fundamentalism and repression, and from an artistic need to go on telling stories.

Notes

1. Jean-Michel Frodon, *La Projection nationale – cinéma et nation*, Editions Odile Jacob/ Le Champ Médiologique, 1998, p.19.
2. Benedict Anderson, *L-imaginaire national. Réflections sur l'origine du nationalism*, Paris, La Découverte, 1996.
3. Ernest Renan, *Qu'est-ce qu'une nation? Et autres écrits politiques*, Paris, Imprimerie nationale, 1996.

FEKRI HASSAN

Conserving Egyptian Heritage: Seizing the Moment

The conditions of archaeological sites in Egypt today are deplorable, in spite of energetic efforts by the Egyptian government to cope with the accelerating impact of the dramatic increase in population, urban sprawl, reclamation, road building and tourism. The assault on archaeological sites is pervasive, virulent and grave. The status quo cannot be maintained for much longer without further serious loss to Egypt and the world. The British Egyptian Association can immediately begin to halt the acceleration of this deterioration by initiating concrete steps in three main areas: (1) capacity building of Egyptian archaeologists, restorers and heritage managers; (2) formulation of a business plan for a strategy of cultural economy; and (3) active contribution to public awareness of Egyptian heritage in Egypt. Such an initiative will contribute to a better appreciation of the relationship between Britain and Egypt. British scholars have contributed immensely over the last 125 years to Egyptology and the promotion of ancient Egypt in the UK. The time has come to extend their contributions more effectively to conservation and development in partnership with Egyptians for the benefit of the peoples of both countries. Inauguration of an Egyptian Heritage Institute and support for a comprehensive business plan for the development of the cultural heritage economy of Egypt will mark this fiftieth commemoration of the Suez war and the one hundred and twenty-fifth commemoration of Amelia Edwards' campaign to save Egyptian antiquities in 1882 as a historical turning point in the relationship between Egypt and Britain.

Ancient Egypt is projected on the screen of history through the cultural filters and prisms of Greeks, Romans, Arabs and European travellers and colonists. The Suez war marked a point in time when Egypt began to reconsider not only its relationship with Britain but also with the dominant political forces in the world. In response to the military aggression, Egypt was provoked into spending a great deal of its resources on creating a strong army and was thus locked into the grip of a military society, and it had to look for sources of arms in a camp that was not ideologically consonant with Egyptian culture. Moreover, it began to aggrandise its affiliation with its neighbouring Arab states in the hope of creating a regional political block.

The Suez war from my perspective on historical writing is relevant only in as much as it is a product of enduring political structures in the relationship between Europe and the Ottoman Orient and its colonial possessions, and a structure of cultural hegemony that buttressed and legitimised its political colonial agenda. It confirmed to Egyptians that a neo-colonial regime was fast replacing the traditional colonial strategy. The Suez war led to the interruption of excavations in Egypt by British archaeologists, but their work resumed after 1972 following an exhibition of the Tutankhamun treasures in London. It was a *critical* transformative event that led to significant changes in the way the world was viewed and constructed by Egyptians. It was not a total break with the past – this would have been very unlike Egypt – but there were political contingencies, and they were expressed and operationalised through cultural pathways that brought many Egyptians closer to the Arab circle, and subsequently many Egyptians began to drift toward a closer identification with their religion. The impact of that transition in the use of archaeological iconography and discourse is clear.[1] Although the cultural manifestations of ancient

Egypt have dwindled, they are still vibrant and evident in state events and the army.

The effective engagement by British archaeologists in Egypt began in 1882 with the establishment of the Egypt Exploration Fund (later the Egypt Exploration Society) by Amelia Edwards. The activities of the society over the last 124 years have focused on excavations primarily in the Delta, Thebes, Abydos, El-Amarna, Saqqara and Nubia[2] and an archaeological survey. The dedicated activities by five generations of archaeologists and Egyptologists have led to spectacular discoveries and substantial contributions to our knowledge of ancient Egypt. Although the initial excavations focused on the discovery of biblical sites,[3] the scope of excavations has since then ranged widely, bringing to light many aspects of Egyptian civilisation. Many texts were retrieved and deciphered, contributing to the efforts by scholars from many other countries – beginning with J. F. Champollion (1790–1832) – to unlock the mysteries of ancient Egypt. One of the main concerns by the founders of the EES was the rampant looting and destruction of Egyptian antiquities. Excavations and documentation were regarded as the primary means of saving valuable information, providing contextual data, and provisioning museums with artefacts for the enjoyment of the public and for promoting knowledge of ancient Egypt. Funding for EES work has been and remains precarious. Donations, supplemented by grants from the British Academy, are the primary means of support. Acquisition of artefacts from excavations to entice donors to contribute to the EES has enriched the British Museum, which has been the main beneficiary, followed by the Museum of Fine Arts, Boston, and other museums in the USA, as well as provincial collections in the north of England and Scotland: Liverpool, Sheffield, Bolton, York and Edinburgh. Antiquities also went to University College London where many EES archaeologists served as professors.[4] Sadly, although this practice has provided in most cases a good environment for the conservation of Egyptian antiquities and exposed many of the British (and American) public to the glory of ancient Egypt, it has led to the dispersal and splitting of collections, undermining their integrity as scientific collections, and has restricted access to the British public and the occasional visitor from abroad, including Egyptians. The emphasis on collecting antiquities from the open market by prominent British archaeologists[5] has definitely increased illicit digging and contributed to the growth of a market for Egyptian antiquities that continues to drain Egypt of its archaeological resources.

It is also regrettable that the exhibitions and display of the trophies from excavations in Egypt appear to have furthered the promotion of ancient Egypt as a remote and exotic land of hidden treasures and artworks.[6] Perceptions of ancient Egypt in Britain, as revealed by a survey undertaken for the Petrie Museum by the Susie Fisher Group (2000), send an alarming signal about how Egypt is perceived. The survey concluded that the public knew very little about Egyptian geography and history. They know that ancient Egypt was death-obsessed, built on slavery, aloof, spiritual and a land of the occult. It was admired because it was powerful and wealthy, creative, and because it produced monumental buildings. The survey revealed that the general public does not have any knowledge of the lives of ordinary people in ancient Egypt, and is not familiar with daily life in ancient Egypt. The icons of Egypt in the public mind were pyramids, sand, heat, tombs, camels, the sphinx, mystery, Cleopatra, kohl and Indiana Jones. Perhaps more saddening was the view that 'Modern Egyptians are largely perceived as a regrettable blight on the ancient landscape'.[7] This survey, which requires further validation and augmentation, indicates that a major effort must be expended to change how Egypt is exhibited and how its cultural history and civilisation are interpreted.

With a few exceptions, British archaeologists and the EES did not place much emphasis on the restoration and conservation of the archaeological sites in Egypt, even after they had been excavated, exposing them to faster deterioration and destruction. In addition, the emphasis on promoting ancient Egypt among the British public, with limited activities in Egypt, often directed to expatriates, has not contributed positively to a broader and increased awareness among the Egyptian public of Egyptian antiquities. No effort has been expended to provide summaries or popular books in Arabic or even to sponsor translations of popular works in English that have recently become one of the main sources of revenue outstanding. More disturbing has been the emphasis on training young British archaeologists, such as F. L. Griffith, who later led an archaeological survey of Egypt; Howard Carter, who made the spectacular discovery of the tomb of Tutankhamun; and W. B. Emery, who later directed excavations in Saqqara and trained in turn other British archaeologists who are now among the leaders of Egyptian archaeology. Egyptians were not included in EES excavations except as diggers, labourers, guards and servants:

> Abdalla brought our supper down to the temple and we sat among the mighty columns and eat [sic] omelets, bread and butter, and chocolate mould, our white robed servants waiting on us like attendant priests.[8]

Donald M. Reid, in the first coherent account of 'Indigenous Egyptology', comments that 'Westerners created Egyptology and eventually taught it to Egyptians. Egypt owes them a debt for that, but the interest on the debt was exorbitant.'[9] In fact, Egyptology, as an Egyptian has just revealed in another ground-breaking study,[10] was initiated and promoted by numerous Egyptian and Arab scholars in medieval times. Reid, nevertheless, aptly observes that already in the 1870s indigenous would-be Egyptologists were seeking careers in the Antiquities Service. 'The French and the British, however, excluded them from Egyptian archaeology almost as effectively as Lord Cromer[11] excluded Egyptians from effective power in national affairs.'[12] This has had a lasting impact and a lingering effect both on Egyptian politics and the practice of Egyptian archaeology. Ahmed Kamal, one of the few Egyptians who struggled to become an Egyptologist and was strongly opposed by the likes of A. Mariette

(1821–81), who was the first director of the Egyptian Antiquities Organisation, was still pleading with the French, who continued to oversee the Egyptian Antiquities Service, to have Egyptians trained as Egyptologists, only to be told that few Egyptologists had shown any interest. 'Ah, M. Lacau,' responded Kamal, 'in the sixty-five years you French have directed the Service, what opportunities have you given us?'[13] Although the Egyptians took control of the governmental Department of Antiquities (the Egyptian Antiquities Organisation and now the Supreme Council of Antiquities) after the 1952 revolution, there is still a huge deficit in the number of well-trained archaeologists, conservators and museum personnel to meet the vast demand in Egypt. This phenomenon requires serious analysis to assess both the social dynamics that contribute to the current shortage and the best strategy to overcome it.

The return of British archaeologists after Suez was not marked, as far as I can tell, with any significant change in the course of the way they operated in Egypt as independent missions who employed local diggers, a tradition that began with Petrie,[14] or with a change in their scholarly missions (that focused mostly on excavation, retrieval of textual material and artefact studies). This reveals, in my opinion, that the lesson of the Suez war was not learned. The way forward to improve British–Egyptian relations to promote a better understanding of ancient Egypt, to contribute to the advancement of science and knowledge and to safeguard Egyptian heritage for Egypt and humanity must include bilateral efforts to support: (1) a public education programme to acquaint the public in Egypt with the fruits of archaeological and Egyptological research through a well-designed programme of public education; (2) the institution of a programme of field restoration and conservation as a major component of archaeological activities in Egypt to complement the current emphasis on restorations of museum specimens; (3) the implementation of a strategy of cultural heritage management through legal and institutional means: (i) to ensure the conservation of Egyptian cultural resources, (ii) to present and interpret appropriately the achievements of Egyptian civilisation in all fields of knowledge and as a dynamic, creative society, and (iii) to provide jobs and improve economic conditions through proper sustainable, economic management of Egypt's archaeological and cultural resources; and, most importantly, (4) allocation of sufficient resources to train Egyptian archaeologists, Egyptologists, restorers, conservators, museologists and heritage managers, and for the creation of an appropriate managerial, scientific and technical infrastructure as the only viable and sustainable means to safeguard and valorise Egyptian heritage. These views have now been voiced by many Egyptologists and archaeologists, such as Haikal,[15] Kamil and Saad,[16] Schulz,[17] McManamon and Rogers,[18] and Saad,[19] and were the focus of many reflections on the prospects of Egyptian archaeology in the twentieth century.[20] Specific emphasis was placed on training, the preparation of an archaeological map of Egypt, more attention to conservation and public education, and an emphasis on the continuity of Egyptian civilisation to the present with greater attention to overlooked periods and to the anthropological and social aspects of civilisation. O'Connor emphasises the Egyptian dimension and asserted that 'Egyptian archaeology in terms of its excavation, documentation and conservation requires a comprehensive approach that foreign institutions can never provide, however productive and important their role may be in other ways'.[21] Mysliwiec emphasises the need for good cooperation with Egyptian colleagues and hopes that archaeological missions will serve as international 'training centers'.[22] Verner, concurring with this view, in addition points out its importance for training foreign students in Egypt.[23]

Egyptian archaeology and the appropriation of ancient Egypt

Changes in political and cultural ideas, outlooks and paradigms are made visible and socially effective through social activities and durable material forms that range from monuments to exhibits. Unlike words, actions and the material products of such actions are a much better proxy to how the world is changing and which are the dominant ideas held.

The appropriation of Egyptian obelisks by Romans, and subsequently by the French and the British,[24] in that order, reveals more than many volumes about the struggle for political hegemony and world dominance by the great powers that wrenched control of the world through trade, war and violence. Rivalries between England and France for world domination were not only manifest in political manoeuvres, but also in the race to acquire Egyptian monuments (among other world treasures including many that are now in the British Museum and the Louvre) by every possible means, including illicit digging and smuggling, bribery, political pressure and deals.[25]

As a child, Amelia Edwards read *The Manners and Customs of the Ancient Egyptians*. It was one of her two cherished books; the other was *The Arabian Nights*. On 29 November 1873, she arrived in Cairo without definite plans, outfit or any kind of 'Oriental experience'.[26] Her visit to Egypt led to one of the most celebrated travel books, *A Thousand Miles up the Nile* (1877),[27] and to a generous contribution to the study of Egyptology: 'the most skilfully written, entertaining, and enthusiastic travel narrative to come out of a voyage up the Nile, ... it quickly became a best seller'.[28] The public in Great Britain became aware of the great monuments of ancient Egypt and many travelled to Egypt to experience first-hand 'the charm of the Nile, the beauty of the desert' and 'the ruins which are the wonder of the world'.[29]

Amelia travelled to Egypt fifteen years before the British troops began a seventy-year occupation of Egypt with the bombardment of Alexandria on 11 July 1882. Amelia and her generation were acquainted with the first fruits of Egyptological learning that were made possible by the deciphering of the hieroglyphic script by Champollion in 1822, almost a decade after the publication of the *Description de l'Egypte*, one of the enduring legacies of the failed Napoleonic military expedition to Egypt in 1798. By 1882, within fifty years of Champollion's discovery, Egyptology had developed into a well-defined discipline popularised by the *Manners and Customs of the Ancient Egyptians* by J. Gardner Wilkinson in 1837–41.

As it happened, the beginnings of Egyptology went hand in hand with the colonial interest in Egypt by the French and the British. In the same year that Alexandria was being bombarded, the Egypt Exploration Fund was established by Amelia Edwards, her friend Stuart Poole and other interested persons, to finance excavations in Egypt. Edwards was alarmed by the ruinous state of Egyptian monuments and had the foresight and will to preserve Egyptian antiquities from destruction by promoting scientific excavations. Edwards and Poole succeeded in March 1882 in calling together the most famous Egyptologists in Great Britain to meet at the British Museum to establish the Egyptian Exploration Fund. Sir Rasmus Wilson, the wealthy philanthropist who had brought the huge obelisk to London, contributed a large sum of money to the fund and was elected president.[30]

At that time, the 'Egyptian Service of Antiquities' was under the control of the French, beginning with Auguste Mariette (1821–81), who was followed then by Gaston Maspero (1846–1916). It was up to Maspero to grant 'foreigners' concessions to excavate in Egypt. Although the first excavations by the Egypt Exploration Fund were entrusted to the Swiss Edouard Naville, they were undertaken by the young British archaeologist, Flinders Petrie (1853–1942), who led many successful expeditions setting the stage for modern Egyptian archaeology. Amelia Edwards was convinced that Petrie was the best contemporary archaeologist. She promoted his work, and when she died provided in her will for the establishment of a chair in Egyptian archaeology at University College London, and named Petrie as her choice for that post.

The invasion by Britain, France and Israel was my first personal taste of the danger to which my own family was exposed. I was learning English as a second language in school and was growing up in a society teeming with different political currents and a definite 'European outlook', a society that was transforming itself from its

'Oriental' past, engendered by generations of Mamluke and Ottoman rule, to a modern, Westernised world, a process that had already been begun by Mohamed Ali (*c*.1769–1849) and was in full swing under Khedive Ismael (1863–79) when Amelia Edwards arrived in Egypt. To Mohamed Ali and Ismael, Egypt's pharaonic past was of far less interest than its future as a modern state. Mohamed Ali was not averse to exchanging the relics of Egypt's past for the fruits of European culture. In 1836, he agreed to allow the French to remove one of the twin obelisks of Rameses II at the Luxor Temple. In 1877, as *A Thousand Miles up the Nile* was released, another obelisk, one of the so-called Cleopatra's needles, made its way to London to rest finally on the banks of the Thames.

By the time Petrie was carrying out his excavations in Egypt it was customary to remove artefacts from Egypt to museums and private collections abroad. Petrie, in fact, managed to secure funding for his excavations in exchange for artefacts discovered in the course of digging in Egypt. This practice was challenged by Egyptians when Howard Carter, the discoverer of the tomb of Tutankhamun, billed as a great Egyptologist at his death in 1939 by *The Times* of London, was about to export the treasures from that tomb to England. Carter and other Egyptologists from Britain and the USA were at that time concerned by a new policy introduced by Pierre Lacau (then the head of the Egyptian Antiquities Service) which stipulated the *partage* of finds between the excavators and Egypt. The Egyptologists represented institutions that were 'only prepared to finance expensive excavations if there was an expectation of good returns of objects'.[31] Alarmed that objects would end up in the Egyptian Museum in Cairo instead of the Metropolitan Museum of Art, Lindsley Hall noted this in his diary on 4 April 1920:

> Mace had a wire 'no division' from Winlock today, whereby we knew that Lacau has seen the sarcophagus and wants it for Cairo. As he wants a great deal of our material too, it has been decided to wait till next year for the division,

as we should come out so badly this year if we accepted Lacau's division.[32]

The pressure by foreign expeditions to secure their privileged acquisition of Egyptian antiquities was not heeded by the administrative authorities in Egypt. The country was gripped with political unrest and a surge of nationalism. Demands by Egyptians for political autonomy in 1918–9 ended with the arrest of their nationalist leader Saad Zaghloul, which led to the outbreak of riots throughout the country. At that time Carter decided to occupy himself in support of Sotheby's sale of Egyptian collections.[33] Upon returning to Egypt to resume excavations, Carter made arrangements to grant *The Times* the right to be the first to report on the Tutankhamun discoveries before they were released to the Egyptian public. This, and his attitude toward the regulation of tourist visits to the tomb during excavations, became bones of contention between Carter and Lacau, who was yielding to his boss, the Egyptian Minister of Public Works, who was in turn representing the sentiments of Egyptians against the control by foreigners of Egyptian antiquities. The main dispute, however, concerned the rights to the antiquities in Tutankhamun's tomb. In 1924, Carter made a deal with the Egyptian government:

> Government willing to give at his discretion Almina (Lord Carnarvon's wife) a choice of duplicates as representative as possible of discovery wherever such duplicates can be separated from whole without damage to science. Almina and executors to at once renounce any claim whatsoever against government.[34]

Six years later, the Wafd government under Nahas Pasha, following up on Zaghloul's nationalist policies, revoked the promise of duplicates and paid the Carnarvon heirs the sum of 35,971 Egyptian pounds, covering the Carnarvon expenses for work rendered commencing from the discovery to the completion of their works in April 1929.

By that time, Carter had decided to act as an agent (with a 10 per cent commission) to purchase Egyptian artefacts for the Cleveland Museum of Arts. The first purchases were made from two well-known Cairo antiquities dealers. Later, he suggested the purchase of an unmatched, wonderful sphinx figure of Amenophis III for £5,000. This statue, among others, was in Carter's private collection at the time of his death.

A new generation of Egyptologists was to follow Carter and his cohort. Petrie had been followed at the Institute of Archaeology by Stephen Glanville (1900–56). As Carter was concluding his career, an opening in the Department of Egyptian and Assyrian Antiquities in the British Museum attracted the attention of I. E. S. Edwards, who was then studying Arabic but who found himself thinking about the excitement that Howard Carter's discovery of the tomb of Tutankhamun had caused. I. E. S. Edwards is well known for his book on the Pyramids of Egypt. His autobiography *From the Pyramids to Tutankhamun* tells us a great deal about the arrangements to mount the Tutankhamun exhibition in London in 1972. In Chapter 16 (covering 1954–60), entitled 'Return to the British Museum ~ Administrative Changes ~ Progress with the Cambridge Ancient History ~ Lodge', nothing is mentioned on the dramatic political events that began in 1952 and culminated in 1956 with the Suez conspiratorial alliance of Britain, France and Israel to invade Egypt with the intention of overthrowing Nasser's regime and regaining control of the Suez Canal.[35] This omission of the political context of Egyptology is perhaps symptomatic of the tendency to regard Egyptology as a world in its own right, unrelated to the life or the politics of the Egyptian peoples, who are no more than a picturesque, if sometimes annoying, backdrop to Egyptological pursuits. A small incident mentioned by I. E. S. Edwards in the period from 1950–4 might have alerted him to the political arena in which Egyptology is situated. The incident concerns Ahmed Fakhry (1905–73), perhaps the most prominent of a handful of Egyptian Egyptologists who have attained international attention. Fakhry visited the Edwards family on a number of occasions and was a favourite with their children. He was described as wildly generous, like so many Egyptians. In the course of one of the visits he brought a bag full of presents for the children, who were more than delighted to see him. When Edwards inquired about Fakhry's son, Ali, Fakhry immediately said that he was proud of him. He was now doing his military service, was an expert sniper and was now assigned to the Suez Canal Zone, where he was sniping at the British soldiers of the occupying force. This was no more than a *faux pas* that neither of them dared to discuss, and in a very short time everything was back on an even keel.[36]

Edwards was not an archaeologist, but he was interested in the texts unearthed by archaeologists. One such archaeologist was Bryan Emery who, together with Stephen Glanville, carried out the missions of the Egypt Exploration Society at the Early Dynastic Cemetery in Saqqara. During World War II, Emery served as Head of Military Intelligence in Cairo,[37] a position higher than that assumed by Howard Carter, who was also attached to the British Intelligence Department of the War Office in Cairo in 1915.[38] Later, Emery was to become involved in the UNESCO Nubia Campaign that was mounted to rescue the monuments of Nubia, which were to be submerged by the water of the proposed Aswan High Dam. In his book on *Nubia in Egypt*, Emery made a disturbing remark about a subject that still seemed then, in the 1960s, to be a sore point for those who represented foreign institutions. Emery explicitly lamented the decision by the Egyptian government after the discovery of Tutankhamun to keep all discovered Egyptian antiquities in Egypt, a decision that he thought deprived foreign expeditions of a source for financing their work in Egypt! He went further to state that Egyptian storerooms were full of 'duplicate' objects that would have greater value in foreign museums where they could be an invaluable source for students:

> Moreover, Egyptologists throughout the world realised
> that archaeological evidence was year by year being

destroyed by the depredations of dealers' agents, who, in ransacking the tombs and other ancient sites, destroyed priceless scientific material. Thus the collector came to depend more on the archaeologist that the dealer (sic.) with the result that ample funds were available for scientific research in the field. And the museums of the world were yearly enriched by the results of the widespread excavation in Egypt. But as a result of the hysteria which followed the discovery of the tomb of Tutankhamun, and influenced by the example of several other Mediterranean countries, the Egyptian government of that time revised the antiquities law so that the excavator was no longer entitled to any of his finds and all the antiquities found by him, at his expense, belong to the State ... And the irony of it was that the storerooms in the basement of the great museum at Cairo and big magazines on the sites of excavations such as those at Sakkara were crammed with duplicate objects, unworthy of a place in the collections of Cairo, but which would have been of great value in foreign museums, where they would have assisted the student in his research and have borne witness to the general public of the greatness and splendour of ancient Egypt.[39]

It was only when Egypt agreed, in appealing to the world to save the monuments of Nubia, to reinstate the policy of giving the excavators half of the objects discovered that Emery was pleased, announcing that 'This new and enlightened policy ... [provides] every inducement for the Egyptologist to return to active field research'.[40] He further pontificated that: 'Of recent years, with the growth of nationalism, there has been a tendency among many nations to consider their past as something exclusively their own, and to ignore the fact that although they indeed may be its legal custodians, it is in reality the heritage of all mankind'.[41]

The Nubia Campaign: a lost opportunity

The contribution by Britain to the Nubia Campaign was much less than that by other countries, to the extent that when I. E. S. Edwards approached Tharwat Okasha, the Egyptian Minister of Culture who was responsible for overseeing the Nubia Campaign, to host the exhibit of Tutankhamun after its time in Paris (1967), Okasha remarked that: 'There is a difficulty. The only reason why Madame Noblecourt has been allowed to have the exhibition is because she has done so much work to assist me in saving the monuments of Nubia. It is a reward for her.' Moreover, he said, 'there have been many other applications for the exhibition from countries which have contributed much more to the Nubia Campaign.'[42]

The construction of the Aswan High Dam galvanised world attention on issues related to the construction of large dams. The UNESCO campaign was a landmark in the history of archaeology, which has often been formulated on nationalistic premises. The appeal by Egypt to the world community, represented by UNESCO, established a precedent in which the concept of 'world heritage' has emerged as a principal notion in archaeological circles. The world owes Gamal Abdel Nasser a great debt for his initiative in the declaration of the principle of world heritage. An ardent nationalist, Abdel Nasser nevertheless realised that 'the preservation of the legacy of mankind is no less important than the construction of dams, the erection of factories and the greater prosperity of the people.'[43]

The success of UNESCO efforts in the Nubia Campaign led to other safeguarding campaigns such as those in Venice in Italy, Mohenjodaro in Pakistan and Borobodur in Indonesia. Consequently, UNESCO initiated, with the help of the International Council of Monuments and Sites (ICOMOS), the preparation of a draft convention on the protection of cultural heritage. The convention, with the inclusion of natural heritage, was adopted by the General Conference of UNESCO on 16 November 1972. The UNESCO World Heritage Center[44] was established to assure the day-to-day management of the convention. Clearly, the convention and the UNESCO World Heritage Center are of great global significance and must be regarded as one of the most prized outcomes of the Nubia Campaign.

The international success of the Nubia Campaign[45] did not, in spite of all its potential, break down the hegemonic structures of Egyptology. A great opportunity to safeguard Egyptian antiquities for humanity has come and gone with no effort to develop a permanent international organisation to continue the international cooperation initiated by the Nubia Campaign. Foreign expeditions came and went, eager to carry back the share of Egyptian antiquities that they could now claim. The French, the Germans, the Czechs, the Italians, the Polish, the Dutch and the Americans have their archaeological institutes or centres in Egypt. By contrast, the British opted not to have an archaeological institute in Egypt; the EES thus operated from the British Embassy. I. E. S. Edwards states that on two occasions (from 1942 to 1943) efforts were made to create a British Institute of Archaeology in Egypt and in both cases they were rejected on the grounds of cost.[46] I doubt that cost was the reason, since institutes were established elsewhere in Rome, Amman, Athens, Ankara, Iraq and Nairobi. Egypt was apparently considered too unstable and the Egyptians too nationalistic. As late as the 1990s, the claim was made that in case of any political turmoil, the Egypt Exploration Society would not have much to lose since it maintains no library or other facilities that can be sequestered by the Egyptians.

Reclaiming responsibilities

Today we face the consequences of decades of Egyptological endeavours. It is now more than a century since Petrie began his scientific investigations in Egypt and since Amelia Edwards inaugurated the Egypt Exploration Fund. We have learned a great deal about ancient Egypt thanks to the efforts of hundreds of mostly foreign Egyptologists who have devoted their lives to deciphering

Egyptian texts and retrieving artefacts as a testimony to the achievements of Egyptian civilisation. Yet, in spite of such wonderful results, we are now at a point when Egyptian monuments are under mounting threats. The Early Dynastic cemetery excavated by Emery (1935–9, 1945–7, 1953–6) is now in a pitiful state of decay and ruin. In spite of efforts by the Egyptian Ministry of Culture to preserve and restore monuments and the sporadic efforts by some expeditions and countries to assist Egypt in its struggle against the dilapidation of its antiquities, the current situation is grim, as the increase in population, urban sprawl, rising water table, pollution, road building, land reclamation, irrigation, quarrying and tourism combine to pose a formidable challenge to the monuments of Egypt. Sadly, the situation is aggravated by the lack of trained archaeologists and conservators who are desperately needed to monitor, document, study, stabilise, restore, protect, preserve and conserve Egypt's invaluable cultural heritage.

Although a documentation centre was created in conjunction with the Nubia Campaign, there was no sustainable effort to train Egyptians to undertake the Herculean task of dealing with the rich archaeological resources of their country, including monitoring the conditions of antiquities in response to the changes in the Nile's hydrographic regime, to mount rescue expeditions in areas which have been threatened as a result of the construction of electric towers, roads, canals, new towns, land reclamation and factories. Special attention must be paid to key sites that bear testimony to the key events and achievements in the long history of Egyptian civilisation.[47]

If this remembrance of the Suez crisis is to have any lasting effect, dignitaries and scholars should resolve to continue the work that was started by Amelia Edwards, whose vision has been eclipsed by petty concerns, colonial pretences and parochial claims. What we need also is a pledge from the Egyptian Civic Society to create an Egyptian Heritage Institute with the main objective of training a new generation of Egyptian archaeologists, conservators, museum curators and cultural heritage managers to bolster the government's efforts. We will also need the pledge from Egyptian and British philanthropists to make generous donations to support this Institute. The Egyptian National Centre for the Documentation of Cultural and Natural Heritage has already prepared, in 2001, in conjunction with UNESCO and the UNDP, a strategic plan for the management of Egyptian heritage, and has drafted plans for such an institute. I hope we can count on the support of the British–Egyptian Association in launching this Institute, and on British scholars in leading an effort to mount international scholarly and financial support for this institution that would not only enhance our knowledge of ancient Egypt but would also safeguard its threatened antiquities from destruction.

The Institute would, in addition, contribute to increasing the awareness of Egyptians with their contribution to world civilisation and to acquainting them with the strands of their cultural ancestry that link them to Coptic and Greek heritage, to Roman and Byzantine cultures, and to Venice, Constantinople and Baghdad. The neglect of the Egyptian public in favour of the general public in England, France or Germany by foreign Egyptologists has led to a curious disparity between public interest in Egyptian antiquities in Europe and Egypt.

The Institute would foster cultural dialogues through a deeper understanding of Egypt's role in cultural exchanges, which were particularly manifested during the New Kingdom and Ptolemaic Alexandria. The continuity between ancient Egypt and Europe through many fields of knowledge from mathematics to medicine could contribute to dispelling the notion of the clash of civilisations.

The Institute could be sustained by promoting sound business management of Egyptian cultural resources, which could lead to a huge increase in revenues from tourism and cultural goods. Egypt at present is not only suffering from lack of archaeologists and conservators, but also from experts in cultural economics. Sites are left to century-old practices that serve more to annoy and repel tourists with no signs or facilities. Try to find the way to the Pyramid at Abu Rawash, assuming that you have heard of it, even though it is less than an hour's drive from Cairo, and do not be alarmed when you get there by the dumps of garbage, some of it on fire.

If Amelia Edwards could get together British Egyptologists and a philanthropist to create the Egypt Exploration Fund in 1882, in the same year that Alexandria was bombarded by the British, how difficult is it today, in a time of peace, to bring together Egyptologists from all over the world to set aside nationalist interests in an effort to save Egyptian heritage for humanity? How difficult is it to invest in developing the cultural economy of Egypt for the benefit of a better understanding of our shared past and for a better life for the poor communities that only see from a distance tourist coaches on their way to archaeological destinations or for the children who beg for a ballpoint pen? In 2007, the EES celebrates the one hundred and twenty-fifth anniversary of its foundation. This is marked with a series of events, including a two-day conference in London on 23 and 24 June and a touring graphics exhibition. Let us expand this anniversary to be more fitting with our times and to point to a new direction in British–Egyptian relations by recognising Egyptians as active partners in the discovery, writing and enjoyment of their own heritage. I. E. S. Edwards used to think that perhaps 'we had a special claim to have the exhibition, because the tomb had been discovered by a British archaeologist'.[48] He was disabused of this idea by Magdi Wahba, a professor of English at Cairo University, who told him that 'The British had been *allowed* to excavate in what had always promised to be one of the richest sites in Egypt. They had made this marvellous discovery thanks to the generosity of the Egyptians in allowing them to excavate there, a sufficient reward in itself'. A request from the Egyptian government (by Minister Morcos Hanna) to include five Egyptian students in Carter's team was refused on suspicion that they were spies.[49] Those five students might by now have created a school of experienced Egyptian archaeologists who were up to the task of safeguarding Egypt's vast archaeological heritage. If only each expedition could train three to five Egyptians, we could have in one year no less than a minimum of 300 to 500 trainees. The Egyptian Heritage Institute could indeed prepare these trainees to be more effective in the field by offering preparatory short courses and specialized modules. The scores of experts that join foreign archaeological expeditions have so far been a wasted human resource for capacity building in Egypt. The Institute could accommodate those experts as guest lecturers.

The Institute, judging from the pilot experiment I conducted at Kafr Hassan Dawood, an Early Dynastic site in the Delta, could be an ideal forum for collaboration among Egyptian and foreign scholars, and a space for promoting friendship between Egyptian students and their counterparts from abroad. International students, often deprived of formal educational opportunities in Egypt, would not only benefit from developing close friendships with Egyptians but would also learn Egyptian archaeology in Egypt. There have been efforts through a new organisation, ECHO (Egyptian Cultural Heritage Organisation, www.e-c-h-o.org) founded by British, Egyptian and international students to promote the training of Egyptians and the promotion of sound cultural heritage management along the lines suggested by Stadelmann,[50] to establish an 'Association for Cultural Heritage' to attract wealthy and educated Egyptians, to make them aware of and care for their monuments. The *Bibliotheca Alexandrina* (www.bibalex.org), a new model for learning centres in the world, is keen to contribute to cultural heritage development issues. It has already started to bring together interested parties in the Arab world to explore these issues and is planning to hold a follow-up meeting in 2007. It would indeed be a signal for a change if a proposal to establish an Egyptian cultural heritage institute was formalised by that time by a task force of prominent Egyptian specialists.

Reflecting upon the Tutankhamun Exhibition, I. E. S. Edwards noted that diplomatic relations between Egypt and England had been severed at the time of the Suez Canal 'incident' and had been resumed only a few months before the Exhibition of Tutankhamun opened in 1972, which led him to understand why the Foreign Office was so anxious to host the exhibition, in order to help in creating closer relations between the two countries. At present, good relationships between governments are not a reliable measure of public sentiments, which can create forceful political tides, as happened in 1919 when the British arrested Egypt's nationalist leader Saad Zaghloul. The situation in Iraq and Palestine not only requires a political solution, but also a change in the cultural relations between Britain, Egypt and the rest of the Arab world. Britain is in an excellent position, because of its greater knowledge of the Middle East, to lead European countries toward the social and economic development of the region for its own benefit and for bettering the lives of those who otherwise will nurture destructive animosities fuelled by fanatical and fabricated notions of history and culture.

The Tutankhamun Exhibition in 1972 added immensely to people's interest in ancient Egypt and raised the prestige of the British Museum. Attendance increased dramatically. In addition, it made available £100,000 for new acquisitions. Egypt received £654,474 for saving the monuments of Philae.[51] Clearly there are many other economic ventures based on Egypt's almost unlimited cultural resources that can contribute to the generation of revenues as a means of funding conservation of Egyptian heritage and improvement of economic conditions. The British Museum continues to gain substantial financial benefits from the publication of Egyptology titles and cultural products based on replicas of Egyptian artefacts.

Investment in the cultural economy of Egypt may range from mounting exhibitions *in* Egypt so that people could not only enjoy viewing treasures that might otherwise be impossible to send abroad but also have the benefit of cultural tours related to the subject of the exhibitions. Might I suggest exhibitions on the 'Age of the Pyramids', 'Akhenaton' and 'The Gold of the Pharaohs'. Revenues from the exhibitions would fund site management and conservation of the neglected pyramid fields outside Giza and Saqqara and the establishment of new cultural destinations such as where Akhenaton founded his capital, and the Red Sea, where gold mines, mining towns and a fascinating natural landscape are spectacular attractions. This could promote the kind of cultural tourism that enhances our knowledge of the cultural achievements of Egyptians in the sciences, technology, statecraft, religion and ethics.

One of the main priorities in light of the dispersion of Egyptian artefacts in a myriad of museums all over the world is to take advantage of currently available information technology to document artefacts so that they can be made available to scholars, students and the public through a virtual global Egyptian Museum. Another priority is to support and join in the development of a definitive archaeological map of Egypt, which is currently underway by the Egyptian National Centre for the Documentation of Cultural and Natural Heritage. This may include contributing the results from the Egypt Archaeological Survey and other mapping data sponsored by the EES to the map. Such a map is a priority for development activities and has been flagged as a priority for Egyptian archaeology in the twenty-first century.[52] Field recording of the conditions and value of archaeological sites using appropriate cultural heritage management criteria is also required to make the map, to establish priorities and guide conservation and development efforts.

As a final note, the engagement by Egyptologists in the contemporary endeavours by other disciplines in the study of state societies and civilisation will not only be a means of countering the criticism of 'insularity'[53] but will also engage Egyptologists in a new era where archaeology plays a significant role in clarifying and contributing to issues of major concern for humanity today, such as connections and continuities of civilisation, the construction of 'others', depletion and pollution of water and other vital ecological resources, violence and armed conflict, civic rights and governance, and spirituality, religion and ethics.[54]

Notes

1. F. A. Hassan, 'Memorabilia: Archaeological Materiality and National Identity in Egypt', in L. Meskell, ed., *Archaeology under Fire: Nationalism, Politics and Heritage in the Eastern Mediterranean and Middle East*, London: Routledge, 1998, pp. 200–16.

2. T. G. H. James, 'The Archaeological Survey', in T. G. H. James, ed., *Excavating in Egypt: The Egypt Exploration Society 1882–1982*, London: British Museum, 1982, pp. 141–59.

3. The first recorded set of objectives was 'To organise excavation in Egypt, with a view to further elucidation of the History and Arts of Ancient Egypt, and to the illustration of the Old Testament narrative, insofar as it has to do with Egypt and the Egyptians; also to explore sites concerned with early Greek history, or with the Antiquities of the Coptic Church, in their connection with Egypt.' (M. Drower, 'The Early Years', in T. G. H. James, ed., *Excavating in Egypt*, Egypt Exploration Society 1882–1982, London: British Museum, 1982, p. 32).

4. Drower, 1982, p. 34; R. M. Janssen, *Egyptology at University College London 1892–1992*, London: UCL Press, 1992.

5. Drower, 1982, p. 19, on Petrie's scheme of paying workers for the fruits of their illicit digging; and T. G. H. James, *Howard Carter: The Path to Tutankhamun*, London: Kegan Paul, 1992, pp. 189, 208ff, 355, on Carter's venture with Sothebys.

6. For additional views on representing Egypt, see Mitchell, 1991; and F. A. Hassan, 'Selling Egypt: Encounters at Khan el-Khalili', in S. MacDonald and M. Rice, eds, *Consuming Ancient Egypt*, London: UCL Press, 2003a.

7. A survey undertaken for the Petrie Museum by The Susie Fisher Group, *Exploring Peoples' Relationship with Egypt*, Mimeograph, London: Petrie Museum, 2000.

8. From the account of the work by Miss Amica Calverley and Miss Myrtle Broome at Abydos in 1932 by James, 1992, pp. 154–5.

9. D. M. Reid, 'Indigenous Egyptology: The Decolonization of a Profession', *Journal of the American Oriental Society*, 1985; Reid, *Whose Pharaohs? Archaeology, Museums, and Egyptian National Identity from Napoleon to World War I*, Berkeley: University of California Press, 2002.

10. O. El-Daly, Egyptology: The Missing Millennium, Ancient Egypt in Medieval Arabic Writings, London: UCL Press, 2005.

11. Who was elected at one time as president of the EES.

12. Reid, 1985, p. 234.

13. Ibid., p. 237.

14. W. M. F. Petrie, *Seventy Years in Archaeology*, London: Sampson, Low, 1931; M. S. Drower, *Flinders Petrie: A Life in Archaeology*, London: Gollancz, 1985.

15. F. A. Haikal, 'Egypt's Past Regenerated by its Own People', in S. MacDonald and M. Rice, eds, *Consuming Ancient Egypt*, London: UCL Press, 2003.

16. J. Kamil and R. Saad, 'Weighing the Issues', *Al-Ahram Weekly*, no. 476, 2000.

17. R. Schulz, 'The Responsibilities of Archaeology: Recent Excavations', in R. Schulz and M. Seidel, eds, *Egypt, The World of the Pharaohs*, Köln: Könemann, 1998.

18. F. P. McManamon and J. Rogers, *Developing Cultural Resource Management in Egypt*, crm.cr.nps.gov/archive/17-3/17-3-11.pdf.

19. R. Saad, 'Fekri Hassan: The Philosophy of Archaeology', *Al-Ahram Weekly*, 2001, no. 536, www.ahram.org.eg/weekly/2001/536.

20. D. O'Connor, 'The State of Egyptology at the End of the Millennium: Art', in Zahi Hawwas and Lyla Pinch Brock, eds, *Egyptology at the Dawn of the 21st Century, Proceedings of the Eighth International Congress of Egyptologists, Cairo 2000*, Cairo: American University in Cairo Press, 2003; R. Stadelmann, 'Response to D. O'Connor', in ibid., pp. 13–114 ; M. Verner, 'Response to D. O'Connor', in ibid., pp. 15–17; K. Mysliwiec, 'Response to D. O'Connor', in ibid., pp. 11–12.

21. O'Connor, 2003, p. 4.

22. Mysliwiec, 2003, p.11.

23. Verner, 2003.

24. F. A. Hassan, 'Imperialist Appropriations of Egyptian Obelisks', in D. Jeffrey's *Views of Ancient Egypt since Napoleon Bonaparte: Imperialism, Colonialism and Modern Appropriations*, London: UCL Press, 2003b.

25. Fagan 1975; P. France, *The Rape of Egypt: How the Europeans Stripped Egypt of its Heritage*, London: Barrie and Jenkins, 1991.

26. A. B. Edwards, *A Thousand Miles Up the Nile*, London: Routledge, 1877, p. 3. Amelia Edwards was a novelist who used her income from novels to travel to Italy. In September 1873 she and her friend Marianne Brocklehurst went to France and on account of inclement weather decided to leave France for Egypt.

27. It is also remarkable that Amelia's excursion up the Nile was at a time when other incursions up the Nile more than 2,440 miles from Cairo were undertaken by the Khedive of Egypt, Ismael and European explorers as a prelude to establishing colonial possession in the interior of Africa.

28. J. D. Wortham, *The Genesis of British Egyptology 1549–1906*, Norman: University of Oklahoma Press, 1971, p. 108.

29. Edwards, 1877, p. xii.

30. Wortham, 1971, p. 109.

31. James, 1992, p. 213.

32. Ibid., p. 214.

33. Ibid., p. 208.

34. Ibid., p. 331.

35. M. Haag, *The Rough Guide to Egypt*, London: Rough Guides, 2003.

36. I. E. S. Edwards, *From the Pyramids to Tutankhamun*, London: Oxbow Books, 2000, p. 205.

37. H. S. Smith, 'Walter Bryan Emery', in *Journal of Egyptian Archaeology*, 1971, p. 194; Edwards, 2000, p. 204.

38. James, 1992, p. 175.

39. W. B. Emery, *Egypt in Nubia*, London: Hutchinson, 1965.

40. Emery, 1965, p. 31.

41. Ibid., p. 32.

42. Edwards, 2000, p. 249.

43. T. Säve-Söderberg, *Temples and Tombs of Ancient Nubia*, London: Thames and Hudson, 1987, p. 90.

44. http://whc.unesco.org/ab_secre.htm#debut.

45. F. A. Hassan, 'The Aswan High Dam and the International Rescue Nubia Campaign', in F. A. Hassan and S. Brandt, eds, *Damming the Past*, London: Westview Press, forthcoming.

46. Edwards, 2000, p. 124.

47. See Hassan, F. A., *The Cultural Legacy of Egypt: A World Legacy*, Paris: UNESCO, 1997, for a tentative list.

48. Edwards, 2000, pp. 271-2.

49. James, 2000, p. 319.

50. Stadelmann, 2003, p.13.

51. Edwards, 2000, p. 296.

52. O'Connor, 2003.

53. D. Jeffreys, 'Introduction – Two Hundred Years of Ancient Egypt: Modern History and Ancient Archaeology', in D. Jeffrey's *Views of Ancient Egypt since Napoleon Bonaparte: Imperialism, Colonialism and Modern Appropriations*, London: UCL Press, 2003, pp. 5-6; T. Champion, 'Beyond Egyptology: Egypt in 19th and 20th Century Archaeology and Anthropology', in P. Ucko and T. Champion, eds, *Wisdom of Egypt: Changing Visions through the Ages*, London: UCL Press, 2003.

54. F. A. Hassan, 'Objects of the Past: Refocusing Archaeology', in R. Layton, S. Shennan, and P. Stone, eds, *A Future for Archaeology*, London: UCL Press, 2006.

MICHAEL JONES

The Conservation and Management of the Coptic Christian Cultural Heritage in Egypt*

This chapter introduces the conservation of historic monuments and sites in the context of community development and suggests that when practised in collaboration with all the stakeholders it can also be an effective form of diplomacy. In the field of cultural heritage management, the words conservation and preservation have different meanings in Europe and North America where they are applied to different processes in the care of historic monuments and sites. They are sometimes even used interchangeably. In this chapter conservation means the work of documenting, recording, cleaning, repairing and presenting buildings, wall paintings or artefacts, while preservation encompasses these interventions into the material remains of the past as well as the care and maintenance needed to ensure their future.[1]

Conventional approaches to cultural heritage preservation have concentrated on the tangible and material features of culture. This has had the effect of isolating monuments from their social and historical contexts and then leaving them to their own devices. Recently a more holistic approach has evolved, identifying intangible aspects that give meaning to material culture. The term cultural heritage acknowledges that culture is a patrimony inherited and held in trust for future generations. This is especially significant for living heritage such as exists in Egypt today. Here the past is ever-present and, in

David Lowenthal's words, 'heritage clarifies pasts so as to infuse them with present purposes'.[2] Origins and affiliations are important as most people identify themselves with a very real imagined past reinforced by its monuments in their midst. These act as powerful reminders and strongly influence present social, political and religious identities. Cultural heritage management, or cultural resource management (CRM) as it is known in America, has advanced greatly in recent years, including more emphasis on management and planning and greater inclusiveness for the interests of everyone involved.[3]

The Copts see themselves as inheritors and guardians of an ancient and unbroken tradition beginning in the first century with the arrival of St Mark in Alexandria. Egyptian resistance to what Copts believe were heterodox and innovative ideas in the fourth and fifth centuries, especially those endorsed by the Council of Chalcedon in AD 451, justify Coptic claims to be defenders of orthodoxy. Coptic material culture comprises archaeological sites throughout Egypt, the collections of the Coptic Museum, and historic buildings still in use such as medieval churches and the desert monasteries. They preserve historic collections of manuscripts, icons, liturgical objects, many still used, and installations from the days before modernisation.[4] Intangible culture includes the liturgy and sacraments of the Church, the Coptic language, music and the Copts' instinctive sense of the spiritual, historic and contemporary meanings of their whole cultural inheritance.

A third kind of heritage, combining both the tangible and intangible, is a deeply-felt sense of sacred ground. According to tradition, Egypt is blessed by having given sanctuary to the Holy Family[5] and as the birthplace of monasticism, and became known as the 'second Holy Land'. Numerous places identified with the Holy Family's journey and with the desert fathers are still occupied by ancient monasteries and churches. They provide guidance to the community and a direct link with the ancestors of the Church. Parishes organise pilgrimages to these sites and visits to the monks whose lives still reflect the biblical past.[6] Visitors experience

The White Monastery near Sohag: the fifth-century church of St Shenoute, still in use, with excavated remains of the archaeological site in the foreground. Photo: Michael Jones. Copyright: American Research Center in Egypt.

spiritual renewal and express social cohesion.[7] For those working in conservation, these factors demonstrate that we are not just dealing with buildings and artefacts but with a vibrant culture heavily charged with cherished symbolism and associations.

This brings us to several important questions; first, what do we conserve, and why and for whom? With a very large amount of material requiring attention but limited resources and specialists to deploy, everything cannot be a priority. An approach now increasingly adopted is based on identifying and assessing the value and significance of monuments and sites for those with direct interests and investments in them; that is, the stakeholders.[8] Since the 1980s, archaeologists have been evaluating sites on this basis and in recent years the same approach has become part of cultural heritage management as the two disciplines have moved closer together.[9] However, it has emotive implications. Suggesting that some aspects of culture are more significant than others implies that some may not be worth keeping when it comes to deciding what to preserve. An élite body of archaeologists and art historians has generally had the final say and in contemporary Egypt it is often politicians, bureaucrats and urban planners who decide; but this process ignores most of the people who use these places.

A fourth question is: who owns these ancient churches and monastic buildings? They are neither museums nor just archaeological sites although many are extremely old and contain museum-class objects. Neither are they private property because although they belong to the church, they are in the care of the Supreme Council of Antiquities, the government body responsible for safeguarding Egypt's historic sites.

Traditionally, the monasteries were desert communities, closely attuned to their harsh environments, often in remote locations of exceptional natural beauty. For centuries, the monks have relied on their own resources and have looked after their buildings using traditional materials. Within living memory this has changed. The seclusion that preserved historic architecture and maintained the old ways of life no longer exists. With improved roads and supplies, water pipelines and a new educated class of monks, the demography is different and the monasteries are expanding to accommodate the current revival in the monastic life. The monks have lost the skills to survive on their own and, when building, prefer steel and concrete over traditional materials. Running water in their cells and in the monastery gardens, and farms on adjacent reclaimed desert land bring problems of increased humidity and poor drainage. This can have disastrous consequences, as when damage caused by flash flooding in the Cave Church at the Monastery of St Paul was repaired with cement in the 1970s. Moisture was sealed in the ground, causing it to rise up the walls behind the mural paintings in the church with potentially catastrophic results. This example provides an answer to Daniel Bluestone's rhetorical question, asked in the context of culture as an ongoing process; 'why should conservators intervene in its dynamic operations? Why shouldn't we accept change with its destructive forces and simply greet new forms with enthusiasm?'[10] Development is important as it emphasises the contemporaneity of the Church. Yet the impact of development on environmental and cultural heritage is often overlooked, and well-meant but ill-advised work jeopardises traditional architecture.

When we consider the range and depth of values and significance of Coptic cultural heritage we can distinguish seven main categories and corresponding groups of stakeholders. The chart below indicates general correspondences between categories of value and significance and stakeholders' interests in them. In reality, they are seldom as fixed as the boxes in the chart might imply. Both sides should be interpreted fluidly so that different stakeholders might have interests in any number of corresponding values.

Categories of value and significance	*Stakeholders*
Spiritual and religious	The Church and the clergy and monks who have preserved the Coptic tradition throughout the centuries
Social and civic	The Coptic community at large, both in Egypt and abroad, who support the Church and its institutions
Symbolic and community identity	Anyone interested in discovering the desert fathers of the Church and developing their own spirituality
Historic and artistic	The Supreme Council of Antiquities with overall caretaker responsibility for all historic sites, artefacts and museums
Academic and research	The academic community, including archaeologists, art historians, historians, Coptologists, sociologists, teachers and students
Natural and environmental	Environmentalists and preservationists
Economic	The tourism industry; donors funding development, infrastructure projects, and conservation; SCA; contractors

Some of the stakeholders representing institutions which have invested in the preservation of the Church of St Anthony at St Anthony's Monastery: from left to right, Bob Springborg (American Research Center in Egypt), Bill Pearson (United States Agency for International Development), Gaballah Ali Gaballah (Supreme Council of Antiquities), Bishop Yustus (Coptic Church and St Anthony's Monastery), Reno and Leslie Harnish (United States Embassy in Egypt) and Fr. Maximus el-Antony (St Anthony's Monastery). Photo: Robert Vincent. Copyright: American Research Center in Egypt.

Working with stakeholders means more than just a one-off meeting to present a plan. It involves continuous communication and involvement. Listening to opinions to reconcile differences is time-consuming and can be stressful; modifying plans to meet diverse and sometimes conflicting needs requires patience and the willingness to compromise. For example, it took three months to decide the fate of the original medieval and eighteenth-century floors in the Cave Church of St Paul, uncovered when the harmful cement was removed. The archaeologists and conservators wanted it kept as the floor of the conserved building. The monks did not for good practical reasons, and some even wanted it removed. The uneven slabs would be cold and difficult to stand on bare-footed during the long services, with

The Red Monastery near Sohag: Conservator Luigi De Cesaris working on cleaning eighth-century mural paintings newly revealed in 2004. Photo: Elizabeth Bolman. Copyright: American Research Center in Egypt.

the risk that they might later be covered again with an unsuitable material. After discussions, it was decided to preserve the original floor under sand and a new lime plaster floor.

The investment in time and flexibility is usually rewarded by the involvement and commitment to maintain the site by those who use it. For example, at the Red Monastery near Sohag, the priest in charge was included from the start in the conservation project and invited to view and discuss the progress of the work regularly. His lengthy homilies delivered to parishioners each evening in the church now include the saints newly revealed by the project and recognition for the conservators doing the work.

An important and contentious constituency with much to offer and also much to lose includes those who have invested economically in cultural heritage. Tourism is estimated to be Egypt's second most valuable source of foreign exchange, with US $7 billion reported for 2005. Seaside resorts and Pharaonic sites attract the majority, but now religious tourism has taken to the 'Holy Family Trail'. Copts in general are proud of this aspect of their heritage and keen to promote it. Furthermore, the Egyptian Tourism Authority plans to use it to increase regional tourism.[11] Yet none of the monasteries and churches on this proposed route through the Nile Delta and between Cairo and Asyut is prepared for an influx of foreign visitors and the region lacks even basic tourism infrastructure.[12] Nevertheless those conditions may not prevent tour operators responding to the potential for a new market.[13] The historic fabric is already distressed by large numbers of Coptic faithful visiting these sites regularly. If mass tourism arrives as well, there will be severe physical damage. The sites need to be conserved and protected in advance and management plans implemented to protect them and enhance visitor satisfaction.[14] The Holy Family tradition illustrates well how culture is a continuous process. It corresponds with all seven of the values listed above, and although there is no archaeological evidence whatsoever, just one literary reference written several decades afterwards recording the event[15] and only a local oral tradition at al-Ashmunain prior to the medieval period,[16] it has created a range of tangible heritage sites, a flourishing pilgrimage and may now become yet another tourist attraction.

There is also the question of how tourism's consuming zeal will affect the socio-cultural environment in which cultural heritage is a significant factor. Many Copts, seeing themselves as a beleaguered minority in their own country, are enthusiastic about raising awareness by presenting themselves to a wider public, a theme particularly strong among Copts abroad.[17]

Foreign governments and international aid agencies can encourage responsible tourism by sharing their experiences and funding appropriate marketing campaigns, research and, above all, training in cultural heritage management and conservation. The United States, the Netherlands and France have traditionally supported work in Coptic heritage and the Levantine Foundation of Great Britain is now conserving manuscripts in the Syrian monastery, Wadi Natrun. Since 1994 the US government, through the United States Agency for International Development (USAID), has devoted considerable funding to cultural heritage preservation in Egypt at all kinds of sites with a substantial percentage allotted to Coptic heritage. The projects have been carried out by the American Research Center in Egypt at monasteries, churches and the Coptic Museum in Cairo.

USAID describes its heritage conservation purpose in four ways: to promote economically sustainable tourism; to encourage public diplomacy; to enhance people's surroundings; and to encourage and perpetuate community relations. These sound grand and idealistic when other aspects of American foreign policy in the Arab world seem so culturally confrontational. Nevertheless, experience shows that cultural heritage can be instrumental in transcending differences just as effectively as it can reinforce them. The value and significance approach in consultation with as many of the interested stakeholders as possible is an effective way of breaking down some of the barriers dividing academics and the public and donors from the beneficiaries.

It is now no longer viable merely to conserve an historic building without investing in effective long-term maintenance. Conservation and site management training must be institutionalised both in the Supreme Council of Antiquities and amongst the monks, priests and laity who are the custodians of the historic monasteries and churches. This can be achieved within the existing systems, by including more talented people in projects to encourage a sense of stewardship and accountability so they develop an appreciation of the quality of their work and an awareness of how to care for their inheritance. Tourism, properly managed, can be a beneficial part of site management by enhancing cultural sites, bringing revenue and promoting awareness, since neglect leads to decline, damage and deterioration. However, in the context of Coptic cultural heritage there is a risk, which needs to be avoided, that touristic interpretation will archaise the Church and its members as though they were a spectacle left over from the past rather than part of modern society. Living religion and living tourism will have to find ways to coexist.[18]

Among the Egyptian public, care of historic cultural heritage is seen as the responsibility of foreigners and a specialised elite, because they have traditionally taken that role. There is also a view amongst the intelligentsia that culture in general and cultural heritage in particular belong in a sphere inaccessible to most people or outside their economic and educational abilities. Yet this attitude ignores participation in both tangible and intangible heritage that takes place without the need to identify, analyse and label it as 'heritage', such as the monastic life of the monks and the experience of Copts as described above. The usual justification is that most Egyptians have far more burning issues to contend with. This is both true and a convenient stimulus for foreign donors to pay, but it is also a catalyst for resentment when donors eventually see their investments eroded in the absence of effective maintenance plans. In the current environment of development and expansion, corresponding with a greater awareness of the fragility of both tangible and intangible heritage, education is needed to promote a widespread historical consciousness. It is to be hoped that Egypt's current economic reform programme will eventually create conditions suitable to encourage more Egyptian donors to feel sufficiently confident to invest in the future of their own cultural heritage.

The conservation projects in the monasteries have transformed the damaged and soot-blackened interiors of the churches so that the buildings are no longer compromised and the mural paintings are clearly visible again. The effect goes far beyond the tangible and is perhaps more vitally intangible. Pilgrims, tourists and residents are no longer presented with what looks like a neglected and debased culture and the monks, who are the custodians, understand better how to protect it. Specialists have access to new material and the

Conservator (Luigi De Cesaris) and monk (Fr. Tomas al-Anba Bula) discussing the preservation needs of the Cave Church of St Paul in front of conserved eighteenth-century mural paintings. Photo: Patrick Godeau. Copyright: American Research Center in Egypt.

Coptic faithful practise in enhanced surroundings. All these elements successfully increase heritage valorisation in the Coptic community and beyond. Publication of the project results provides access to a far wider public than will ever see the sites themselves. Successful preservation of cultural heritage can be understood and practised as a benefit to the whole community and therefore as a significant contribution to social development.

Notes

*   I would like to acknowledge the support received from the Supreme Council of Antiquities, in particular the Secretary General, Dr Zahi Hawass, former Secretaries General, Dr Abd al-Halim Nur al-Din and Dr Gaballah Ali Gaballah, and the Head of the Coptic and Islamic Sector, Dr Abdallah Kamil and his predecessor Abdallah al-Attar. The projects in this field are carried out in collaboration with the Coptic Orthodox Church with the blessing of His Holiness Pope Shenouda III. The conservation projects at the Monastery of St Paul and the Red Monastery near Sohag, mentioned in this paper, are funded by the United States Agency for International Development and implemented by the American Research Center in Egypt. I would also like to thank Fr. Maximus el-Antony and Dr Laila Iskander for their helpful suggestions during early drafts of this paper.

1. Anthony M. Tung, *Preserving the World's Great Cities, The Destruction and Renewal of the Historic Metropolis*, New York: Three Rivers Press, 2001, pp. 3–4.
2. David Lowenthal, *The Heritage Crusade and the Spoils of History*, Cambridge, 1998, p. xv.
3. Martha Demas, 'Planning for Conservation and Management of Archaeological Sites', in *Management Planning for Archaeological Sites*. Proceeding of an international workshop organised by the Getty Conservation Institute and Loyola Marymount University, May 2000, Corinth, Greece. Los Angeles: Getty Conservation Institute Los Angeles, 2002, pp. 27–54.
4. Massimo Capuani, *Christian Egypt; Coptic Art and Monuments Through Two Millenia*, Cairo: American University in Cairo Press, 2002.
5. William Lyster, 'Coptic Egypt and the Holy Family', in Gawdat Gabra, ed., *Be Thou There; The Holy Family's Journey in Egypt*, Cairo: American University in Cairo Press, 2001, pp. 1–29.
6. Georgia Frank, *The Memory of the Eyes; Pilgrims to Living Saints in Christian Late Antiquity*, Berkeley: University of California Press, 2000, pp. 53–9.
7. Elizabeth E. Oram, 'In the Footsteps of the Saints; The Monastery of St. Antony, Pilgrimage, and Modern Coptic Identity', in E. Bolman, ed., *Monastic Visions; Wall Paintings in the Monastery of St. Antony at the Red Sea*, New Haven: Yale University Press and American Research Center in Egypt, 2002, pp. 203–13.
8. Randall Mason, 'Theoretical and Practical Arguments for Values-Centered Preservation', in *CRM: The Journal of Heritage Stewardship* 3, no. 2, Summer 2006, pp. 21–48. Neville Agnew and Janet Bridgeland, eds, *Of the Past, For the Future: Integrating Archaeology and Conservation*, Proceedings of the Conservation Theme at the Fifth World Archaeological Congress, Washington DC, 22–6 June 2003, Los Angeles: Getty Conservation Institute Los Angeles, 2006, pp. 85–142, Part Four, 'Finding Common Ground: The Role of Stakeholders in Decision Making'.
9. Robert C. Dunnell, 'The Ethics of Archaeological Significance Decisions', in E. Green, ed., *Ethics and Values in Archaeology*, New York: Free Press, 1984, pp. 62–74. Timothy Darvill, 'Value Systems in Archaeology' in M. Cooper et al., eds, *Managing Archaeology*, London: Routledge, 1995, pp. 40–50.
10. Daniel Bluestone, 'Challenges for Heritage Conservation and the Role of Research on Values', in Marta de la Torre and Erica Avrami, *Values and*

Heritage Conservation, Research report, Los Angeles: Getty Conservation Institute, 2000, p. 65.

11. British Egyptian Business Association (BEBA); H.E. Dr Mamdouh el-Beltagui, Minister of Tourism, business luncheon on Monday, 15 December 2003 in Cairo at the Marriot Hotel, 'The Challenges of Sustainable Tourism Development in Egypt', online at http://www.beba.org.eg/resources/html/15-12-2003Speech.asp (consulted 18 September 2006).

12. Sherine El-Madany, 'Trail of Tears', *Business Today/Egypt*, online at http://www.copts.net/detail.asp?id=948 (consulted 18 September 2006).

13. Barbara Kirshenblatt-Gimblett, *Destination Culture; Tourism, Museums, and Heritage*, Berkeley: University of California Press, 1998, pp. 149–53.

14. Bob McKercher and Hilary Le Cros, *Cultural Heritage Tourism, the Partnership Between Tourism and Cultural Heritage Management*, New York: Haworth Hospitality Press, 2002, pp. 65–99. Bernard M. Feilden and Jukka Jokilehto, *Management Guidelines for World Cultural Heritage Sites*, Rome: ICCROM, 1993.

15. The Gospel of St Matthew, 2:13–15.

16. Stephen J. Davies, 'Ancient Sources for the Coptic Tradition', in Gawdat Gabra, ed., *Be Thou There*, pp. 133–53.

17. Issandr El Amrani, 'The Emergence of a "Coptic Question" in Egypt', Middle East Report Online, 28 April 2006. Online at http://www.merip.org/mero/mero042806.html (consulted 27 August 2006).

18. Thomas S. Bremer, *Blessed with Tourists, The Borderlands of Religion and Tourism in San Antonio*, Chapel Hill: University of North Carolina Press, 2004, pp. 117–46.

STEPHEN QUIRKE

Interwoven Destinies: Egyptians and English in the Labour of Archaeology, 1880–2007

Cotton tells a distinctive tale as capital in nineteenth- and twentieth-century history. Cotton binds workers in the fields, factories and docks of Egypt with the history of the English working-class. The history of relations between Egypt and England may be directed, or presented, by businessmen, diplomats and generals, and the tourist industry may have blinded modern Egypt to the existence of a class of manual labour in Europe and North America. Yet it should not be as hard as it is to recall that managers did not unload Egyptian cotton at Liverpool, and that merchants were not enslaved in Lancashire mills to produce the textiles for a colonised global market.

In the 1860s the American Civil War had blocked the main source of cotton for English capital, forcing industrialists to the land their bankers were ruining with the repayments of credit for the Suez Canal.[1] Within the generation, alongside the cotton, the freight included excavated and purchased antiquities, destined for collections, including a concentration around the textile cities of northern England. Shipping-lists are not yet a regular source for history of archaeology and the museum, but the transport of material and personnel was a precondition for the external funding of digs, as well as for populating galleries. Cotton created the shipping lane for archaeology: funds for excavation came from mill-owners in

Lancashire towns such as Bolton, at the heart of the colonial global production.[2] Social historians could unveil another connecting strand: sponsor lists and museum visitor records everywhere readily privilege the privileged, but they might still reveal the presence of textile industry workers both among subscribers to excavation funds, and in the audiences attracted to the presence of Egypt in the museums. That vaster social history linking the Nile Valley and alien museum cities remains to be written for archaeology, along lines drawn from European and North American stances in anthropology.[3] First, though, an immediate history of labour within the acts of archaeology can be identified, and documents brought forward for writing one immediate part of that web.

Despite a strong disciplinary focus on materiality, histories of archaeology sometimes seem to reserve study of the past to a dematerialised History of Ideas, specifically through the genre of biography, so perpetuating a 'great (white) man' theory of history.[4] Biography is a powerful frame, and in this chapter I draw extensively on one magnificent example, the evocative life of Flinders Petrie by Margaret Drower.[5] Yet, if biography dominates, archaeological theory and method appear as brainchildren of uniquely talented men from metropolitan centres of capitalism. Reactions against colonial archaeology have offered little resistance to this historiographical tendency. Nationalist revisions of nineteenth- and early twentieth-century archaeology pursue the important task of emending the name-list of great men,[6] but do not delve further into the political economy of archaeological labour. As a result, the history of how pasts are recovered remains a hermetically sealed affair of the middle (sometimes upper) class. This article proposes a return to specific practices and practitioners upon which the great ideas-men of today and yesterday depend. The men, women and children who move the mounds of earth for excavation directors, and usually tell directors where to dig, are not anonymous: like the Lancashire mill workers, these are the named, and taxed, populations of civil census and the policed state. Equally, at the other end of the export-trail, it seems unlikely that sociological resources can provide no information at all on the working-class visitors to museum displays of archaeological finds, and subscribers to excavating bodies. Both excavating/ producing and visiting/consuming working-classes have been omitted by multidisciplinary design, not from a lack of resources. In response, we can ask which skills are only generically acknowledged, to be excluded from the aristocracies of theory and method? And what breadth of class is present in both retrieval and reception of material from the past?

This enquiry might address archaeological excavation in any context; 'metropolitan', for example English, archaeology probably follows the same recruitment methods, low payment and political exclusion whether in its local nation territory or in colonised territory abroad.[7] I explore here the way in which England and Egypt share and conceal working-class destinies, because the volume focus is on relations between those two countries, and because I am an Egyptologist with immediate access to the archives of the Petrie Museum of Egyptian Archaeology, UCL – not because the story is substantively different elsewhere.

Ali Gabri and the Petrie Survey of the Great Pyramid at Giza, *1880–1882*

On 14 December 1880 the then twenty-six-year-old enthusiast William Matthew Flinders Petrie arrived in Alexandria on his first mission to Egypt, to survey the Great Pyramid, testing in particular a theory popularised by one Charles Smith ('Piazzi Smyth') that the pyramid was constructed on a divinely-inspired unit of measurement, the pyramid inch. At twenty-six, the age of Petrie seems to place him, for us, among the heroically young, befitting a history of pioneers: in the 1880s, though, he may have seemed rather old not to have been married, and even a little late for global exploits. Perhaps he saw himself as heroic outsider, growing up in mid-Victorian England; his father belonged to the Exclusive Brethren, a non-Establishment

Protestant group that might have fostered such a self-image of outsiderness in an officially Anglican land. This self-image may have given him the energy he needed for his work. With hindsight, the Petrie 1880–2 survey and, most importantly, its 1883 publication *The Pyramids and Temples of Gizeh* marked the triumphant start of a career in which Petrie dedicated his life to rescuing information about the past of Egypt. Here biography can trump any radical doubt: unquestionably, and to marked appreciation among Egyptians too ever since, Flinders Petrie dedicated his life to the study of Egypt with exceptional energy, and achieved astonishing results on remarkably limited resources. However, his first season back in 1880–1 also reveals much of the pragmatics of this far from Anglocentric encounter with the past, and some of the choices in self-imaging by archaeologists in constructing their own past. According to the biography by Margaret Drower, Petrie arrived in Cairo with an introduction to a well-connected Scottish physician resident in the city, Dr James Grant, and the first practical step on his advice was to employ Ali Gabri, the man who had 'assisted' Charles Smith in 1864. As Drower outlines the start of the expedition:

> Ali went with him to the station, loaded the precious boxes
> on to carts, and spent the night guarding them. He turned
> up with them early the next morning and found Flinders
> a donkey to ride ... Flinders planned to occupy the tomb
> Waynman Dixon had lived in, for which Ali had the key.[8]

Ever practically-minded, Petrie then constructed his own bedstead of wood. His guard is said to have been a black 'slave' (status reported, not verified) of Ali Gabri, named Muhammad, the second non-European to frame the start to the career of this English guest in Egypt.

During this first season, Petrie received a chance visit from a heroised figure of the previous generation in the history of archaeology, Augustus Henry Lane Fox, named from 1880 Pitt-

Rivers.[9] The two men had much in common, pursuing the social Darwinian model of evolution of 'civilisation'. In 1862–6, Colonel Fox, as he then was, served as Assistant Quartermaster General in the British military occupation of Ireland.[10] In his evolutionary scheme for archaeology, he relegated to the bottom of the pile the stubbornly unconverted Catholic-believing, Celtic-living, Irish-speaking inhabitants. According to his interpretation of skulls, they could be placed scientifically in this place along with the Tasmanians being exterminated by settlers of Tasmania in the British rule of Australia (1876: death of one of the last inhabitants, Truganini, after a move to Flinders Island; her skeleton displayed in the Tasmania Museum until 1947).[11] These are not side issues in the history of relations between Egypt and England. Colonialism and the social evolutionary ideology which grew from that had genocidal impact, as strong in the nineteenth as in the twentieth century.[12] As a branch of the ideological developments, and as keen commentators in their time on political and social issues, the big figures in archaeology belong to this story too. Like Pitt-Rivers, Petrie might easily have belonged to an English middle and upper class exasperated by the Ireland they occupied and blaming it for the million deaths in the mid-century Famine.[13] This, though, is not noted in histories of archaeology, and must be researched from the correspondence and publications on questions of race. By contrast, Petrie's views on contemporary Egyptian politics are more visible. Writing home, Petrie witnessed the damage caused by modernisation to the monuments, and wrote in the vein generally used to justify orientalist attitudes about destruction levels that were in fact being inflicted everywhere, including 1880s England:

> The savage indifference of the Arabs, who have even stripped the alabaster off the granite temple ... is only surpassed by a most barbaric sort of regard for the monuments by those in power ... It is sickening to see the rate at which everything is being destroyed.[14]

For building demolition in Victorian London, we would presumably write 'The savage indifference of the English ...' – and Petrie was often to deride the manners and tastes of public-school society. On the positive side, horror at destruction motivated Petrie to what we would now call rescue archaeology. On the negative side, its choice of wording exposes the easy culture of blame between 'European' and 'Arab' over matters of technical specificity and difficulty, in the extraordinarily costly task of preserving remains from a past as rich as the Egyptian. Curiously to our minds sensitised by the accelerating pace of destruction of monuments by a rapacious antiquities trade, Petrie saw no opposition between his aims of preservation and his collecting. Like many other freelance travellers of the time, he collected both for his own personal collection, and for sale back home to recoup travel costs.[15] This was within the law of the day: the antiquities legislation of Egypt permitted sale and export of antiquities until decades after Petrie had died in Jerusalem in 1942, through the Nasser period and well into the Sadat era. Again, though, the career of Petrie as collector and antiquities dealer has been omitted from the history of archaeology, as though the economic dimension of his work would infringe on his scientific achievements, rather than forming a part of a whole and complex life.

Petrie packed up at Giza in May 1881, when the heat became too great; he returned to Cairo on 14 October 1881 for a second survey season. This time he visited the French head of the Antiquities Service of Egypt, Gaston Maspero, and was advised to obtain a work permit nominally as temporary official of the Museum, to avoid the necessity of a firman or official work-permit.[16] That week, Petrie was robbed by soldiers in the Cairo City of the Dead; evidently the following trial, in which Greek and Coptic witnesses 'abandoned' him, brought him no satisfaction, as his biographer reports: 'He wrote an account of the incident for *The Times* and *The Globe* in England, both of which newspapers published the item.'[17] Petrie here seeks to use the media, the public sphere of politics, at an ominous moment in Anglo-Egyptian relations. This presentation makes no mention of the political and social context of increasing tensions within the armed forces in Egypt, still nominally under Ottoman suzerainty, against the background of the accelerating Suez Canal debt crisis imposed on Egypt under Khedive Tawfiq.[18] In these years, Egyptian officers were seeking a greater role, against the resistance of government ministers inclined to entrench the Turco-Circassian officer control rooted in centuries of Mamluk and Ottoman power.[19] There was a world of difference between the Turkic-speaking military and Arabic-speaking Egyptians, but, in the Petrie reminiscence, the 'soldiers' and their 'officer' become generalised orientalist types, strategically detached from the larger forces at play.

On a more humane note, Ali greeted him warmly at Giza, and Petrie refused the offer from the museum to live in urban accommodation, with the words 'I am *ibn el beled*, a son of the country: all the Arabs are my friends and I know them all'. *Ibn el beled*: in these remarkable words, at the most optimistic, we glimpse a history of archaeology that might have been – or perhaps this is only the anthropological field encounter, hosted humanely at a local level to be written up anonymously in a distanced report.[20] That season Petrie made his first journey upriver to Upper Egypt, in a private charter boat, a *dhahabiya*, at the invitation of well-to-do English friends. Purchases and researches continued hand-in-hand, and, returning to Cairo, Petrie reported that Maspero advised him against declaring the minor antiquities at customs: 'he recommends me to carry the little things away in my pockets'.[21]

Military occupation, 1882

By the time Petrie was back in Cairo on 23 October for his third archaeological season, this time for excavation, catastrophe had struck Egypt: British military occupation.[22] Shortly after Petrie had left in May, Khedive Tawfiq dismissed the nationalist Colonel Urabi. Popular uprisings reinstated him, but too much was at stake for British financial, industrial and strategic interests, and on 11 July the British fleet bombarded Alexandria. On 13 September, the Urabi army was defeated by British invasion forces: the occupation was to last over seventy years, across several constitutional changes, until 1954 – twelve years after Petrie died in Jerusalem. Petrie could be cast, and perhaps energised himself with the image, as heroic outsider pitted against the monolith of official bureaucracy. In the harsher light of this military history, though, the entire Petrie excavating career from 1883 in Egypt and from 1925 in Palestine places him not as an unresourced guest, but as citizen of the occupying power, a man in close contact with the colonial administration. In political history, this phase of scientific archaeology seems far more the central story of colonial dispossession, than does the more publicly visible and deplored antiquarian export of large sculptures to Paris and London earlier in the century.[23] The bulk of the early collections of colossal sculpture, even obelisks, coffins and furniture, arrived in Europe from the much more threatening Egypt of the 1820s and 1830s. Their export was permitted by the semi-independent governor of Egypt, Muhammad Ali, in pursuit of his own goals. This gulf between early and late nineteenth-century history of Egypt is ignored in the self-image of archaeology. Field archaeologists may find it safe to echo public distaste at the visibly powerful, in this case a national institution of the power and prestige of the British Museum. Yet their home university departments are more complicit in dismantling all knowledge-production beyond the metropolitan centre.

Shortly before the fateful events of that summer of 1882, a new society had come into existence in London, to channel funds for excavation into Egypt from Britain and anglophone North America. The driving force behind this new venture was the wealthy novelist Amelia Edwards, since a Nile journey in 1873 spurred by her own sense that everything was being destroyed.[24] On 27 March 1882 she saw her selfless aspirations become reality, as a meeting in the British Museum agreed to constitute a new society, the Egypt Exploration Fund, on the model of the similarly London-based Palestine Exploration Fund founded in 1865. Again, biography fairly credits

Edwards with matchless creative, generous energy, a woman who literally wore herself to death in the struggles to build up the society in England and North America. However, the biographical triumph is not the full story: correspondence with Maspero reveals the intense politicisation of cultural policy within Egypt. At the suggestion that English excavators might explore the Delta, Maspero sought to warn off the creators of the new society, in a letter sent from the Egyptian Museum then at Bulaq in Cairo on 20 May 1882. This document sets out the nationalist position clearly on the eve of the fall. Its date and contents effectively undermine the premises on which foreign archaeologists came to contribute to the archaeology of Egypt, a contribution already naturalised in the minds of the English foreigners:

> ... comme une souscription entraine une Société, il ne s'agit plus aujourd'hui de rien moins que d'une Société analogue à celle qui explore la Palestine. Ceci présentait quelques difficultés. Je ne crois pas qu'en Angleterre on songe à former une Société destinée a explorer la Gaule antique: l'Egypte est un peu dans les conditions où se trouve la Gaule, nullement dans les conditions où se trouve la Syrie. En Syrie, il n'y a point de service des antiquités, point de gardiens des monuments, point de musées: en Egypte tout cela existe comme en France. Je vous présente en ce moment la thèse du gouvernement égyptien. Ce gouvernement dit: Nous dépensons tous les ans une somme de ... pour l'entretien et la découverte des monuments. Sans doute cette somme est insuffisante, mais quelle serait la somme qui suffirait à l'exploration d'un pays comme l'Egypte? Vous me disez qu'ici la disproportion entre la somme allouée et les besoins du service est telle, que les monuments ne peuvent etre entretenues et périssent. Qui détruit les monuments? Les étrangers qui tous les ans parcourent le pays, achètent des antiquités, enlèvent des blocs de pierre, pour le Louvre et le British Museum: ils font ici ce qu'ils ne feraient ni en Allemagne, ni en

Angleterre, ni en Espagne, ni en France, ni en Italie. Ce
n'est pas une conversation imaginaire que je vous invente
là: je ne fais que vous répéter des conversations que j'ai eu
avec tous les ministres qui se sont succedés depuis que je
suis en Egypte.[25]

This is a critical document in the history of archaeology, revealing
within the nineteenth century the plurality of views that modernity
considers its exclusive right. In May 1882, 'Egypt for the Egyptians'
was to apply to archaeology as well as to army, finance and the
government: a national budget and infrastructure existed to protect
monuments, and the main blame for destruction lay with the foreign
'metropolitan' cultural institutions themselves. Nationalist aims
were thwarted by the British military occupation, following which
direction of archaeological policy became a point of negotiation
between the two main European colonial powers in the region,
Britain and France.[26] The Egypt Exploration Fund began its support
for fieldwork the following year, appointing Petrie on the strength
of his 1883 publication of the Giza survey. The archaeology to which
many aspire today – ethical, locally-embedded, locally-owned – was
struck from reality.

The eyes and hands of archaeology: Sheikh Ruhuma discovers Naukratis, 1883, and 'an old reis of Mariette' continues to uncover Tanis

In 1883 Petrie enlisted the support of Ali Gabri again, relocating him
to the new excavation site assigned to the Egypt Exploration Fund:
San al-Hagar, in the north-eastern Delta. Just before the start of the
season, a brother of Ali, Sheikh Ruhuma, brought Petrie to the site of
Naukratis. Although he did not realise the significance until explicit
inscriptional evidence was brought to light by farmers removing the
archaeological earth for fertiliser, the Petrie rediscovery of the site
is the first great moment in his excavating career. Yet it was in fact
Sheikh Ruhuma who showed him where the material of interest lay.[27]

That week among the British community in Cairo, Petrie mentioned the discussions over the future under occupation, siding with the view of one Colonel Gibbons that Egypt be split 'into independent little states, each under the absolute autocracy of an Englishman'.[28] He left Cairo for Faqus, with Mahmoud, nephew and adopted son of Ali Gabri, and Mursi, also from Giza. At Tanis, as in the pyramid survey, and at Naukratis, Egyptian knowledge led the way on this first excavation. 'An old reis of Mariette's turned up, who had worked at San and knew the site well, and exactly where things had been found'.[29] The season was to see the only fatality recorded at a Petrie dig, when a cutting collapsed on two boys, killing one; Petrie paid the compensation and wrote 'I cannot tell you all the misery this has been to me, it has undone me altogether'.[30] The details missing in this history of an accident, outside the control of Petrie himself, are the reminder that compensation was paid at a time of foreign military occupation. The reportage and reaction to the event in the Faqus area and in Egyptian newspapers remains to be researched. In later work, Petrie made sure that he took the greatest risks himself, as when he explored the subsiding subterranean corridors and chambers at pyramid sites such as Hawara.

At San al-Hagar in 1883 workers too had names:

> Like many other Europeans in a similar situation, Petrie found it difficult to remember the names of some of his workpeople; so often they were combinations of the most usual: 'Ali Hassan, Hassan Muhammad, Muhammad 'Ali, Ibrahim Ahmad, Ahmad Hassan, and so on; but others had less usual patronyms to distinguish them, and his memory was good; by the end of March he could put a face to every one of the 183 names on his payroll.[31]

Many were children, and there were girls as well as boys; in name-lists from later seasons that is not so evident, though clear in photographs. This biographical observation on naming workers introduces one of the most valuable sources for the social history of archaeology in the Petrie Museum archives: the payroll accounts in the pocket notebooks. Across the 163 notebooks preserved in the museum, the following contain name-lists of workers with the sums paid to them:

Delta sites, 1883–6: 74a, 74e, 98c–d, h
Hawara, Lahun, Ghurob, 1888–90: notebooks 39b, 48a
Tell Hesy, Palestine, 1890: notebooks 77, 78
Meydum, 1891 or 1910: notebooks 58, 60, 63
Quft, 1894: notebook 54
Naqada, 1895: notebooks 69, 71
Qurna (Thebes West), 1896: 84, 110
Dendera, 1897: notebooks 16, 17a
Hu, 1898: notebook 40a
Abydos, 1899–1902: notebooks 1–4
Tell el-Yahudiya and Wadi Tumilat, 1906: notebooks 104, 105
Rifeh, 1907: notebooks 85–9 (E. Mackay)
Memphis, 1908–13: notebook 7b (and Athribis), 68a, 68b (and Meydum)
Kafr Tarkhan, 1912–3: notebook 100
Qau, 1923–4: notebook 79

In addition, in the same series of pocket notebooks, the lists and the all-important sketches of ancient burials sometimes include a note of the name of the man or boy responsible for clearing the soil carefully enough from the burial for it to be drawn by Petrie or another European. Sketches of burials give name of finder for the sites Naqada (1895: notebooks 8–9, 11, 69–70, 136–40, 142–7), Zoweyda (1906: notebook 113), and Meydum (1912: notebook 67c). Lists of finds by tomb are marked with name for the sites of Tell el-Yahudiya and Saft (1906: notebooks 90–2, 104–6), Zaraby (1907: notebook 112), Sidmant (1920: notebook 95a). From 1912 to 1924, the recording of cemetery finds was formalised using printed index cards, and again many of these preserve the name of the man or boy who uncovered the finds (Harageh, 1914, Ghurob, 1920, some Abydos, 1922). Together with the rare archaeological photographs with captions recording names of non-Europeans, these pages should be enough to repopulate the archaeology of Egypt with people who provided its labour and brought in its harvest for study.

Notebook 98c provides the 'excavator's wage book San 1884'.[32] This roll-call restores the names of women and girls as well as men and boys, comes from the first Petrie mission to excavate in Egypt and contains an unusual number of annotations to names. For these reasons, although otherwise an unillustrated name-list, the 1884 litany of Egyptian names deserves initial presentation here, for all the uncertainties in reading the Latinised forms of names in the rather challenging handwriting of Petrie.[33] My annotations are enclosed in square brackets; round brackets are in the original. The references to 'brick', 'pylon' and 'stone' may imply different rates of pay for those clearing brick structures and those moving heavy stone at the Tanis temple gateway ('pylon') and elsewhere; if so, it would be interesting to determine which were paid more. These references to materials and workplace return the focus to the hard labour in this archaeology.

[Scan 2 right]*
Muhd Abu Abdeen
Ahmed Adib
Ahmed Muhd
Ahmed es Said
Aid Abdu
Fatimeh um Afi
Ali abu Afi
Ali Muhd (too quick [?])
Ali Salim (brick)
Muhd Alik [?]
Amneh Ali (small)
Amneh Salim (tall)

---

* 'Scan' refers to the individual page or double-page spread of Petrie's notebook as scanned on the published CD-ROM.

Arab Ali (one eye)
Salam Amtawa (on stone)
Ibrahim Ata
Auad + Ali Jafir Muhd
Aziz[a?] um Ibrahim tattoo

[Scan 3 left]
Said Bakhsheed [?] boatman's son
Balassi abd en Nabi
Balassi Mustafa
Ali abu Basha
Muhd abu Basha
Ali Baz
Said Bedawi
Ali Bedawi
Bedawi Muhd
Buhadadi Mursi (tall)
Buhadadi Said (small)
Buharieh Um Usuga
Ali Dafallah
Ibrahim Dafallah

[Scan 3 right]
Ahmed Daud
Daud Muhd
Muhd Daud (grey)
Muhd Dafani
Khadri Dafani
Muhd Hassan Dahabiyeh
Yusuf Dahabiyeh
Hassanen Etman
[here note 'Donkey 5 days at 3 ½']
Ibrahim el Faghi
Ahmed El Faghi (blue)
Farha (tall, bright)
Farag Hassanen
Hassan abd el Fatah
Ali [?] abd el Fatah

Fatimeh um Basha
Fatimeh um Ahmed

[Scan 4 left]
Abd el Gader (Mutwali)
Abd el Ad [?] Gandur
Hassanen Gandur
Ali Ganeb
Gazam Ali
Ahmed Hainawi (good, tall)
Hassan Abdullah (guard)
Hassan Ali (fresh)
Hassan Ahmed (big)
Hassan Muhd (Sharqawi)
Hassan Muhd (good)
Hassanen Ali (blue)
Ali abu Hassanen
Halimeh or Ibrahim Ali

[Scan 4 right]
Ibrahim Ali
Ibrahim abu Ali
Ibrahim Muhd
Ibrahim Salim
Ihfaim [?] Abdu (poor eyes)
Ali Jafer
Muhd Jafer
Jafer Hassanen
Khadijeh um Ibrahim (pink)
Khallil Hassein + substitute
Khallil Omar
Lamir Ahmed
Mabruka um Ali
Medallala [?] um Hassan
Derwish Mansoor
Khamsi Mansur
Salim Mansur (beard)

[Scan 5 left]
Abdullah Mansur + Mutwali
Ali Mansur
Abd el Ati Mansur
Salimeh Um Maraka [?]
Mattah Sad
Abul Saif Muftah
Muhd Ali discordant + Khallil
Muhd Hassan
Muhd Hassan [no note distinguishing from preceding]
Muhd Ibrahim
Muhd Um [?] Ibrahim
Muhd Abu Said (small)
Muhd Said Abdullah
Muhd Salim
Mursi Muhd
Muhd Mursi
Mursi Abu Shati
Mursi Mansur

[Scan 5 right]
Mustafa abu Said
Mutwali Muhd
Asharieh Mutwali
Muhd Nur
Osmali
Abd er Rahman Muhd
Fatimeh Um Rakha
Rakha Salameh (nose)
Muhd abder Rahman (on stone)
Abdu Riani (sharp)
Ali Salim Riani
Fatimeh Riani
Ali Sad (black)
Said Ali (French)
Said Ali ['+ Basha' erased]

[Scan 6 left]
Said Abu Ise
Said Abdullah
Said Hassan on pylon
Said Hassan (black rags)
Said Muhd + Fathy
Salam Ali
Salim Hassan big (open)
Mahmud Salameh (fat face)
Hassan es Salihi (stupid)
Sabha Muhd (gold ring)
Sabha Mustafa
Sabha Ali Salmeh + Sidahmed
Abd es Satur Ali (small)
Shalabi Ali
Sabha Sharqawi
Ahmed Shirbini
Said Abu Shindi
Said Sidahmed

[Scan 6 right]
Ibrahim Sidahmed (pretty)
El Grawi Sidahmed
Said ... [illegible] high
Sidahmed Abduh (ugly)
Smain Hassan (one eye, bright)
Smain Salim (pitted)
Ahmed Ismain Maskuta
Muhd es Suleiman
Ali Suleiman
Suleiman Ahmed
Suleiman ali ed din
Muhd Timras [?]
Umalkher Hassanein
Umalkher um Daud
Umbaraka um Ibrahim
Said Umgrawadi (bright)
Said Um es Said squint

Ibrahim abu Yusuf paint [?]
Yusuf Muhd + Riani
Yusuf abu Said

Ali as-Suefi from 1880s Lahun to 1920s Qau

It will be a great pleasure to have him with me again, for
I feel that all must go well with such a faithful, quiet,
unselfish right hand to help. As far as character goes he
is really more to me than almost any of my own race. Few
men, I believe, have worked harder for me or trusted me
more. Perhaps none are sorrier at parting, or gladder when
we meet again. A curious link in life but a very real one, as
character is at the bottom of it. Kipling's 'East and West' is
the only expression of such a link that I know.[34]

With these words Petrie recorded the arrival of Ali as-Suefi at
Bahnasa (Oxyrhynchus) in 1896, with his wife Fatma, their son, and
his younger brother Mahmud. On his way to excavate Amarna in
1891–2, Petrie had previously selected him and four other workers
from the freelance seasons in the Fayum, 1888–91:[35] Petrie describes
the enthusiasm of the men in a way that does not square with the
Western myth that Egyptians had no taste for either labour in
general, or digging the past in particular. Ali is credited with the eye
for detecting ancient remains at sites critical to understanding the
prehistory of Egypt.[36] His thirty years of archaeological labour were
noted as a *sed* (ancient Egyptian thirty-year kingship festival) when
Guy Brunton, succeeding Petrie, dug with his help in the Badari region
in the 1920s. Another essential worker was Erfai, one of the dozens of
men recruited at Quft and renowned in Egyptian archaeology ever
since as the Quftis. Of Ababda nomadic stock, Erfai was among the
only workers prepared to join Petrie on the expedition out of the Nile
Valley to the turquoise and copper mines of the Egyptians in Sinai in
1904–5, and his connections with Bedouin were crucial in the success
of the expedition.[37]

Yet, when Petrie came to write his own manual on archaeological method, halfway through his career, the 'workforce' and the 'archaeologist' are on two separate planets.[38] The workforce are trained, and good separated from medium and from unreliable: qualities of keen eyes and dexterous hands are, self-evidently, prerequisites for first uncovering and then preserving any fragile remains in the ground. These indispensable qualities were not enough to earn them the role of archaeologist: Petrie stated in a separate section that the latter should display scholarly and engineering skills, sense of history, strong visual memory, drawing skills. Petrie is a fascinating writer on archaeological method here, because he pays such unusual attention to practical skills, such as crating finds and transporting them safely, or the conservation of monuments, including back-filling. To appreciate such mundane skills, it should be noted how much has been, and continues to be, destroyed in transport of fragile antiquities, from site to store, store to museum, or museum to museum on the current global trade in exhibitions. Similarly, the non-archaeological reader needs to be aware that failure to cover over monuments has destroyed most, and continues to destroy them today. Petrie was a lone voice in emphasising the importance of physical dexterity, and so, if anyone was going to recognise the importance of worker skill, it should have been Petrie. Yet the Egyptian workers, in a class barred from formal education, remain outside his sight. In its failure to reward skill with training and opportunity, the Petrie manual amounts to an indictment of archaeological practice in enforcing class divisions, by Egyptians and foreigners alike. The corollary in the political economy of archaeology is the payroll, where earlier archaeologists again effectively condemn themselves in complaints over the piastres lost in minimal wages. It can always be countered that, practically, a foreign archaeologist cannot change class structures even under colonial military rule, and that the rural and regional workforce had no possibility of entry into the urban university environment. Against such claims stands the social mobility achieved in Egypt as in other countries, generally against the same structural odds; Saad

Zaghloul himself was, after all, of Egyptian farmer stock, and could enter al-Azhar university in 1873. The claims of impotence are also belied by the knowledge that few foreign or nationalist archaeologists seem to have tried or cared much in practice. Hopefully, here, there is some social history to be written of archaeologists or philologists finding grants to enable the ablest workers to enter university, and this negative history can be offset, but it seems unlikely to be more than a minority gesture.

Strike, 1920; Tutankhamun, 1922; the flight out of Egypt, 1924

In the interwar years, the last Petrie seasons in Egypt, labour and politics come to dominate and derail archaeological strategy. Here the workforce ceases to play the passive role assigned it by professionals, and archaeology has to recognise where it stands at the political divide. During the season at Lahun, 1919–20, for one day the local workforce went on strike, as their contribution to the nationalist protests sweeping Egypt under Zaghloul and his Wafd Party. This is an exceptional irruption of the political into the apolitical terrain dear to academic archaeological sensibility. More loyal (to Petrie, that is) Qufti workers did not join the strike.[39] One, Muhammad Osman, was mugged on his way from market the next season. Petrie remarked that 'had every Arab squatter within two miles of us been arrested at once, the cook could have recognised which of them attacked him, and the case would have been settled in twelve hours', but that the colonial administration of justice did not or could not intervene. No political dimension to the incident need be present on the Egyptian side, but the tone and vocabulary of the English response carry their own political dimension in the context of 1920s Egypt.

On 28 February 1922 the English ended their 'Protectorate' of Egypt by unilateral proclamation of independence for the land as a, still militarily occupied, kingdom. Petrie was among those reacting strongly against proposals to change the law on division of finds between excavator and Antiquities Service.[40] Providence intervened with a miracle. On 26 November 1922 a working-class Englishman, Howard Carter, with his not particularly wealthy aristocratic backer Lord Carnarvon, opened the tomb of King Tutankhamun in the Valley of the Kings. Division of such an extraordinary find would be an affront to the national sense of justice and to science alike. In 1923 the British establishment recognised Petrie on the occasion of his seventieth birthday with knighthood and a medal; the award was said to be 'for services to Egypt', an ambivalent honour on the terms of the colonial power.[41] In 1924 the legislative assembly elections swept Zaghloul and the Wafd Party to power, and the nationalist agenda was set finally to become law, even under continuing colonial domination. In the summer of 1926, Petrie gave up on divisions of finds in Egypt (in fact, for UCL they continued for six decades, throughout the presidencies of Gamal Abd al-Nasser and Anwar Sadat, and into the early years of the present president Hosni Mubarak, under whom one last division of finds, a potsherd sample from Mit Rahina, was assigned to the Egypt Exploration Society, and is now housed at the Petrie Museum). He requested his British School of Archaeology in Egypt to fund new work over the border with Palestine, along the Wadi Gaza, work that he would direct. In this final shift of excavating focus, Petrie moves ahead of a political wind, to a territory still colonial and so less distracting for archaeological fieldwork. In doing so, he makes transparent the place of politics at the heart of his work in enabling its existence.

The find that caused the political debate over divisions, Tutankhamun, had been a moment when Egypt had a chance to see an Englishman of a different class holding the reins of archaeological direction: Howard Carter.[42] For his first mission to Egypt as a teenager, in 1891, Carter had been employed for his artistic talent and for his humble background, making him cheaper for the Egypt Exploration Fund. Petrie found him amiable but not worth training. Perhaps class loses its distinctive edge across linguistic and cultural borders, and one English colonial would be much like another. It seems unlikely that the working-class soldiers of the army of occupation would have struck their unwilling hosts as particularly close. Yet archaeology and history are so closely guarded as part of the machinery of hegemony, that perhaps this intruder could have made, perhaps did make a difference. Perhaps class consciousness rather than Anglo-French rivalry lay behind the episode in which Carter was sacked for supporting Egyptian Antiquities Service workers against French-speaking tourists at Saqqara back in 1905. Apart from such rare biographical intrusions, there seems little prospect outside uniform for a working-class person of one country to meet a working-class person of another. The encounter has to be conjured as a fantasy. Here both museum and historian can use their powers. The museum can explore the politics of archaeology, as indeed the Ruhrlandmuseum Essen plans a major exhibition on archaeology and politics from the 1880s to the 1930s. In research and its publication, social historians might turn to the current popularity of 'object biography' in archaeology, extending the life history of an artefact as it moves from the eye and hands of its immediate excavator – man, woman or child (the digger: not the director or supervisor) – through the vagaries of freight, along with all the cotton pouring out of the Nile Delta towards Bolton and other northern English mill towns, to arrive before the hands and eyes of a faraway other man or woman or child in the same socially structured circumstances where manual labour is indispensable to a polity but brings no opportunity and slight reward.

Egyptian archaeology in English mill towns – and back?
Towards full circle

When Amelia Edwards encouraged the Egypt Exploration Fund to employ Petrie, she set the English museum-going public on the course of appreciating the small beside the large: the great monuments of stone, and the dramatic coffins and mummified bodies, were now guaranteed a new life beside the myriad objects of daily existence that archaeological fieldwork restores to human memory. In the 1820s, museums and their audiences in Europe had benefited from the discovery in Thebes of intact elite burials dating to the Eighteenth Dynasty (about 1550–1290 BC), a period at which furniture and musical instruments were placed in the tomb.[43] Crowds reacted with the same astonishment and delight at these very familiar and extremely refined works of 'decorative arts' from Egypt, as they had in the previous century to the uncovering of Pompeii and Herculaneum.[44] Subverting the nineteenth-century reign of historicism, these objects could suspend, even reverse, time. The archaeology of Petrie attended equally to all ancient work, whatever its quality or scale, because it served a new, later nineteenth century global map, social evolution in the path of Darwin. A crude work could be just as useful as an artwork, to illustrate the rise and fall of civilisations, as long as you knew where to put it. That, at least, was the ideology of the chronological display showing Victorian Man the path he had had to traverse to become so very great.

Yet the museum gallery can subvert its own framing story, simply because it links the previously unlinked among the powerless. Just as the factory-owner is forced to organise workers, raising their class-consciousness and promoting trade union militancy, the museum authority is forced to install a simple direct link between viewer and object, and cannot, in the end, hold back unwanted reactions – for example, an unintended sense of appreciation of what is held up as inferior on the authoritative evolutionary scale imposed by chronological order. Is there any chance that it might subvert the structured order still more powerfully, by drawing a line for the disadvantaged viewer out to not only the ancient users and makers, but to her and his contemporary disadvantaged finders along the Nile? Is there a metaphysics to the object that allows viewers in one place to see the viewers in another, those in one time to see those in another, and through all the permutations? Audiovisual gallery aids, most recently with webcam and audio guide are attracting attention among museum designers anxious to develop a new poetics in this public sphere. They may be the most direct means, but they remain mediated, and perhaps still rather depersonalised, unless the mobile develops its own new etiquette for greeting strangers. Performative encounters of a more traditional dramatic timbre may offer greater empowerment, and more variation in the media of delivery. However these routes are taken forward, they are acts of correction that the disciplinary institutions of museum, history and archaeology need to take for their own survival and for their redemption. For nowhere else does it feel more strongly that all monuments to culture are also monuments to barbarism.

Notes

1. J. Beinin, 'Egyptian Textile Workers: From Craft Artisans Facing European Competition to Proletarians Contending with the State', International Institute of Social History, conference 2004, online at http://www.iisg.nl/research/egypt.doc (consulted 18 March 2007), p. 6.
2. From the perspective of worker organisation: A. Fowler, 'British Textile Workers in the Lancashire Cotton and Yorkshire Wool Industries', International Institute of Social History, conference 2004, online at http://www.iisg.nl/research/britain.doc (consulted 18 March 2007), pp. 6–9.
3. Particularly the co-evality thesis expounded in J. Fabian, *Time and the Other. How Anthropology Makes its Object*, New York, 1983, noting the caution from Edward Said, see note 20 below.
4. C. Renfrew and P. Bahn, *Archaeology: Theories, Methods and Practice*, 3rd edition, London, 2000, chapter 1, 'The Searchers: The History of Archaeology', pp. 19–48.
5. M. Drower, *Flinders Petrie, A Life in Archaeology*, 1985.
6. E.g. Z. Hawass, 'Excavating the Old Kingdom: the Egyptian archaeologists', in D. Arnold, ed., *Egyptian Art in the Age of the Pyramids*, New York, 1999, pp. 155–65.
7. M. Wilmore, 'Landscapes of Disciplinary Power: An Ethnography of Excavation and Survey at Leskernick', in M. Edgeworth (ed.), *Ethnographies of Archaeological Practice: Cultural Encounters, Material Transformations*, Lanham, 2006, pp. 114–26.
8. M. Drower, *Flinders Petrie*, pp. 37–8.
9. Ibid., pp. 40–1.
10. E. Twohig, 'Pitt-Rivers in Munster (1862-65/6)', in *Journal of the Cork Historical and Archaeological Society*, 92, 1987, pp. 34–46.
11. On this famous Tasmanian woman, see V. Ellis, *Trucanini, Queen or Traitor*,

Canberra, 1981. For Pitt-Rivers on Irish and Australians, see M. Bowden, *Pitt Rivers. The Life and Archaeological Work of Lieutenant-General Augustus Henry Lane Fox Pitt-Rivers, DCL, FRS, FSA*, Cambridge, 1991, p. 56, and also on p. 10; 'the General abused the Irish not only in his overtly political speeches ... but also in his archaeological writings', citing from the classic archaeological excavation report *Excavations in Cranborne Chase*.

12. For the consequences of the ideology, and the engagement of higher education in England as elsewhere in Europe, see D. Stone, *Breeding Superman: Nietzsche, Race and Eugenics in Edwardian and Interwar Britain*, Liverpool, 2002, especially pp. 103–6 on Karl Pearson, Petrie's colleague directing the Eugenics Laboratory at UCL, to whom Petrie sent about two thousand examples of human remains from the 1890s to 1930s; now preserved at the Duckworth Collection, Cambridge University, these form today an essential resource for study of the ancient populations, as one of the only larger preserved population samples from the hundreds of thousands of burials unearthed during archaeological excavations; see http://www.human-evol.cam.ac.uk/Duckworth/history.htm.

13. A recent succinct, somewhat revisionist account of the famine is given by E. Purdon, *The Irish Famine 1845–52*, Cork, 2000. On the 'commonplace' English view, see B. Kinzer, *England's Disgrace? J. S. Mill and the Irish Question*, Toronto, 2001, pp. 67–8.

14. Cited in Drower, *Flinders Petrie*, p. 43.

15. Ibid., p. 47.

16. Drower, *Flinders Petrie*, pp. 48–9.

17. Ibid., p. 49.

18. In general, see A. Schölsch, *Egypt for the Egyptians! The Socio-Political Crisis in Egypt 1878–1882*, London, 1981.

19. R. Harrison, *Gladstone's Imperialism in Egypt: techniques of domination*, Westport, 1995, p. 57, on the Turco-Circassian officer issue as immediate cause of the Orabi rising.

20. Fabian, *Time and the Other*. For doubts over even the possibility of self-critical anthropology, see E. Said, 'Representing the Colonized: Anthropology's Interlocutors', in *Critical Inquiry*, 15, 1989, pp. 205–25, with the partial reply of Fabian, 'Dilemmas of Critical Anthropology', in his *Time and the Work of Anthropology: Critical Essays 1971–1991*, Amsterdam, 1992, pp. 245–64.

21. Cited in Drower, *Flinders Petrie*, p. 64.

22. Harrison, *Gladstone's Imperialism in Egypt*.

23. P. France, *The Rape of Egypt: How the Europeans Stripped Egypt of its Heritage*, London, 1991; B. Fagan, *The Rape of the Nile: Tomb Robbers, Tourists and Archaeologists in Egypt*, London, 1977. Although these accounts correct the heroising tendency, the use of the word 'rape' by white Western men unwittingly perpetuates an orientalist *leitmotif* of the 'Orient' as powerless female.

24. J. Rees, *Amelia Edwards: Traveller, Novelist and Egyptologist*, London, 1998.

25. Cited in M. Drower, 'Gaston Maspero and the Birth of the Egypt Exploration Fund (1881–3)', in *Journal of Egyptian Archaeology*, 68, 1982, pp. 299–317, on p. 309. '... as a subscription implies a Society, now it is a matter of nothing less than a Society analogous to that for the exploration of Palestine. This presents some difficulties. I do not imagine that anyone in England is thinking of forming a society to explore ancient Gaul: Egypt is rather in the position to be found in Gaul, not at all that to be found in Syria. In Syria, there is no antiquities service, there are no guards for monuments, no museums: in Egypt all that exists just as in France. Let me present you with the attitude of the Egyptian government. This government says: every year we spend a sum of so much for the maintenance and discovery of monuments. Doubtless, this sum is inadequate, but what would be the sum adequate for exploring a country like Egypt? You might tell me that in this case the disproportion between the allocated sum and the needs of the service is such that the monuments cannot be maintained and are perishing. Who destroys the monuments? The foreigners who scour the land year by year, buying antiquities, removing stone blocks, for the Louvre and the British Museum: they practise here what they never would, not in Germany, not in England, not in Spain, not in France, not in Italy. I am not inventing some imaginary conversation for you here: I am doing no more than repeating to you conversations that I have had with all the ministers who have succeeded one another since the time I arrived in Egypt.'

26. A particularly dismal incident in 1899, in which Petrie played his part, concerns the manoeuvring to replace Victor Loret with the more pliable and Anglophile Gaston Maspero, over the question of moving the body of Amenhotep II from his tomb to a museum, as Loret wished for security reasons, or leaving it in its tomb, as argued by press and public opinion, then as now. Loret duly lost his job, and the body of Amenhotep II was rifled within two years, and the remains finally removed to the safety of the Egyptian Museum, Cairo; see P. Piacentini, *La valle dei re riscoperta: i giornali di scavo di Victor Loret (1898–1899) e altri inediti*, Milan, LII–LVI.

27. Cited in Drower, *Flinders Petrie*, pp. 74–5.

28. Ibid., p. 75.

29. Ibid., p. 77.

30. Ibid., p. 79.

31. Drower, *Flinders Petrie*, p. 82.

32. Published in the *Petrie Museum Archive CD-ROM*, 1999, Notebook 98c, scans 2–6.

33. I am grateful to Rashid Elsheikh for his assistance in reading the names in the list. I have followed the spelling by Petrie, with unmarked long 'i' (e.g. Abdin) and Muhd as the abbreviation of respect for Muhammad.

34. Cited in Drower, *Flinders Petrie*, p. 226.

35. Drower, *Flinders Petrie*, p. 188.

36. Drower, *Flinders Petrie*: p. 247 on the area from Nag' Hammadi to Hu; p. 361 on the identification of the earliest farming culture of Upper Egypt

at Badari and Hemamia. The importance of Ali Suefi at the latter sites is acknowledged in G. Brunton, *Qau and Badari I*, London, 1927, p. 1: 'Our old Fayumi workman, Ali es Suefi, was with us as usual, and his experience was invaluable in detecting the sites of the cemeteries, which were often almost invisible on the surface'.

37. Drower, *Flinders Petrie*, p. 288.

38. W. M. F. Petrie, *Methods and Aims in Archaeology*, 1904.

39. Drower, *Flinders Petrie*, p. 349.

40. *Ibid.*, pp. 355–6.

41. P. Ucko and S. Quirke, 'The Petrie Medal', in *Living Symbols of Ancient Egypt = Public Archaeology*, 5.1, 2006, pp. 15–25.

42. N. Reeves and J. Taylor, *Howard Carter before Tutankhamun*, London, 1992.

43. Deposition of such material is not regular across time, but a distinctive phase in the burial customs of Egypt, see W. Grajetzki, *Burial Customs in Ancient Egypt: Life and Death for Rich and Poor*, London 2003.

44. S. Moser, *Wondrous Curiosities: Ancient Egypt at the British Museum*, Chicago, 2006, pp. 157–9, pp. 166–7 and pp. 228–9 on the impact of the display of 'objects of daily life' in the British Museum Egyptian Room, opened in 1837.

Nicholas Warner

Food for the Soul: the Restoration of the Gayer-Anderson Museum in Cairo

In the first half of the twentieth century, Egypt was home to a variety of British colonial administrators, many of whom fell in love with the country. John 'Bimbashi' MacPherson and Thomas Russell 'Pasha' have both left substantial written accounts of their life and times beside the Nile. There was, however, another Englishman who left, perhaps, an even more impressive visual reminder of his forty years in Egypt: R. G. Gayer-Anderson 'Pasha', known to his familiars as 'John'. Gayer-Anderson arrived in Cairo in 1906 to work as a doctor in the Egyptian Army. His career included medical commissions in Sudan and Libya and active service in Gallipoli, after which he was employed as the chief recruiting officer of the Army. He ended his government career in 1924 as Oriental Secretary to Allenby, but continued to make Cairo his home until his death in 1945. During this time, he devoted himself to his principal passion: collecting antiquities of the Pharaonic, Coptic and Islamic periods. He regularly transmitted his immense knowledge of the past to readers of *The Sphinx* magazine in entertaining articles with such titles as *How to Buy a Scarab* and *The Care of the Oriental Carpet*. Although he lived for much of his life in the downtown and Zamalek neighbourhoods of the city, he was always on the lookout for the opportunity to live in an 'Arab-style' house in what was then termed the 'native' quarter.

The museum in context, seen from the north-west. Photo: Tim Loveless.

His opportunity finally came in the 1930s, when his contacts enabled him to take up residence in an Ottoman house next to the famous ninth-century mosque of Ibn Tulun. This house, named the Bayt al-Kritliyya or 'House of the Cretan Woman' after its last owner, had been purchased by the Antiquities Department and restored to a safe structural condition. Gayer-Anderson continued that restoration, and furnished the house with his vast collection of objects, making it a delight for all those who visited him there. Upon his death, he bequeathed this collection to the Egyptian people, leaving the house as a museum. In recognition of this gift, King Farouk granted him the title of 'Pasha', and the museum bears his name until this day. It remains a place of enchantment, due to the architectural richness of its interiors and the fantastic variety of its contents.

The Museum had been one of my first stops in Cairo in 1992 when I came to live there and research the Islamic architecture of the city. For me, as an architect, it represented an Egyptian version of the Sir John Soane's Museum in London: one of those rare 'house-museums' where the character of the creator remains stamped upon the interiors, and is recalled by an often overwhelming collection of artefacts. My professional involvement with it began in 1998, when I met the grandson of the illustrious founder: Theo Gayer-Anderson, a building-fabric conservator. Together we toured the house, which must have been uncanny for him since it contained so many reminders of his family. And together we conceived a project to try to restore the museum and its displays. For the intervening years since the founder's death had not been kind ones: a sea of steel desks and filing cabinets – symbols of Egyptian bureaucracy – threatened to overwhelm the interior, and many of the collections were hidden away in cupboards, unseen by the visiting public.

An initial grant was given in 1999 by the 'Challenge Fund' of the British Foreign and Commonwealth Office, with which we constructed a new two-storey conservation laboratory and storage facility in dead space adjoining the house. This was the essential base for our operations, and the home of the existing team of Egyptian conservators working at the Museum. A variety of training workshops were held here, at the same time as work on the collections continued. The Museum is, in fact, not one house but two, linked by a bridge over an alley that leads to the outer precinct of the mosque of Ibn Tulun. Each house dates to the sixteenth century, and has a courtyard. In combination there are a total of thirty-five rooms of differing sizes and degrees of grandeur: some no bigger than a cupboard, and some of lofty proportions housing polychrome inlaid marble fountains. Many spaces have painted wooden ceilings rescued by Gayer-Anderson from traditional houses in course of demolition, as well as built-in architectural features. Some rooms bear surprising names: 'Byzantine', 'Chinese', 'Persian' and 'Queene Anne' can be found alongside the more expected harem rooms and winter and summer reception spaces. These testify to the range of collecting interests of the founder. Yet at the time of the commencement of the project, many rooms were shut, and there was no basic orientation information for visitors. To rectify this situation was, therefore, an immediate objective.

Into the first room to be restored went archival photographs of the house as it was in the 1930s, and a presentation of its history and architecture. The next room was the *sabil* or charitable water-dispensary attached to the house, originally designed with an enormous cistern beneath it, and a magnificent carved and painted wooden ceiling above. Neither had ever been seen before. Other rooms followed with entirely new displays using objects in storage (some 40 per cent of the collection), which were all conserved prior to their exhibition with improved lighting. These displays were mostly created within reclaimed storerooms and offices. Gayer-Anderson's study was rehabilitated with a biographical display including family photographs and life masks he made of his acquaintances – among them Freya Stark, the traveller and writer, and K. A. C. Creswell, the doyen of Islamic architectural historians. One room was set aside for a display of the esoterica of Islam: a unique collection of *sufi* paraphernalia such as crutches and begging bowls. Other rooms were dedicated to the past lives of women and children. These feature collections of portable birthing chairs, charms, fertility dolls, bath clogs, combs, spoons and jewellery. The Library, rich in volumes related to the history and topography of the Near East, was catalogued and given new bookcases. A room dedicated to Pharaonic art, with 150 previously undisplayed pieces, was established. It has been a continual delight to rediscover the full extent of the collection and to share it with others.

Work was not only limited to the interiors of the Museum. One of the courtyards was cleared of an accumulation of filing cabinets,

The restored library. Photo: Tim Loveless.

which were replaced by a Muhammad Ali period marble fountain and display of Roman, Coptic and Islamic column capitals. Perhaps the most complex project in terms of restoration was that undertaken in 2002–3 on the roof terrace which overlooked the mosque of Ibn Tulun. Sadly, this most magnificent panorama of the mosque had been blocked by the construction of a wall in the 1960s that was intended to deter burglars from breaking and entering. With the agreement of the Supreme Council of Antiquities the wall was removed, allowing the terrace to be redesigned to fully exploit the magnificent collection of *mashrabiyya* (turned-wood) screens displayed there. These screens had been salvaged by Gayer-Anderson from demolished houses in the 1930s, and installed on the perimeter of the terrace. All needed steam-cleaning, soaking in linseed oil, physical repairs and reframing in new supports that allowed for their future individual removal for conservation treatment. New trellis sunshades and lighting were introduced to enable the terrace to serve as a venue for cultural events. The large collection of Ottoman-period marble sink-backs, carved in a variety of floral patterns, were painstakingly cleaned and coated

The restored roof terrace with the mosque of Ibn Tulun to the left. Photo: Francis Dzikowski.

Detail of the mashrabiyya *wooden screens on the roof after restoration. Photo: Francis Dzikowski.*

New landscaping and outdoor theatre in the garden of the museum. Photo: Tim Loveless.

with microcrystalline wax to preserve them from the worst of the effects of the polluted atmosphere. Today the roof terrace is one of the most popular parts of the Museum, where visitors pause to enjoy the highlights of the Islamic architecture surrounding them, and the dappled light as it passes through the *mashrabiyya* screens.

The garden of the Museum has been another area of intensive activity. A significant piece of land extends to the south of the Museum, which had been already partially developed with new buildings for the police and a cafeteria block. These buildings, however, made no attempt to integrate themselves with the historic architecture of their context, and the garden lacked plants. The area was re-landscaped with two goals in mind: to provide better amenities for both the staff of the Museum and visitors, and to create a venue for cultural events. The former goal was achieved by constructing new offices and toilets (replacing the single functioning toilet within the Museum that served eighty-six staff as well as visitors), and creating a new shaded terrace for outdoor seating. The latter was achieved by gently terracing the site to form an outdoor theatre. This was framed by hedges, bougainvillea on trellis-work, and a collection of Ptolemaic and Greco-Roman stone capitals mounted on plinths. These capitals, made of limestone, granite and basalt, were transported here from the Citadel where they had been in storage since the 1960s when the Mamluk mosque that they were reused in was demolished.

I hope that one day the Museum will play host to an increased range of cultural events that exploit its full potential. The possibility for it to function in this manner now exists for the first time. This would certainly be very much in accordance with the founder's wishes, who intended his home to celebrate the best of the artistic traditions of both East and West. He took pains, during his lifetime, to collect and publish the plethora of legends surrounding the house and the mosque of Ibn Tulun that had been handed down by oral tradition. He also reinvigorated the local *mawlid* (saint's day celebration) of the Sheikh buried in a tomb adjacent to the house. Such goals may be difficult to achieve, but remain worth striving for.

The restoration of the Gayer-Anderson Museum has been executed while the Museum has remained open to visitors at all times. All work has been carried out with the full endorsement of the Supreme Council of Antiquities, under whose authority the Museum falls. The project has been funded by a variety of sponsors during the last six years. As these sponsors receive little in the way of public acknowledgement for their contributions, apart from a discreet notice on new visitor information panels, it is appropriate to record their generosity here. Our work would not have been possible without the support of the Barakat Trust, the Cultural Fund of the Royal Netherlands Embassy, the Ford Foundation, the Egyptian Antiquities Fund of the American Research Center in Egypt, BP Egypt, Daimler Chrysler Corp., Oriental Weavers, and the British Egyptian Business Association. Much work still needs to be done, however, to maintain and improve the Museum. Only a third of the spaces within the building have been restored. Egypt has many needs, both social and economic, as it embarks on a new century. It also has a need for places such as the Gayer-Anderson Museum, which offer delight to the eye and food for the soul.

PETER MACKENZIE SMITH

On Education: UK–Egypt Relations Since 1956

My objective is to look at some of the ways in which Egypt and the UK have worked together in the general areas of education, training and learning over the past fifty years or so, since relations were restored after Suez, and to suggest a theme or two for future cooperation and some ways of working.

Egypt sequestrated all British assets in the country when the invasion started in 1956. One of the effects of this was extraordinary: the British Council, under sequestration and with its British staff expelled, continued its activities in Egypt under the enlightened leadership of its appointed sequestrators, Rashad Rushdi and Morsi Saad ud Din. Perhaps the only example of an invaded country continuing the cultural and educational activities of the invaders.

This augured well for the educational relationship, and a start was made in the early 1960s when the Egyptian government instituted a scholarship programme that brought some 2,000 postgraduate students to British universities. Such a dramatic commitment also helped to restore some of the academic links that had existed before Suez. This was particularly true of the medical profession, which in many ways, along with Egyptology, forms the most enduring link there is between the two countries. Egyptian students sat the exams of the UK Royal Colleges, and faculties of medicine renewed their connections after the briefest of interludes.

The other theme was the English language.

The 1960s saw the restoration of UK connections at school level, with teachers from Voluntary Service Overseas taking up posts in the English-medium schools in Cairo and Alexandria and in government secondary schools in Luxor and Aswan (foreigners were not, until 1975, allowed to live anywhere else). UK specialists in English language and curriculum development were also appointed to Ministry of Education teaching centres in Cairo (Manshiet El Bakry) and Alexandria (Bulkeley).

In the late 1960s English language teaching projects were set up in the English Departments at Ain Shams and Alexandria Universities with UK and Egyptian lecturers working together with additional resources provided by both sides. These operations, very large by today's standards, continued for some years and exercised great influence over the teaching of English at Egyptian universities. They were funded, in part, by the Overseas Development Administration (now the UK's Department for International Development, DFID). There was also a smaller, but important, effort in English literature with visits by authors like P. H. Newby and Iris Murdoch and fellowships for Egyptian English literature students to do part of their research in Britain.

By the time of the 1973 war, and especially after President Sadat's 'Open Door' policy was introduced, relationships were on a much steadier footing and more significant programmes began to develop as Egypt started to expand its links away from the USSR and the Warsaw Pact countries.

The first major UK effort was in developing a new kind of technician training school at Moharem Bey in Alexandria. This was done through a twinning arrangement, one of the first of its kind, between Moharem Bey School and Bradford College. Teachers from both sides worked on new curricula, teaching methods and equipment in a wide range of engineering subjects and Egypt began to produce high quality technicians by the mid to late 1970s.

The Moharem Bey example (which was supported by substantial funds under the British aid programme) was followed by a range of other technical training initiatives as Egypt began to draw upon World Bank finance. This led to new partnerships, as illustrated below:

Twinning: the Ministry of Education's Five Year Technician Schools

	Egypt	UK	Subject specialisation
1.	Moharem Bey	Bradford	All
2.	Zawia al Hamra	Oldham	Teacher Training
3.	Dar es Salaam	Humberside	Building Trades
4.	El Wardian	Teesside	Petrochemicals
5.	Zagazig	Bradford	Diesel
6.	Galal Fahmy	Bradford	Mechanical/Electrical
7.	Girga	Bolton	Teacher Training
8.	Ismailia	Worcestershire	College of Agriculture
9.	Port Said	Anniesland	Shipbuilding/Marine
10.	Aswan	Humberside	Refrigeration and A/C
11.	Minia	Humberside	Refrigeration and A/C

These links not only produced standards and curricula for new skills in Egypt, but developed ways of working in international technical education which were innovative and had a wider impact than on the individual schools involved. These activities broadened significantly in the 1980s and 1990s with UK engagement with education in Egypt at the secondary and higher education levels. A number of research links between universities in the two countries were initiated and supported under the UK government's Academic Links Scheme and there was much UK engagement in reform programmes in different university faculties (for example the Cairo University Faculty of Agriculture). Egyptian students continued to benefit from the Egyptian and the British governments' scholarships and technical assistance programmes, and these reinforced a widening range of professional and academic relationships. Today the Egyptian Ministry of Higher Education supports some 500 postgraduate and PhD students in the UK at any one time.

Parallel investments were made in the 1980s on the vocational training side through the Ministry of Labour's training institutes, also with UK involvement. I'm not sure these were as effective as the education programmes and I would like to return to this subject. Another example of cooperation in those days was the reform of the Egyptian Electricity Authority's training activities through a partnership with the UK's Central Electricity Generation Board.

On the foundations built by these operations and the professional relationships and ways of working they initiated, Egypt and the UK have, over the past ten years, begun to focus on the drastic requirements of educational reform itself. There have been exchanges concentrating on the achievement of international standards in qualifications and on how to improve teaching methods, research capacity, and curriculum development and updating.

One of the most significant investments in this area of educational exchange has been the Egyptian Ministry of Education's teacher training programme, initiated in 1992. Since then an average of 350 school teachers a year from primary, preparatory and secondary schools have visited the UK for three-month training programmes at British universities (Strathclyde, Edinburgh, Exeter and East Anglia among them) with the objective of studying teaching methodology, curriculum development and the use of information technology in schools. The programme focuses on maths, science and English language teachers. The teachers follow an initial orientation programme at the Mubarak Academy in Sixth October City before travelling to the UK. For 2006–7, the budget for this programme has been doubled to £4 million per year, and 800 Egyptian teachers will be participating.

One new development we have seen in the past few years is the significant growth in the role of the private sector in education in both countries. The British University in Egypt opened for business earlier this year and there are now a number of private universities in Egypt with UK links, as well as those oriented more towards Canada, the US, France and Germany. This ought to introduce greater flexibility into the system as a whole and help with my proposal below.

What next? It looks as if one of Egypt's (as well as Britain's) biggest challenges is to make the whole education and training process better attuned to the needs of business and industry. This doesn't just mean vocational training. It means looking much more carefully at what schools and universities do too. The complaints we hear from the Egyptian private sector are common in the UK as well: why doesn't the education system produce people who are much more immediately employable, who know how to work with others as much as they do about their academic subjects. I know from my own experience of working at the interface between industry and education how difficult the relationship can be between the two, and I do not have any easy answers. I believe we should start to look for action in this area and that it would be a fruitful field for British Egyptian cooperation.

HODA RASHAD

Youth and Education: Proposals for Collaborative Activities

This essay is divided into three parts, covering: introductory remarks; proposals for collaborative activities as well as a call for integrating a gender and equity perspective in the planning and implementation efforts.

I) Introductory remarks

My opening remarks provide three brief reflections commending both the objectives of this publication and the relevance of framing part of the discussion therein around youth and education.

1. The current context

The objectives and orientation of this publication draw on a changing paradigm. There is an assumption, as summarised in the title, of a shift from conflict, war, tension symbolised in the Suez war, towards a move for present and future collaboration.

Unfortunately, the current context of bilateral relations is clearly different from the underlying paradigm of this discussion. There is clearly a separation between the formal view and public and societal perceptions. The recent political developments on a number of fronts have alienated large groups in both of our societies. The vocabulary of occupation, aggression, fear, threat, isolation and marginalisation is much more predominant nowadays than a decade or two ago.

The wounds that we thought were healed are being reopened. Roger Owen's chapter comments on the wisdom of the Egyptian public in differentiating between people and policies. I do agree with this stand and I would argue that the question of 'Why do they hate us?' should have been 'Why do they hate our politics?' I would, however, warn that recently the lines between people and policies have started to become blurred.

It is indeed a welcome sign that we (the authors of this volume) as a group are trying to address these recent tendencies and to open a space and bring to the debate a breath of fresh air.

The difficulties we are currently feeling should encourage rather than discourage a frank discussion. It should guide us towards action rather than lead us to passive inaction.

2. *The term collaboration*

This term should be interpreted to be built around mutual benefits rather than a sugar coat for welfare assistance. Both of our societies stand to benefit from sound bilateral relations that are built on understanding, respect and fairness.

The fact that DFID decided to stop its programme in Egypt based on a conceptualisation of development cooperation as welfare assistance should be revisited. Welfare is very different from development. Cooperation is different from assistance.

3. *The focus on youth and education*

Youth and education are excellent entry points for a discussion of collaborative bilateral ties. They both capture the core of the challenge facing the development processes in our countries but also both hold the promise of a better future.

We need to admit we are facing serious problems on both fronts. The fact that our youth are regressing and not progressing should not go unnoticed. The resurgence of intolerance and fanaticism among the young and educated in both of our societies is a real cause for concern.

Youth is truly a stage in life that mirrors the functioning of the society. Indeed, a sign of development and success is the ability of societal organisations to provide space for inclusiveness and participation for its youth, a space where the legitimate needs and aspirations of the emerging leaders of the next generation are catered for and where the promise of a better future is not an elusive dream.

Education determines the content and the boundaries of such a space. It is an arena where values are influenced, skills are shaped and through which opportunities are grasped.

II) Proposals for collaborative activities

The proposed activities have two clear features. First, they respond to key challenges facing youth and education. Second, they draw on practical examples that have demonstrated their values.

The challenges can be summarised by the limited success of the educational system, particularly in developing countries, to adequately address the three building blocks of development: values, skills and opportunities.

The proposed ideas emphasise one or more of these key ingredients. They draw on ideas that have already been tried and have shown their worth. They are down-to-earth and simple, and we can find many examples of them already applied nowadays. But my message is that they are few, scattered, receiving neither the support of our two governments nor the attention of the private sector.

The first few examples, allowing for interpersonal exposure and acquisition of general skills, include:

Exchange of high school students who will reside for a year with a host family in the other country. A programme of personal ties and cultural understanding that can never be replicated by any educational curriculum. Penelope Lively's chapter is excellent testimony to the value of these types of programmes. The American Field Service Program, which goes back as far as the seventies, is but one example of a more systematic and sustained programme. There are also similar illustrations, but which may be less well-known, in some European countries that we can draw upon.

The programme of student interns implemented by the American University in Cairo with collaborating universities in the United States is also a promising model. In this programme, fresh graduates at the top of their classes in American universities work for a year in an Egyptian academic setting learning new skills while mingling in society. This programme could be easily replicated with the newly established British University in Egypt or any other university in Egypt where English is the language of teaching.

Other models targeting the building of specialised skills could take a number of formats, including:

The very much appreciated higher education scholarships and links already offered by the British Council.

These could be easily complemented and expanded in scale by offering scholarship opportunities for high-quality university education within Egypt. An example of a very promising programme offered by USAID in Egypt is the two scholarships per governorate in Egypt (a total of fifty-six scholarships) for high school students graduating from national schools to study at the American University in Cairo. This leadership programme is a valued opportunity to level the playing field and allow a competitive edge for less advantaged students unable to afford the cost of high quality education.

Another programme of the British Council that could be easily expanded and modified is the Bridge Programme. The programme connects some projects run in Egypt and the UK. This programme could be implemented as an add-on to every collaborative activity involving Egyptian and UK counterparts.

For example, the Social Research Center of the American University in Cairo is currently part of a research consortium generously funded by DFID. This consortium can include the exchange of young trainees from Egypt and the UK.

Another initiative cited at the British Council site under vocational/technical training deserves much more investment and expansion. The Khol-Mubarak initiative in Egypt, targeting high-quality vocational training catering for the needs of Egypt's industry, is an initiative that demands replication, particularly in the tourism and nursing fields. These are sectors where the expertise and relative advantage of the UK is well established.

DFID could return to Egypt holding that banner, or we could call on the private sector to get more involved. Indeed, the private sector could adopt an initiative such as the BG/Orascom Alliance for Development.

Another programme that could be discussed is a programme which benefited from private/public partnership; the Egypt–US parliamentary exchange programme involving collaboration between the privately-established technical bureau of a member of the Egyptian Parliament (Badrawi Technical Bureau) and the American Council of Young Political Leaders. The exchange is designed to develop skills and understandings between young congressional staffers/volunteers in the two countries.

These are a few ideas that we could choose from and prioritise. My personal preference would push to the forefront the formation of values and the shaping of morality based on interpersonal exposures and relations.

I am intentionally not emphasising the task of education to prepare young people to enter the labour force. My concern is the task of education to prepare young people to embrace and contribute to life.

I am a believer in Martin Luther King Junior when he points out that education has a two-fold function. The first is the utility function of providing efficiency and intelligence and allowing the transmission of accumulated knowledge. The second function is that of morality, the building of character, the choice of purpose in life, the respect for differences and plurality. He warns that 'education which stops with efficiency may prove the greatest menace to society' and that 'the most dangerous criminal may be the man gifted with reason, but with no morals'. He also noted that: 'The complete education gives not only power of concentration, but worthy objectives upon which to concentrate.'

A cursory look at both of our societies would reveal the increasing danger that is taking hold: our societies, which were once proud of their multiculturalism, inclusiveness, assimilation and tolerance, are being invaded by fear, divisive stereotyping, misunderstanding and extremism.

Indeed, it is the veiling of the mind that should be targeted as our common enemy. The recent discourse in Britain around the face veil should alert us to the fictitious divide between 'us and them'. The polarities of the discourse should never have been portrayed as between the West and Muslims; the face veil, as a religious symbol not as a dress code, invites even stronger negative reactions from within the Muslim community. I could easily illustrate this point with concrete evidence from Egypt.

This example demonstrates the clear need for a more sophisticated and differentiated discourse that recognises that within our different cultures we have commonalities and alliances that should not give way to polarisation.

III) Integrating an equity perspective

Finally, let me conclude by calling for the collaborative programme not just to be targeting ideological and value changes but also to be explicitly guided by a value position.

The call is for an equity perspective to be a central feature in all our collaborative activities. Our collaborative programme must reflect a moral position. It needs to adopt equity as a core value and to place this explicitly in the mainstream of all its activities.

Both of our societies suffer from the marginalisation and alienation of large groups. In the UK, a very recent report introduced by Ken Livingstone, the Mayor of London, on 'The Situation of London Muslims in 2006', documented worrying inequities and biases as well as stereotyping.

In Egypt disparities by social class and examples of gender discrimination are abundant. Let me take the example of technical education in Egypt to illustrate the inequity dimension. This type of education is simply the place where the underprivileged cluster. They do not get an education or a job. The Egyptian government has recognised this problem and is exerting a lot of effort and allocating resources to reform technical education. The reform until now has been insensitive to the gender bias that is dominant in this type of education. Girls are clearly disadvantaged on all fronts. They are concentrated in the least competitive branches (commercial as compared to industrial) of this type of education. The reform efforts do not address their needs or encourage them to change specialisations and, more importantly, their prospects for employment and decent work are significantly lower than those of their male counterparts. A gender-sensitive reform programme is badly needed.

PAUL SMITH

Beyond Bilateralism:
Globalising Education for Future Security

It is a privilege for me to be asked to contribute to the most substantive appraisal of the bilateral UK–Egyptian relationship since Suez. For a Brit, like myself, who happened to be born in 1956, this volume is resonant with recognition about the trajectory of learning that my country has passed through in this half-century, a half-century against which my own life has been plotted. Anecdotally it has been interesting to register, over the decades, the common response to my declaring my year of birth, '56? Ah, Suez!', followed by a regretful sigh, a coupling of embarrassment and lost opportunity, the contemporary taintedness of the-way-we-were.

I'm delighted to be invited to contribute in my capacity as Director of the British Council in Egypt because this book concentrates on exploring a *relationship*, a fifty-year relationship of increasing collaboration. I would like to think that the British Council's prominent presence in Egypt itself continuously signals the UK's fullest commitment to on-the-ground fuelling of that relationship educationally, culturally and professionally. And we thrive on the knowledge that this support is mutual and reciprocated, perhaps especially through the work of the Egyptian Cultural Bureau in London and the imaginative initiatives stimulated by the Egyptian Embassy in the UK:

We should remind ourselves at the outset that, though the British Council works from centres in 110 countries, we have been operating in Egypt for longer than in any other. In 1938 when, for the first time, a British Council sign was put over a foreign front door, that door was in Cairo.

We work in closest liaison with the British Embassy and are indeed part funded by the UK Foreign and Commonwealth Office – as is our sister organisation, which has also contributed so much to the evolving relationship between the UK and Egypt: the BBC World Service. But we work between peoples rather than between governments and we engage in long-term relationship building for mutual benefit and try to avoid the shorter-term diplomatic imperative.

I do not believe it is my place to deliberate on what the education reform process in Egypt or in Britain independently should be focusing on. Though I would note that the British Council in Egypt is encouraging more UK support at those primary points – curriculum development, quality assurance, teacher development, HE sectoral growth and innovative method in the classroom – than has been seen for many years, and all in the strongest cooperation with the Ministries of Education and of Higher Education and Scientific Research. The British Council will shortly be enabling the Minister of Education to make his second visit to the UK in some six months with a practical agenda relating to comparison of quality assurance programmes and the introduction of ICT in the classroom.

Instead I want to plot my short contribution via two main assertions.

The first is that education policy for the future, and for our bilateral educational relationship, must be increasingly conceived within a regional and global embrace. Merely national or bilateral policy will more and more condemn nations to be left lagging in a newly fast-paced world of educational exchange and collusion.

The second point is that there have traditionally been two core missions to education. But now there are three. The third draws to the heart of the new trust and security that we must achieve in a transformed domain of international relations and interdependence and within which we *all* need to be re-educated.

Suez '56 – it is that place in Egypt and that date which has given the history of modern Britain its ironic slant. In some ways, 1956 is the definitive date in contemporary British history, as 9/11 may become the iconic defining moment for the contemporary US's sense of its place and reason in the world. Similarly the phrase 'East of Suez' – laden with Orientalist baggage – still retains an atavistic potency as we manoeuvre our way through a newly fractured East–West world.

So, to focus on this bilateral relationship in 2006 is salutary. But this book has already revealed that the days have now passed in which it makes sense solely to consider the future in terms of a bilateral past. The same applies to the relations between any two countries in the twenty-first-century world. In the past decade of these last five decades – maybe in just the past five years – the world has shown itself to be ungraspable, and unmanageable, except in regional and, increasingly, in global terms. It is now impossible intelligently to disaggregate to the bilateral – and the implications for education are manifold.

It is essential to look at education primarily in the context of the new demands and opportunities offered by the world's newly evolving sense of international relations. Looking at the front pages of any newspapers in Cairo or in London in October 2006, it was immediately evident what the informing global issues of the day were. Essentially there are two and both will inform, and increasingly govern, nearly every aspect of our, and all other paired countries' relationships. Any responsible educational policy must be reoriented in line with these two worldwide scenarios and it will be the intrinsic purpose of education to determine whether these scenarios turn to opportunity or threat.

The first dominating issue is, literally, how we manage, protect and share the natural resources of our planet. Our future overriding global concern will be the way we care for, or gradually destroy, the earth itself, our only home. This is the global concern that is gradually drawing all aspects of international economy, industry, commodities, resourcing and wealth creation into its grasp.

And the second aspect of globalisation which must be the domain for our bilateral relationship, including its educational parameters; is this not our natural *context* (climate and resources) but, even closer to home, our human *text*?

In particular, as globalisation generates homogeneity, how shall we address and uphold the levels of mutuality, distinction, cultural trust and respect, shifting identities and, above all, the values we must attain in common, as a single human species, and the differences that we must celebrate as a diversely evolved pattern of cultures, conditions and faiths? How are we going to live plurally and tolerantly as one world?

I suggest that education's new imperative must be the re-skilling of a world to protect and sustain itself by teaching each individual to realise his or her global identity. All of us committed in the past to the progressing of bilateral relations and regional collaborations must now stretch the arc of our embrace to its circumference. The increasing regionalisation and globalisation of nationalistic concerns must cause all nations to reconsider the mission of education in the modern world. This perhaps particularly applies to countries, such as Egypt, which feel that their values, cultures and faiths are being widely misrepresented and misunderstood, and perhaps wilfully demonised, and to other nations, such as Britain, which feel themselves to be newly constituted of multiple cultures and identities.

A few years ago people would probably have spoken of two main missions for education. One would be vocational – that education which directly prepares young people for the world of work. This centres on professionally and technically oriented learning which meets individual career ambition but which is in danger of seeing the human resource of a country as just that, a resource – to realise the country's socioeconomic potential. In Egypt, as throughout the Middle East, this remains government's key educational imperative, particularly in developing an educational system capable of filling the one hundred million new jobs which need to be found to fulfil the growing young workforce of the next fifteen years. The second main mission of education would traditionally be seen as the need to recognise the human dignity and the human right of personal growth through learning. This is an education which plays to the Latin origins of the word – education which brings out from the individual that which is latent within them.

Unlike vocational learning, this is an educational principle which thrives in interpretative and analytical cultural contexts, particularly such as grew in Britain after the Reformation moved minds from Catholic dictate to Protestant conscience, which increased again after the so-called Enlightenment gave more central prominence to human over divine interpretation and, further in the nineteenth century, when science and secularism rigorously questioned inherited pedagogy. In the UK, such education finally blossomed during the twentieth century when postmodernist questioning undermined the status of the fixed curriculum and the set text.

It remains a question of importance, but also of sensitivity, to continue to research the impact of differing contemporary faiths, political ideologies and value systems on educational policy and method. The central consideration of the teacher/student relationship and the possibilities of enlightened pedagogy need researching through some relevant pairings, including: the impact of Islamic and Christian hermeneutical methods, inclusive or exclusive authority and participation, and tendencies to the autocratic or to the democratic.

Traditionally, then, there have been two highways through education: the vocational, particularly bringing directly useful knowledge and skills, and learning for personal growth, bringing self-realisation and fulfilment in life. But our newly regionalising and globalising world is constructing a third highway through education, a third purpose which it is essential that educationalists in Egypt, and the UK, and everywhere else, should accept as a critical task of lifelong learning. It will lead not so much to an emphasis on skills and expertise, self-realisation and personal fulfilment, but will help deliver worldwide networks of trust and a continually open space for the changing conversation of mankind. Beyond trust, this education must deliver future security – from conflict prevention to the demolition of radicalisation and fundamentalism as exclusive means of learning and knowing. And beyond trust and security, the new education, this third way, may turn out to be our key hope for survival. This is an educational mission which must make our children, and in fact all living generations of men and women, more globally knowing and interculturally aware. It is a continuing education in world citizenship – a phrase which reeked until recently of platitudinous aspiration and somewhat do-gooding after-school activity such as running model student United Nations. But, again, in the last five years or so, seeking to make communities of world citizens of all our populations has become a seriously intelligent directive. Education has traditionally taught us all to survive and thrive in our local habitat and with full emphasis on playing our part in our national society. But that is now a scale and scope of education which is insufficient for the singular, fragile and now totally networked planet that we inhabit.

There may not be a 'clash of civilisations' as such but we all know that the dynamics that are going to determine our children's futures ignore national boundaries and have to be realised, understood and engaged with in a globally plural way. Education as international appreciation and the nurtured will to collaboration is the education critical to world security and survival. Our children, as globally responsible and responsive citizens, must learn to understand:

- How to recognise and discuss universal values;
- How to discern relativism in cultures and belief systems;
- How to celebrate the diversity of world traditions and cultures;
- How to allow their appropriately energising patriot-

isms to embrace the responsibilities of collaboration creative of community on a shared planet;
- How to champion rightful citizenship and to stretch the embrace of civil society from the parochial to the global.

One of the chief sponsors of the conference upon which this book is based, HSBC, has an inspiring motto: 'the world's local bank'. That's a concept which needs to be similarly constitutional in our educational systems and in our educational method. In the twenty-first century, global and local are becoming completely symbiotic.

Common, and therefore responsibly shared, international responsibilities and the new global terrors are not going to be solved by the imposed short-term foreign policy actions of governments or by the outrages of terrorist or factional groups. The move to globalisation and world citizenship – a move which must still celebrate local identity and belief – must also be a move towards a new nurturing of, and by, our peoples themselves. This must be, in the broadest sense, an educational venture, taking place at all levels of all societies, and it must increase exponentially from these times onwards.

Yet it is ironic to realise that this aspect of internationalising education is not so new – certainly not so new for Egypt and the Middle East in their relations with Britain and Europe. We have to take a long trajectory over the centuries of nationalism to draw this circle. But we can – from the viewpoint of the Egypt–UK bilateral relationship – look to a time before national self-consciousness and commitment to patriotic cause so strongly determined people's sense of their place in the world. We can look to a time when cultures, faiths and shared identities played a greater role in determining place, meaning and reputation in the world. This was the time of a more fluid sense of demographic profile and constituent identity, a time and sense of geographic space which was not so threatened, for instance, by immigration, and in which the processes of learning and research were framed more by larger-scale regional cultural commitments than by any country loyalty.

The spread of Islam, the European and Levantine gestation of Christianity, continent-wide monastic scholarship, the parameters of Empire and the transforming centuries of Renaissance and Reformation – these were the contextual environs of education, knowledge and learning in our pre-modern world. Our fullest understanding of the engagement of the West, of the UK, with the Middle East, the Arabic and Islamic world today, might be informed by our still evolving knowledge and appreciation of the intellectual and spiritual infrastructures of these worlds between 500 and 1,500 years ago.

Let us remind ourselves that collaborative study, research and knowledge advocacy has this long trajectory of historical association between the Middle East and Europe.

The roots lie deep in time. At the period of the earliest growth of universities in Europe – Bologna and Paris, Oxford and Cambridge, the first Scottish universities – many of the scholarly disciplines in which they were founded derived from the influences, retentiveness and well-established academic leadership of the Middle Eastern and North African world, with Egypt, then as now, as cultural hub and place of academic interchange. The growth of universities in Britain and Europe ran parallel to the Western rediscovery of learning and the growth in Europe of more scholastic and interpretative endeavour. Inspirational to that revival of learning were sources of established patterns of learning from the Middle East – Arabic mathematics, scientific method, astronomy, logic, philosophy, geometry, rhetoric, aesthetics and even comparative theological hermeneutics. In addition to this Arabic and early Islamic scholasticism, there is the historical fact that, as Europe passed through its so-called Dark Ages, it was the centres of learning across the Middle East – and particularly Cairo and Alexandria – that retained, protected and nurtured much of the learning of other Mediterranean cultures, including the classical knowledge and texts of the Graeco-Roman world. Many of the disciplines of the newer universities, in England and Scotland, in France and Italy and in Iberia, were based on the scholastic traditions deriving particularly from the disciplinary method of Aristotle whose works had been, in part, lost to Europe but explored and studied across the Middle East and particularly in the Egyptian centres of learning throughout those centuries.

So the classical learning foundation of European higher education was, from inception, part of a regional bilateral dependency, reliant on the partnership with and dissemination from the Islamic world. The migration of knowledge and learning was primarily achieved through the dedication of many Arabic scholars. In 2006 we might cite just the one example of Ibn Khaldun who migrated from Spain across North Africa to his final place of study in Cairo where he died exactly six hundred years ago. The way our new century, our new millennium is taking us, should encourage us to remember anew this longer historical panorama so as to see our national and bilateral relationships and platforms as typical of just a five-hundred year-lacuna in a two-millennia stretch of otherwise regionally fluid, staunchly intercultural, globally migrational education and scholarship. It is this that we must re-conceive for our own times.

There is then an imperative to internationalise our educational policies and directives. National systems and bilateral initiatives must understand themselves within this broader embracing context. Indeed, the internationalising of education in the current Egypt–UK partnership can already be seen to be moving in this direction.

There is the evident involvement in each other's university structures. A range of the newer private universities in Egypt are – playing to the 'universality' inherent in the 'university' concept – seeking quality assurance and international benchmarking through accreditation and academic infrastructural merger with UK universities, which already operate more within an international paradigm. Thus we see new partnerships between the British University in Egypt and with Loughborough, Exeter and others, between Modern Science and Arts University and Middlesex and

Greenwich, between the Future University and a Scottish higher education consortium and, most recently, we have seen overtures between the Pharos University in Alexandria and the University of Wales.

Looking far beyond the historical trajectory earlier described, it is inspiring to see new European, and particularly British, partnership with the al-Azhar University where, through the British Council's support with quality assurance systems and the implanting of a new department to teach English to faculty and students, al-Azhar is again growing able to negotiate the discussion of Islamic theology, teachings and jurisprudence with a Western world within which it had for too long lost its voice.

The last two years have seen robust consolidation of the determination to get young people of the variant cultures of the UK and Egypt into conversation through new emphasis on school linkage and shared curricula. This is not just through the wider dissemination of the IGCSE and A-level portfolio which is offered by some one hundred Egyptian schools to 10,000 to 15,000 Egyptian students each year, but also through the new protocols being introduced to encourage regular school linkage and exchange, most notably the *Global Gateway* programme run by the British Council worldwide for the UK Department for Education and Skills and signed by the Egyptian Minister of Education just a few months back.

The processes of accreditation described here involve the opening of overseas campuses of national universities, the franchising of reputed higher, professional and vocational educational qualifications to foreign universities and the increasing provision of school qualifications of global surety. All these are critical to the process of establishing international standards of teaching and assessment which will continuously move towards consensus on what are the values which must underpin the choice of syllabus and curricula contents and the methods of exploring and interpreting these.

From the UK side, much of the progressive content of the educational agenda between Egypt and Britain has been placed in the facilitating care of the British Council and it is therefore important to recognise the policy context in which new initiatives are being developed. Increasingly – almost exclusively – the British Council's educational focus is on those younger people who will bear the responsibility for the Egypt of the future, with youth employability as the primary empowering motivation. Large projects targeting model schools from which best practice can be cascaded concentrate on innovative methods of teaching and learning in the classroom, practical processes for the introduction of enabling quality assurance and the imaginative but realistic introduction of ICT learning and teaching.

Running parallel to substantive school projects is a portfolio of interventions in support of continuous and lifelong learning, including: the continuing provision of scholarships; the sustenance of UK–Egypt alumni networks; higher institutional linking in support of achieving ever-higher quality assurance thresholds in universities; assistance in building new platforms of scientific research and development within the tertiary sector, and the provision of professional and technical qualifications, and support to achieve these, particularly in the medical, business and financial fields.

The provision of business-oriented English, for which there is currently an unstemmable demand in Egypt, continues to underscore the bilateral educational partnership as catalysed by the British Council. The Council continues to teach directly up to 20,000 mostly young professional students each year at its Cairo centres, but it is also reaching out to Alexandria and greater Egypt through English teacher training projects and the provision of the Cairo-maintained free Arabic/English go4english.com website, which is now providing self-access English study to some 100,000 Egyptians, 5,000 to 10,000 of these themselves being teachers.

The purpose of the educational agenda is to fulfil all three of the educational missions described earlier: to enhance vocational capability and employability of more Egyptians nationally, regionally and internationally; to help meet the needs of a myriad stories of individual aspiration and the search for skilled and knowing fulfilment; and to help grow an organically conceived new world of mutuality and shared learning in the interests of constructive intercultural dialogue, planetary appreciation and sensitivity. Above all the resolve must be to envision and achieve a future of trust, security and survival based on mutual understanding and shared possession of the world's humanly-induced threatening agendas.

And mutuality must be the watchword; cultural imposition is anathema to this evolving imperative. Thus, in this one bilateral – Egypt–UK – and in just the past six months, we have seen large groups of UK school teachers visiting Egyptian schools to learn new methodologies in differing cultural contexts, followed by groups of head teachers to Cairo to share management ideas. Young Muslim professionals, including journalists and student leaders, have been on public platforms in Egypt to share the experience of their faith in widely divergent national scenarios. And teenagers from schools in Britain have been learning immersion Arabic, again at the British Council's invitation, at state schools and in Egyptian homes in Alexandria.

This short chapter on education falls at the end of a substantial section addressing the nature of the cultural relationship between Egypt and the UK. But the continuities are more important than the distinctions as, in a tightening twenty-first-century context, education is the key subset for the growth of cultural relations and cultural understanding. Glancing from the past post-Suez fifty years to the next fifty in our planet's history, we must educate ourselves to move from confusion to fusion and determine to create of ourselves guarantors of our own social and environmental survival.

Understanding the cultural future first involves grasping the current conditions and conditioning for learning as experienced particularly by the 70 per cent of Egyptians who are under the age of thirty. How can we simultaneously understand and provide for their individual and group aspirations and how can we enable them to develop the understanding and sensitivities which alone might promise progress in a seriously threatened world?

The historical trajectory of the educational and scholarly relationship between Egypt and Britain – between the Middle East and Europe – still has a powerful, if poorly realised, undertow of resonance and relevance. The early centuries of Islam not only developed the philosophies and theologies specific to what Europe saw as the Near East, but also guarded and nurtured Western academic traditions and resources during a long period when the European narrative of inherited learning had fragmented.

The history of the educational relationship continued to be one of shifting dependencies giving way, today, to new concepts of partnership and mutuality and within a necessarily international domain of new responsibility. Global opportunity and the international determinants of national development now insist on worldwide networked partnerships, understanding, benchmarking and consensus on taught values, all of which must now become critically formative of national educational policies and strategies.

Notes on Contributors

Noel Brehony completed his PhD on Libya and undertook postdoctoral research on the West Bank before he joined the Foreign and Commonwealth Office where he worked for twenty-six years, with postings to Kuwait, Yemen, Egypt and Jordan. He was Director of Middle East Affairs for Rolls-Royce plc from 1992 to 1999 and is currently Chairman of Menas Associates. Dr Brehony is Chairman of the Council for British Research in the Levant and a former chairman of the Middle East Association and president of the British Society of Middle East Studies. He is a member of the British Egyptian Society Executive Committee and the Advisory Council of the London Middle East Institute.

Ayman El-Desouky is Lecturer in Modern Arabic and Comparative Literature at the School of Oriental and African Studies (SOAS), the University of London. He studied Comparative Literature at the American University in Cairo and the University of Texas at Austin, and lectured on Arabic Language and Literature at Johns Hopkins and at Harvard. He has published on Egyptian literature and comparative hermeneutics and is currently preparing a book-length study on the conception and practice of Sacred Discourse in modern Arabic literature.

Ali E. Hillal Dessouki is Professor of Political Science at Cairo University, Editor-in-Chief of the quarterly journal *Al Nahda* (Renaissance), and Chairman of the Arab Association of Political Science. He served as Egypt's Minister of Youth from 1999 to 2004 and Dean of the Faculty of Economics and Political Science, Cairo University, from 1993 to 1999. He has been a visiting professor at the American University in Cairo, Calgary University, the University of California at Los Angeles and Princeton University, and has served on the editorial board of many academic journals in Egypt and abroad. He has published extensively in Arabic and English on issues related to political development and social change in the Arab world.

Mostafa El-Feki has had a long and distinguished diplomatic and academic career. Dr El-Feki is currently President of the British University in Egypt (since 2005) and a Member of Parliament (during which time he has been Chairman of the Foreign Relations Committee of the Egyptian People's Assembly and a Member of the Middle East Committee of the International Parliamentary Union). He is Deputy Chairman of the Arab Parliament and a Member of the Supreme Council for Policies of the ruling National Democratic Party. During his diplomatic career he represented his country at the League of Arab States, in Austria, at the IAEA, as a non-resident ambassador to the republics of Slovakia, Slovenia and Croatia, and held many senior posts in Egypt, culminating in his work as First Assistant Foreign Minister in 2000. He has published widely on Egyptian politics, Arab nationalism, Islamic politics and international relations.

Heba Handoussa is currently Director and Lead Author of the Egypt Human Development Report (EHDR), which she also directed in 2004 and 2005. Previously, and for ten years, Dr Handoussa was Managing Director of the Economic Research Forum (ERF), established in 1993 to promote policy-relevant research on the MENA region. As Research Director she began the regional Gender Economic Research and Policy Analysis (GERPA) initiative in 2006. Dr Handoussa obtained her PhD in Economics from the University of London and taught at the American University in Cairo where she was twice elected as chairperson of her department and was subsequently appointed as Vice Provost. She has also served as adviser to the Egyptian government and consultant to the World Bank. Dr Handoussa is a former member of Egypt's Upper House of Parliament, and a former member of the Board of the Central Bank of Egypt. She has served on the board of international and regional research-related institutions including CEDEJ, IFPRI, UNRISD and WBI. Her publications cover the areas of industrial policy, productivity growth, institutional reform and development.

Fekri Hassan has been Petrie Professor of Archaeology at the Institute of Archaeology and Department of Egyptology at University College, London, since 1994, following a career in universities in North America and Europe. From 1988 to 1990 he was also adviser to the Egyptian Minister of Culture. He obtained his first degree in geology and chemistry from Ain

Shams University, Cairo, and followed this with an MS in geology from Ain Shams, an MA and a PhD in anthropology from Southern Methodist University in Dallas, Texas. His academic interests centre on the origins of agriculture and civilisation, geoarchaeology, demographic and ecological archaeology, modelling and computer simulation, cognition and the philosophy and theory of archaeology throughout North Africa and the Middle East. Professor Hassan has published a large number of articles and books on his subjects.

Michael Jones has worked in Egypt for more than twenty-five years as a field archaeologist both on excavations and in recording, documentation and conservation of historic monuments and sites of all periods. These include Qasr Ibrim, Luxor, Quseir, Tell el-Amarna, Memphis, Giza, Siwa Oasis and Wadi Firan in Sinai. Since 1996 he has directed the USAID-funded conservation projects carried out by the American Research Center in Egypt at the Red Sea monasteries of St Anthony and St Paul and the so-called Red Monastery (Dair al-Anba Bishai) at Sohag. He is particularly interested in cultural heritage management and ways of displaying, presenting and preserving heritage in its modern contexts.

Penelope Lively has written novels, short stories and children's books. Her novel *Moon Tiger* – set partly in Egypt during the early 1940s – won the Booker Prize in 1987. Her memoir *Oleander, Jacaranda: A Childhood Perceived* looks at her early years in Egypt and is a discussion of the way in which a child interprets the world as well as a view of Egypt and the Middle East at that time. Penelope Lively is a former chairman of the Society of Authors, and has served on the boards of the British Library and the British Council. She was awarded the CBE in 2002.

David Lubin has a BA (philosophy, politics and economics) from Oxford University and a Master's degree focusing on development economics from the Fletcher School at Tufts University in the US. He has almost twenty years' experience researching the relationship between developing countries and international financial markets. Most of his career has been spent with the HSBC Group, which he joined in 1989 and where he worked in various capacities as an emerging markets economist. Since September 2006 he has been at Citigroup in London, where he is responsible for economic research and market analysis on Eastern Europe, the Middle East and Africa. He also represented Midland Bank in debt-restructuring negotiations with the governments of a number of developing countries. He has contributed to a number of academic studies including chapters in *The Road to International Financial Stability* (Palgrave, 2003) and *From Capital Surges to Drought: Seeking Stability for Emerging Economies* (Palgrave, 2001).

Gamon McLellan started journalism in Ankara in the mid-1970s as editor of a political and economic weekly. While there he travelled extensively in the Eastern Mediterranean and the Middle East, returning to London in 1978 to become Deputy Editor of *Arab Month* magazine. A year later he joined the BBC to run the Turkish Service and developed its output to provide much-needed news and analysis in the years following the 1980 military coup in Turkey. He also appeared regularly on the BBC World Service as an analyst of Eastern Mediterranean affairs. After four years as Deputy Head of the Central European Services, he became Head of the BBC Arabic Service in 1992. During his time the radio output more than doubled to become a twenty-four-hour news service, and the award-winning Arabic news website bbcarabic.com was launched. His work in the Arabic Service culminated in directing its output during the 2003 invasion of Iraq. He retired from the BBC in 2004 and now lectures and writes about Turkey, the Eastern Mediterranean and the Middle East.

Fiona Moffitt is a Senior Associate with the UK-based consultancy firm MENAS Associates, specialising in Egypt's political and economic risk. Previously, and for sixteen years, she was the Egypt author for the Economist Intelligence Unit and edited MENAS's *Egypt Focus* monthly report. She has written for numerous publications over the years including *The Times*, the *Financial Times* and *The Economist*. Prior to moving to Cairo, she worked in the documentary unit of the leading UK independent television station, Granada, and won an Emmy for a documentary exploring the causes of militant Islam, covering Egypt, Lebanon and Iran. She has played tennis at a professional level, competing on the senior international tournament circuit and has played for England in both senior and junior internationals.

Ahmed El-Mokadem was born in Egypt but moved to the UK in 1963 and has held dual British and Egyptian nationality for thirty-five years. He was educated in Egypt (BA Econ., 1961, Cairo University) and the UK (PhD, 1968, Manchester University). He has spent more than thirty-five years in academic consultancy and a business career worldwide. He has been adviser to many governments on economic policy, oil and defence. He has published or supervised books, articles and research projects in economics, econometrics, management and systems engineering. He contributed to the early economic thinking of Margaret Thatcher in the early 1970s. Dr Mokadem was one of the founders of the British Egyptian Society and has been Vice Chairman since the society's inception. He is a member of many professional bodies and charitable societies. He recently retired to focus on writing, lecturing, public services and social and charitable work.

Yousry Nasrallah was born in Egypt in 1952. He has a degree in statistics from the Faculty of Economics and Political Sciences at Cairo University where he was an active member of the film club movement in Egypt. In 1978 he moved to Beirut where he lived for four years, working as a film critic for *As-Safir*, one of Lebanon's most important daily newspapers. In 1987 he wrote and directed his first feature film, *Summer Thefts*, which was selected in Cannes for the Directors' Fortnight. The film received more than twenty awards in various international film festivals. He has since worked on several films which have been critically acclaimed; *Mercedes, On Boys, Girls and the Veil, La Ville, The Gate of the Sun*, and *The Aquarium*. He is currently shooting a video installation for the Musée du Quai Branly on the Nubian Diaspora.

Roger Owen is currently the A. J. Meyer Professor of Middle East History at Harvard University and was formerly director of the Center for Middle Eastern Studies at the same university. Previously he taught Middle East political and economic history at Oxford University where he was also Director of St Antony's College Middle East Centre. His books include *Cotton and the Egyptian Economy, The Middle East in the World Economy: 1800–1914*, and *State, Power and Politics in the Making of the Modern Middle East* (3rd edition, revised, 2004). He is also the co-author (with Sevket Pamuk) of *A History of the Middle East Economies in the Twentieth Century*. Roger Owen has also written a biography of Evelyn Baring, the first Lord Cromer, *Lord Cromer; Victorian Imperialist, Edwardian Proconsul*, which was published by Oxford University Press in January 2004 and an Arabic edition of which appeared in Cairo in 2006. Professor Owen has written a regular column for the Arabic newspaper, *Al-Hayat*, since the late 1980s and an occasional one for *Al-Ahram Weekly* (Cairo) since 1999.

Stephen Quirke is Curator at the Petrie Museum of Egyptian Archaeology, UCL, and Reader in Egyptian Archaeology at the Institute of Archaeology,

UCL. Previously he was Curator in the then Department of Egyptian Antiquities at the British Museum, with special responsibility for hieratic manuscripts. His doctoral dissertation at the University of Cambridge was on the administration of Egypt during the late Middle Kingdom, about 1850–1700 BC, and his research since then has extended to other written evidence from ancient Egypt, and to the ethics of archaeology and the museum. His monographs include *The Administration of Egypt in the Late Middle Kingdom: The Hieratic Documents* (1990), *Titles and Bureaux of Egypt 1850–1700 BC* (2004), *Egyptian Literature 1800 BC* (2004), and, with Mark Collier, *The UCL Lahun Papyri: Letters* (2002), *The UCL Lahun Papyri: Religious, Literary, Legal, Etc* (2004) and *The UCL Lahun Papyri: Accounts* (2006).

Hoda Rashad is Director and Research Professor in the Social Research Center of the American University in Cairo. She is also a member of the Senate, one of the two parliamentary bodies in Egypt. In addition she serves on the National Council for Women, is a member of the Higher Council for Policies of the National Party and is Chair of the Committee on Women in the Policy Secretariat of the National Party. She is also a member of the Ethical Research Council, and the Egyptian Academy of Scientific Research and Technology. She acts as a resource person and consultant to a number of regional and international organizations: Commissioner to the WHO Commission on Social Determinants of Health, Vice Chairman of the Dutch Development Assistance Research Council and member of the Advisory Committee on Health Research to the Director of WHO and the International Union for the Scientific Study of Population.

Hugh Roberts is Director of the North Africa Project for the International Crisis Group, having joined the Crisis Group in October 2002. Based in Cairo, he has been responsible for a series of Crisis Group reports on 'Islamism in North Africa' and on the problems of political reform in Egypt, Algeria and Mauritania. From 1997 to 2002 he was a Senior Research Fellow of the Development Studies Institute at the London School of Economics. Between 1976 and 1997 he lectured in politics and history at the universities of East Anglia, Sussex, California (Berkeley) and London (SOAS). Educated in London, Oxford and Aix-en-Provence, he received his DPhil from Oxford University in 1980 for a thesis on the Kabyle question in Algeria. He has continued to work on Algeria, visiting the country repeatedly, and has published many articles on Algerian politics. He has also worked and published articles and papers on the cooperative movement in Jordan, the Western Sahara question, the Northern Ireland question, the history of Islamism in North Africa and the political anthropology of Berber society. His book, *The Battlefield: Algeria, 1988–2002. Studies in a Broken Polity*, was published by Verso in March 2003. Further books on Berber politics and on North African Islamism are currently in preparation.

Ahmed Maher El Sayid is the former Minister of Foreign Affairs in Egypt. During a long and distinguished career in the Egyptian Foreign Service he served as Director of the Arab Fund for Technical Assistance to African States, League of Arab States, from 2000 to 2001; during the period 1980 to 1999 he was Egyptian ambassador to Portugal, Belgium, the Soviet Union and finally the United States. During his postings in Egypt he has been Director of the Legal and Agreements Department of the Ministry of Foreign Affairs, Director of the Department of Political Planning at the Ministry of Foreign Affairs and Chief of Cabinet of the Minister of Foreign Affairs, in addition to serving at the Office of the National Security Adviser to the President from 1972 to 1974. Ahmed Maher obtained his LLB from the Faculty of Law at Cairo University.

Mustapha Kamel al-Sayyid is Professor of Political Science at Cairo University. He obtained his PhD at the Graduate Institute of International Studies in Geneva. His doctoral thesis was entitled 'Social Inequality, Collective Protest and Political Violence in Some Social Formations of the Periphery 1960–1973'. He taught at Cairo University, the American University in Cairo, Harvard Law School and Colgate University. He also spent a year as visiting scholar at the University of California in Los Angeles and the summer months of 2002 as a fellow of the Carnegie Endowment of International Peace in Washington. He founded and directed the Center for the Study of Developing Countries at Cairo University (1995–2004), and in 2005 helped to establish Partners-in-Development, a think-tank specialising in development research, of which he is the executive director. His publications in Arabic, English and French deal with issues of the political economy of development, democratisation, civil society and human rights in Arab countries, and Egyptian politics and political theory. He has served as a member of the Executive Board of the Arab Political Science Association (1992–2001) and of the Executive Board of the Egyptian Human Rights Organisation (1989–91).

Mohammed Shaker has been Vice Chairman of the Board of the Egyptian Council for Foreign Affairs since 2003, having previously been its Chairman. He has been Chairman of both the Regional Information Technology Institute since 2002 and of the Sawiris Foundation for Social Development since 2001 and has been a member of the Higher Council for Policies of the National Democratic Party since 2002. Dr Shaker was Egypt's ambassador to the UK (1988–97); ambassador to Austria and Egypt's Governor on the Board of the IAEA (1986–8); Egypt's Deputy Permanent Representative to the UN in New York (1984–6); and Deputy Representative to the UN (1984–5). He was President of the Third Review Conference of the Parties to the Treaty on the Non-Proliferation of Nuclear Weapons, Geneva, in 1985; President of the UN Conference for the Promotion of International Cooperation in the Peaceful Uses of Nuclear Energy, Geneva, in 1987; and a member of the UN Secretary-General's Advisory Board on Disarmament Matters from 1993 to 1998. Dr Shaker graduated in Law from Cairo University in 1955 and obtained Docteur des Sciences Politiques, University of Geneva, in 1975. His published works include *The Nuclear Non-Proliferation Treaty: Origins and Implementation 1959–1979* (three volumes), published by Oceana Publications, Dobbs Ferry, New York, 1980.

Paul Smith has been Director of the British Council in Egypt, and Cultural Counsellor at the British Embassy, since August 2005. He was born in 1956 and educated at King Edward's School, Birmingham, and Queens' College, Cambridge, where he gained a double first in English. From 1978 to 1980 he lectured in English Literature at St Stephen's College, University of Delhi. He then pursued doctoral studies in Renaissance Literature at Cambridge University and worked as an academic supervisor for Cambridge BA honours students. He joined the British Council in 1983 and has had postings in Nigeria, Myanmar, Chile, Germany, Bangladesh and as Director of the British Council in New Zealand. He then returned to the UK as Director of Arts, before taking up a five-year posting as Director, West India, based in Mumbai. His interests include all the arts, especially drama, history and international cultural relations. He has directed plays, particularly Shakespeare, in various countries and has published articles in academic volumes.

Peter Mackenzie Smith, the Deputy Chairman of the British Egyptian Society, is a consultant on international education and training. His previous career was with the British Council and this included two periods at the Council's office in Cairo, from 1972 to 1977 and 1983 to 1987, during which his responsibilities included education and training development programmes and bilateral cultural relations. From 1997 to 2003 he was Director of Education at GEC plc and Marconi. Recent links with Egypt include the management of a strategic forum in Cairo in 2005 on higher and further education strategy between the UK and the countries of the Middle East.

Robert Springborg completed a PhD in political science at Stanford University in 1974. Since that time he has held academic positions at Macquarie University in Sydney, Australia, the University of California, Berkeley, the University of Pennsylvania, and at the University of Sydney. In the late 1990s he served as Director for the Middle East for Development Associates and was based in Cairo. From 2000 until 2002 he was Director of the American Research Center in Egypt. In 2002 he was appointed the MBI Al Jaber Chair in Middle East Studies at the School of Oriental and African Studies and Director of the London Middle East Institute. He has published two monographs and numerous articles on the history, politics and/or economics of Egypt and has served as consultant on those subjects with various departments of the governments of Australia, Great Britain, New Zealand and the United States, as well as with the EU and numerous private clients.

The Rt Hon Baroness Symons of Vernham Dean is a senior Labour member of the House of Lords and a business leader. Formerly Deputy Leader of the House of Lords, Baroness Symons was a minister in the UK government from 1997 until stepping down in 2005. Among her government posts she was Minister for the Middle East, Minister for International Trade and Minister for Defence Procurement, and the Prime Minister's envoy to the Gulf. She has a wide range of experience in the Middle East in particular, and currently chairs the UK Parliament's all-party group on Qatar, the Saudi–British Joint Business Council and the British Egyptian Society. Previously a trade union general secretary, she was an Equal Opportunities Commissioner and a governor of the London Business School. As well as working closely with DLA Piper, Baroness Symons is now involved with a number of other commercial organisations, including roles as a non-executive director of British Airways and as an adviser to other companies, including those with strong Middle East links, and with a number of not-for-profit organisations, including the International Red Cross.

Nicholas Warner is an architect trained at Cambridge University, UK. He came to Egypt in 1992 to conduct research on the Islamic Architecture of Cairo. Since then he has participated in or directed a number of projects related to the documentation, preservation and presentation of historic structures and archaeological material throughout Egypt. These include surveys (ranging from a new map of Historic Cairo to recording prehistoric rock art in the Western Desert), physical conservation of Pharaonic tombs in Saqqara and Roman remains in Dakhleh, as well as restoration and presentation activities at the Egyptian Museum and the Gayer-Anderson Museum in Cairo.

Bibliography

Agnew, Neville, and Bridgeland, Janet, eds, *Of the Past, For the Future: Integrating Archaeology and Conservation*, Proceedings of the Conservation Theme at the Fifth World Archaeological Congress, Washington DC, 22–6 June 2003, Los Angeles: Getty Conservation Institute Los Angeles, 2006, pp. 85–142, Part Four, 'Finding Common Ground: The Role of Stakeholders in Decision Making'.

El Amrani, Issandr, 'The Emergence of a "Coptic Question" in Egypt', Middle East Report Online, http://www.merip.org/mero/mero042806.html, 28 April 2006 (consulted 27 August 2006).

Ayubi, N., *Over-stating the Arab State: Politics and Society in the Middle East*, London: IB Tauris, 1995.

Beinin, Joel, 'Egyptian Textile Workers: From Craft Artisans Facing European Competition to Proletarians Contending with the State', International Institute of Social History conference 2004, http://www.iisg.nl/research/egypt.doc (consulted 18 March 2007).

Bluestone, Daniel, 'Challenges for Heritage Conservation and the Role of Research on Values', in Marta de la Torre and Erica Avrami, *Values and Heritage Conservation*, Research Report, Los Angeles: Getty Conservation Institute, 2000.

Bowden, Mark, *Pitt Rivers. The Life and Archaeological Work of Lieutenant-General Augustus Henry Lane Fox Pitt-Rivers, DCL, FRS, FSA*, Cambridge: Cambridge University Press, 1991.

Bremer, Thomas S., *Blessed with Tourists, The Borderlands of Religion and Tourism in San Antonio*, Chapel Hill: University of North Carolina Press, 2004.

British Egyptian Business Association (BEBA); H. E. Dr Mamdouh el-Beltagui, Minister of Tourism, 'The Challenges of Sustainable Tourism Development in Egypt', address at business luncheon, 15 December 2003, Marriot Hotel, Cairo, http://www.beba.org.eg/resources/html/15-12-

2003Speech.asp (consulted 18 September 2006).

Brunton, Guy, *Qau and Badari I*, London: British School of Archaeology in Egypt and Bernard Quaritch, 1927.

al-Bughdadi, Abd al-Latif, *Mudhakkirat* (Memoirs), 2 vols, Cairo: al-Maktab al-Misri al-Hadith, 1977.

Capuani, Massimo, *Christian Egypt; Coptic Art and Monuments through Two Millenia*, Cairo: American University in Cairo Press, 2002.

Champion, T., 'Beyond Egyptology: Egypt in 19th and 20th Century Archaeology and Anthropology', in P. Ucko and T. Champion, eds, *Wisdom of Egypt: Changing Visions through the Ages*, London: UCL Press, 2003, pp. 161–85.

Darvill, Timothy, 'Value Systems in Archaeology', in M. Cooper et al., eds, *Managing Archaeology*, London: Routledge, 1995, pp. 40–50.

Davies, Stephen J., 'Ancient Sources for the Coptic Tradition', in Gawdat Gabra, ed., *Be Thou There; The Holy Family's Journey in Egypt*, Cairo: American University in Cairo Press, 2001, pp. 133–53.

Demas, Martha, 'Planning for Conservation and Management of Archaeological Sites', in *Management Planning for Archaeological Sites*. Proceedings of an international workshop organised by the Getty Conservation Institute and Loyola Marymount University, May 2000, Corinth, Greece, Los Angeles: Getty Conservation Institute Los Angeles, 2002, pp. 27–54.

Dessouki, Ali E. Hillal, and Korany, Bahgat, eds, *The Foreign Policies of Arab States*, Boulder, CO: Westview Press, 1991.

Drower, M., 'The Early Years', in T. G. H. James, ed., *Excavating in Egypt: The Egypt Exploration Society 1882–1982*, London: British Museum, 1982, pp. 9–36.

Drower, Margaret, 'Gaston Maspero and the birth of the Egypt Exploration Fund (1881–3)', in *Journal of Egyptian Archaeology*, 68, 1982, pp. 299–317.
—— , *Flinders Petrie: A Life in Archaeology*, London: Gollancz, 1985.

Duckworth Collection, http://www.human-evol.cam.ac.uk/Duckworth/history.htm (consulted 20 March 2007).

Dunnell, Robert C., 'The Ethics of Archaeological Significance Decisions', in E. Green, ed., *Ethics and Values in Archaeology*, New York: Free Press, 1984, pp. 62–74.

Edwards, A. B., *A Thousand Miles Up the Nile*, London: Routledge, 1877.

Edwards, I. E. S., *From the Pyramids to Tutankhamun*, London: Oxbow Books, 2000.

El-Daly, O., *Egyptology: The Missing Millennium, Ancient Egypt in Medieval*

Arabic Writings, London: UCL Press, 2005.

Ellis, Vivienne, *Trucanini, Queen or Traitor?*, Canberra: Australian Institute of Aboriginal Studies, 1981.

Emery, W. B., *Egypt in Nubia*, London: Hutchinson, 1965.

Fabian, Johannes, *Time and the Other: How Anthropology Makes its Object*, New York: Columbia University Press, 1983.

—— *Time and the Work of Anthropology: Critical Essays 1971–1991*, Amsterdam: Harwood, 1992, pp. 245–64.

Fagan, Brian, *The Rape of the Nile: Tomb Robbers, Tourists and Archaeologists in Egypt*, London: MacDonald and Jane's, 1997.

Fahmy, Ninette S., *The Politics of Egypt: State-Society Relationship*. London and New York: Routledge Curzon, 2002.

Feilden, Bernard M., and Jokilehto, Jukka, *Management Guidelines for World Cultural Heritage Sites*, Rome: ICCROM, 1993.

Fowler, Alan, 'British Textile Workers in the Lancashire Cotton and Yorkshire Wool Industries', International Institute of Social History conference 2004, http://www.iisg.nl/research/britain.doc (consulted 18 March 2007).

France, P., *The Rape of Egypt: How the Europeans Stripped Egypt of its Heritage*, London: Barrie and Jenkins, 1991.

Frank, Georgia, *The Memory of the Eyes; Pilgrims to Living Saints in Christian Late Antiquity*, Berkeley: University of California Press, 2000.

Gayer-Anderson Pasha, R. G. 'John', *The Legends of the House of the Cretan Woman*, Cairo: American University in Cairo Press, 2001 (Arabic version, Cairo: Sharqiyat Press, 2002).

El-Ghonemy, Riad *Egypt in the Twenty-first Century: Challenges for Development*, London: Routledge Curzon, 2003.

Gorst, Anthony, and Johnman, Lewis, *The Suez Crisis*, London: Routledge, 1997.

Grajetzki, Wolfram, *Burial Customs in Ancient Egypt: Life and Death for Rich and Poor*, London: Duckworth, 2003.

Haag, M., *The Rough Guide to Egypt*, London: Rough Guides, 2003.

Hahn, Peter, *The United States, Great Britain and Egypt, 1945–1956: Strategy and Diplomacy in the Early Cold War*, Chapel Hill: University of North Carolina Press, 1991.

Haikal, F. A., 'Egypt's Past Regenerated by its Own People', in S. MacDonald and M. Rice, eds, *Consuming Ancient Egypt*, London: UCL Press, 2003, pp. 123–38.

Harrison, Robert, *Gladstone's Imperialism in Egypt: Techniques of Domination*, Westport: Greenwood Press, 1995.

Hassan, F. A., *The Cultural Legacy of Egypt: A World Legacy*, Paris: UNESCO, 1997.

Hassan, F. A., 'Memorabilia: Archaeological Materiality and National Identity in Egypt', in L. Meskell, ed., *Archaeology under Fire: Nationalism, Politics and Heritage in the Eastern Mediterranean and Middle East*, London: Routledge, 1998, pp. 200–16.

—— 'Selling Egypt: Encounters at Khan el-Khalili', in S. MacDonald and M. Rice, eds, *Consuming Ancient Egypt*, London: UCL Press, 2003a, pp. 111–22.

—— 'Imperialist Appropriations of Egyptian Obelisks', in D. Jeffrey's *Views of Ancient Egypt since Napoleon Bonaparte: Imperialism, Colonialism and Modern Appropriations*, London: UCL Press, 2003b, pp. 19–68.

—— 'Objects of the Past: Refocusing Archaeology', in R. Layton, S. Shennan, and P. Stone, eds, *A Future for Archaeology*, London: UCL Press, 2006, pp. 217–27.

—— 'The Aswan High Dam and the International Rescue Nubia Campaign', in F. A. Hassan and S. Brandt, eds, *Damming the Past*, London: Westview Press, forthcoming.

Hawass, Zahi, 'Excavating the Old Kingdom: The Egyptian Archaeologists', in D. Arnold, ed., *Egyptian Art in the Age of the Pyramids*, New York: 1999, pp. 155–65.

Haykal, M. H., *Malafaat al-Suwais* (Suez Archives), Cairo: Dar al-Shuruq, 2004.

Haykal, Muhammad, *'Ala shatt al-qanah: muwatinun ikhtaru al-watan*, Cairo: Dar al-Hilal, 2006.

Heikal, M. H., *Cutting the Lion's Tail*, London: Andre Deutsch, 1986.

Hinnebusch, Raymond, and Ehteshami, Anoushiravan, *The Foreign Policies of the Middle East States*, London: Lynne Rienner, 2002.

Hourani, Albert, Khouri, Philip S., and Wilson, Mary C., eds, *The Modern Middle East: A Reader*, Berkeley: University of California Press, 1993.

Ikram, Khalid, *The Egyptian Economy, 1952–2000: Performance, Policies and Issues*, London and New York: Routledge Curzon, 2002.

Institute of National Planning and United Nations Development Program, *Egypt Human Development Report*, Cairo, 2005.

James, T. G. H., *Excavating in Egypt: The Egypt Exploration Society 1882–1982*, London: British Museum, 1982.

—— 'The Archaeological Survey', in T. G. H. James, *Excavating in Egypt: The Egypt Exploration Society 1882–1982*, London: British Museum, 1982, pp. 141–59.

—— *Howard Carter: The Path to Tutankhamun*, London: Kegan Paul, 1992.

Jameson, Fredric, *The Political Unconscious: Narrative as a Socially Symbolic Act*, London: Routledge, 1983.

Janssen, R. M., *Egyptology at University College London 1892–1992*, London: UCL Press, 1992.

Jeffreys, D., 'Introduction – Two Hundred Years of Ancient Egypt: Modern History and Ancient Archaeology', in *Views of Ancient Egypt since Napoleon Bonaparte: Imperialism, Colonialism and Modern Appropriations*, London: UCL Press, 2003, pp. 1–18.

Kamil, J., and Saad, R., 'Weighing the Issues', *Al-Ahram Weekly*, no. 476, 2000, www.Ahram.org.eg/weekly/2000/476/tr1.htm.

Kassem, Maye, *Egyptian Politics: The Dynamics of Authoritarian Rule*. London: Lynne Rienner, 2004.

Khalidi, Rashid, 'Consequences of the Suez Crisis in the Arab World', in A. Hourani, P. S. Khoury and M. C. Wilson, eds, *The Modern Middle East: A Reader*, Berkeley: University of California Press, 1993, pp. 535–50.

Kinzer, Bruce, *England's Disgrace? J. S. Mill and the Irish Question*, Toronto: University of Toronto Press, 2001.

Kirshenblatt-Gimblett, Barbara, *Destination Culture; Tourism, Museums, and Heritage*, Berkeley: University of California Press, 1998.

Kyle, Keith, *Suez, Britain's End of Empire in the Middle East*, London and New York: IB Tauris, 2003.

Louis, W. Roger, *Ends of British Imperialism: The Scramble for Empire, Suez and Decolonization*, London: IB Tauris, 2006.

Lowenthal, David, *The Heritage Crusade and the Spoils of History*, Cambridge: Cambridge University Press, 1998.

Lyster, William, 'Coptic Egypt and the Holy Family', in Gawdat Gabra, ed., *Be Thou There; The Holy Family's Journey in Egypt*, Cairo: American University in Cairo Press, 2001, pp. 1–29.

El-Madany, Sherine, 'Trail of Tears', *Business Today/Egypt*, http://www.copts.net/detail.asp?id=948 (consulted 18 September 2006).

Mar'i, Sayyid, *Awraq siyasiyya* (Political Papers), 2 vols, Cairo: al-Maktab al-Misri al-Hadith, 1978.

Marlowe, John, *Arab Nationalism and British Imperialism, A Study in Power Politics*, London: Cresset Press, 1961.

Mason, Randall, 'Theoretical and Practical Arguments for Values-Centered Preservation', in *CRM: The Journal of Heritage Stewardship* 3, no. 2, Summer 2006, pp. 21–48.

McKercher, Bob, and Le Cros, Hilary, *Cultural Heritage Tourism, the*

Partnership Between Tourism and Cultural Heritage Management, New York: Haworth Hospitality Press, 2002.

McManamon, F. P., and Rogers, J., *Developing Cultural Resource Management in Egypt*, crm.cr.nps.gov/archive/17-3/17-3-11.pdf.

Mitchell, T., *Colonising Egypt*, Cambridge: Cambridge University Press, 1988.

Moser, Stephanie, *Wondrous Curiosities: Ancient Egypt at the British Museum*, Chicago: University of Chicago Press, 2006.

Mysliwiec, K., 'Response to D. O'Connor', in Zahi Hawwas and Lyla Pinch Brock, eds, *Egyptology at the Dawn of the 21st Century, Proceedings of the Eighth International Congress of Egyptologists, Cairo 2000*, Cairo: American University in Cairo Press, 2003, pp. 11–12.

National Centre for Documentation of Cultural and Natural Heritage, *National Heritage 2001: Strategic Approach to Egypt's Cultural Heritage*, Cairo, 2001.

Nonneman, Gerd, ed., *Analyzing Middle East Foreign Policies and the Relationship with Europe*, London and New York: Routledge Curzon, 2005.

O'Connor, D., 'The State of Egyptology at the End of the Millennium: Art', in Zahi Hawwas and Lyla Pinch Brock, eds, *Egyptology at the Dawn of the 21st Century, Proceedings of the Eighth International Congress of Egyptologists, Cairo 2000*, Cairo: American University in Cairo Press, 2003, pp. 1–12.

Oram, Elizabeth E., 'In the Footsteps of the Saints; The Monastery of St. Antony, Pilgrimage, and Modern Coptic Identity', in E. Bolman, ed., *Monastic Visions; Wall Paintings in the Monastery of St. Antony at the Red Sea*, New Haven: Yale University Press and American Research Center in Egypt, 2002, pp. 203–13.

Oweiss, M. Ibrahim, ed., *The Political Economy of Contemporary Egypt*, Washington DC: Centre for Contemporary Arab Studies, Georgetown University, 1990.

Owen, Roger, 'Egypt and Europe: From French Expedition to British Occupation', in A. Hourani, P. S. Khoury and M. C. Wilson, eds, *The Modern Middle East: A Reader*, Berkeley: University of California Press, 1993, pp. 111–24.

—— *Lord Cromer: Victorian Imperialist, Edwardian Proconsul*, Oxford: Oxford University Press, 2004.

—— and Louis, W. Roger, eds, *Suez 1956: The Crisis and its Consequences*, Oxford: Oxford University Press, 1989.

—— and Louis, W. Roger, eds, *A Revolutionary Year: The Middle East in 1958*, London: IB Tauris, 2002.

Petrie, W. M. F., *Seventy Years in Archaeology*, London: Sampson, Low, 1931.

—— *Methods and Aims in Archaeology*, London: Macmillan, 1994.

Petrie Museum Archive CD-ROM, London: Secure Data Services, 1999.

Piacentini, Patrizia, *La valle dei re riscoperta: i giornali di scavo di Victor Loret (1898–1899) e altri inediti*, Milan: Università degli Studi di Milano.

Purdon, Edward, *The Irish Famine 1845–52*, Cork: Mercier Press, 2000.

Rees, Joan, *Amelia Edwards: Traveller, Novelist and Egyptologist*, London: Rubicon Press, 1998.

Reid, D. M., 'Indigenous Egyptology: The Decolonization of a Profession', *Journal of the American Oriental Society*, 1985, vol. 105, pp. 233–46.

—— *Whose Pharaohs? Archaeology, Museums, and Egyptian National Identity from Napoleon to World War I*, Berkeley: University of California Press, 2002.

Ricoeur, Paul, *Memory, History, Forgetting*, trans. Kathleen Blamey and David Pellauer, Chicago: University of Chicago Press, 2004.

Saad, R., 'Fekri Hassan: The Philosophy of Archaeology', *Al-Ahram Weekly*, 2001, no. 536, www.ahram.org.eg/weekly/2001/536.

Said, Edward, 'Representing the Colonized: Anthropology's Interlocutors', in *Critical Inquiry*, 1989, vol. 15, pp. 205–25.

—— *Culture and Imperialism*, London: Vantage, 1994.

Säve-Söderberg, T., *Temples and Tombs of Ancient Nubia*, London: Thames and Hudson, 1987.

al-Sayyid, Afaf Lutfi, *Egypt and Cromer*, New York: Praeger, 1969.

Schölsch, Alexander, *Egypt for the Egyptians! The Socio-Political Crisis in Egypt 1878–1882*, London: Ithaca Press, 1981.

Schulz, R., 'The Responsibilities of Archaeology: Recent Excavations', in R. Schulz and M. Seidel, eds, *Egypt, The World of the Pharaohs*, Köln: Könemann, 1998.

Shaker, Mohamed I., *The Nuclear Non-Proliferation Treaty: Origins and Implementation*, 3 vols, Dobbs Ferry, New York: Oceana Publications, 1980.

Smith, H. S., 'Walter Bryan Emery', in *Journal of Egyptian Archaeology*, 1971, no. 57, pp. 190–201.

Stadelmann, R., 'Response to D. O'Connor', in Zahi Hawwas and Lyla Pinch Brock, eds, *Egyptology at the Dawn of the 21st Century, Proceedings of the Eighth International Congress of Egyptologists, Cairo 2000*, Cairo: American University in Cairo Press, 2003, pp. 13–114.

Stephens, Robert, *Nasser: A Political Biography*, New York: Simon and Schuster, 1971.

Stone, Dan, *Breeding Superman: Nietzsche, Race and Eugenics in Edwardian and Interwar Britain*, Liverpool: Liverpool University Press, 2002.

The Susie Fisher Group, *Exploring Peoples' Relationship with Egypt*, Mimeograph, London: Petrie Museum, 2000.

Thornhill, Michael T., *Road to Suez: The Battle of the Canal Zone*, London: Sutton, 2006.

Troen, Selwyn Ilan, and Shemesh, Moshe, eds, *The Suez–Sinai Crisis 1956: Retrospective and Appraisal*, London: Frank Cass, 1990.

Tung, Anthony M., *Preserving the World's Great Cities, The Destruction and Renewal of the Historic Metropolis*, New York: Three Rivers Press, 2001.

Turner, Barry, *Suez 1956: The Inside Story of the First Oil War*, London: Hodder and Stoughton, 2006.

Twohig, Elizabeth, 'Pitt-Rivers in Munster (1862–65/6)', in *Journal of the Cork Historical and Archaeological Society*, 1987, no. 92, pp. 34–46.

Ucko, Peter, and Quirke, Stephen, 'The Petrie Medal', in *Living Symbols of Ancient Egypt = Public Archaeology*, 2006, no. 5.1, pp. 15–25.

Utvik, Bjorn Olav, *Islamist Politics in Egypt: The Pious Road to Development*, London: Lynne Rienner, 2006.

Vatikiotis, P. J., *The History of Modern Egypt: From Mohammad Ali to Mubarak*. 4th edn, London: Weidenfeld and Nicolson, 1991.

Verner, M., 'Response to D. O'Connor', in Zahi Hawwas and Lyla Pinch Brock, eds, *Egyptology at the Dawn of the 21st Century, Proceedings of the Eighth International Congress of Egyptologists, Cairo 2000*, Cairo: American University in Cairo Press, 2003, pp. 15–17.

Warner, Nicholas, *Guide to the Gayer-Anderson Museum in Cairo*, Cairo: Supreme Council of Antiquities Press, 2003.

Wilkinson, J. G., *Manners and Customs of the Ancient Egyptians*, 6 vols, London: J. Murray, 1837–41.

Wilmore, Michael, 'Landscapes of Disciplinary Power: An Ethnography of Excavation and Survey at Leskernick', in M. Edgeworth, ed., *Ethnographies of Archaeological Practice: Cultural Encounters, Material Transformations*, Lanham: Altamira Press, 2006, pp. 114–26.

Woollacott, Martin, *After Suez: Adrift in the American Century*, London: IB Tauris, 2006.

Wortham, J. D., *The Genesis of British Egyptology 1549–1906*, Norman: University of Oklahoma Press, 1971.

Index

SOAS MIDDLE EAST ISSUES

Published by
SAQI
in association with
The London Middle East Institute (LMEI)
School of Oriental and African Studies (SOAS)
University of London

SOAS Middle East Issues is an authoritative, internationally refereed series of in-depth analyses of contemporary political, economic and social issues in the region stretching from Morocco to Iran.

The series takes no editorial stand on issues and requires material published to be sound and presented without bias. All opinions expressed are those of the authors and not necessarily those of the editorial board of SOAS Middle East Issues or the London Middle East Institute.

About the London Middle East Institute

The London Middle East Institute (LMEI) of SOAS is a charitable, tax-exempt organisation whose purpose is to promote knowledge of all aspects of the Middle East, both among the general public and to those with special interests in the region. Drawing on the expertise of over seventy SOAS academic Middle East specialists, accessing the substantial library and other resources of SOAS, and interacting with over 300 individual and corporate affiliates, the LMEI since its founding in 2002 has sponsored conferences, seminars and exhibitions; conducted training programmes; and undertaken consultancies for public and private sector clients. The LMEI publishes a monthly magazine – *The Middle East in London* – and with Saqi it publishes four books annually in the SOAS Middle East Issues series. These activities are guided by a Board of Trustees on which is represented SOAS, the British Academy, the University of London, the Foreign and Commonwealth Office and private sector interests.

Professor Robert Springborg

MBI Chair in Middle East Studies
Director, London Middle East Institute
School of Oriental and African Studies
Russell Square, London WC1H 0XG
United Kingdom

www.lmei.soas.ac.uk